THE LOYALISTS
IN THE
AMERICAN REVOLUTION

Claude H. Van Tyne

The Loyalists in the American Revolution

Simon Publications

2001

Copyright © 1902 by The Macmillan Company

First published in 1902 by The Macmillan Company

Reprinted in 1929 by Peter Smith

Library of Congress Card Number: 02026761

ISBN: 1-931313-44-X

Distributed by Ingram Book Company

Printed by Lightning Source Inc., La Vergne, TN

Published by Simon Publications, Safety Harbor, FL

TO MY MOTHER

PREFACE.

The formation of the Tory or Loyalist party in the American Revolution; its persecution by the Whigs during a long and fratricidal war, and the banishment or death of over one hundred thousand of these most conservative and respectable Americans is a tragedy but rarely paralleled in the history of the world. The consequences of their banishment are not so easily seen as were the results of the expulsion of the Moors from Spain or the exile of the Huguenots from France, but that there were penalties and, perhaps, rewards consequent upon their removal is a conclusion hardly to be denied. In the case of the Moors and of the Huguenots the loss to their abandoned fatherland was economic and tangible, but in the case of the Loyalists the speculations of the historian are made more dangerous, because the probable political and social results are of so much subtler a nature. We may only venture the suggestion that the youthful errors of the American republic in the matters of finance, diplomacy and politics might have been in part corrected by the presence of that conservative element which had either been driven into exile, or, if permitted to remain, was long deprived of political and social influence, because of an unremitting intolerance. Whatever may have been the result of their elimination, however, the story of the origin and evolution of the party can lose none of its dramatic interest.

In the preparation of this work on the Loyalists there was a temptation to go over the usual ground of a history of the Revolution, and, doubtless, the dramatic interest could have been attained only by so doing; but such a treatment would have greatly increased the volume of this work, and would have buried the real contributions to our knowledge of the American Revolution in a mass of well-known facts concerning the campaigns and historic personages. Except, therefore, in chapters one, two, four and five, there is a departure from the regular treatment of the logical growth of the Revolution. In those chapters the activity of the Loyalists can be best understood in the regular setting of the revolutionary history The remaining chapters treat of matters necessary for an understanding of the Revolution, but hitherto, for the most part, neglected, and in many cases inaccessible.

The material out of which the work has been constructed has been gathered in the main from original sources. The laws of each of the thirteen colonies during the whole period of the Revolution have been carefully examined. The Charlemagne Tower collection of laws in the Pennsylvania Historical Society Library, supplemented by that of the New York Bar Association, made a complete inspection of the laws possible. The "Transcript of the Manuscript Books and Papers of the Commission of Enquiry into the Losses and Services of the American Loyalists, etc.," recently undertaken at the expense of the Lenox Library of New York, has made it possible to learn whether the laws were really carried out in all their severity. The public records of the original states, so far as they have been published, have also greatly aided in this verification. In addition to consulting the newspapers of the time to establish definite facts, I have made a thorough examination of the files of *Rivington's Gazette*, the greatest Loyal newspaper, from 1774 until the close of the war. The letters and journals of the Loyalists such as Curwen, Van Schaack, John Murray and Hutchinson, and the pamphlets of Galloway and others have been valuable sources for their political arguments and sentiments. Mr. Flick's "Loyalism in New York," gives a bibliographical note, which, supplemented by that in Winsor's "Narrative and Critical History of America," in the article on the Loyalists, renders it unnecessary to include a bibliography in this book.

CONTENTS

CHAPTER I
THE "SONS OF DESPOTISM" . . . 1–26

CHAPTER II
THE FIRST EXILES 27–59

CHAPTER III
THE INQUISITION 60–86

CHAPTER IV
THE DOWNFALL OF THE OLD FAITH . . 87–107

CHAPTER V
THE OVERTHROW OF THE LOYAL STRONGHOLD . 108–128

CHAPTER VI
THE POLITICAL SHIBBOLETH . . . 129–145

CHAPTER VII
TRYING TO PRESERVE THE UNION . . . 146–164

CHAPTER VIII
UNDER THE STANDARD OF THE KING . . 165–189

CHAPTER IX
UNDER THE BAN OF THE LAW . . . 190–212

CHAPTER X
RECONCENTRATION CAMPS AND BANISHMENT . 213–242

CHAPTER XI
LIVING IN EXILE 243–267

CHAPTER XII
CHARGED WITH TREASON 268–285

CHAPTER XIII
EXPATRIATION 286–307

APPENDIX A 309–317

APPENDIX B 318–326

APPENDIX C 327–341

INDEX 343–360

CHAPTER I.

THE "SONS OF DESPOTISM."

IN the early days of the American Revolution, when the companies of patriots were rallying from every part of the country to repel the British, a regiment of militia, coming up from the south, crossed the James river at the little town of Richmond in Virginia.[1] While they were passing through the town, a shoemaker stood in his door and cried: "Hurrah for King George." No one took any notice of him; but after halting in a wood, a little distance beyond, the soldiers were cooking and eating some fish, when the shoemaker came to them and began again to hurrah for King George. When the commanding officer and his aids mounted and were starting on, the shoemaker still followed, hurrahing for King George. Thereupon the officer ordered the pertinacious Tory to be taken back to the river and "ducked." The soldiers brought a long rope which they tied, about the middle, around the shoemaker's waist, and seesawed him backward and forward in the stream until they had him nearly drowned; but every time he got his head above water he would cry for

[1] "State Records of N. C.," Vol. XI., p. 835.

King George. The officer finally ordered him to be tarred and feathered. A feather-bed was taken from the shoemaker's own house, where his wife and four daughters were crying and beseeching the father to hold his tongue; but still he would not. The soldiers tore the bed open, knocked the top out of a tar barrel, and plunged the king-worshipper in headlong. He was then drawn out by the heels and rolled in the feathers until he was a sight; but still he would hurrah for King George. The officer, now thoroughly aroused, ordered the fellow to be drummed out of town with the warning that if he plagued him any more he would have him shot. The sentence was executed and the soldiers saw no more of the shoemaker.

There was a ludicrous element in the shoemaker's obstinate loyalty, but in a more dignified character the same determined allegiance could have been found in the hearts of thousands of Americans in the early days of the Revolution. With these loyal subjects of the British king, Samuel Adams and John Adams had to contend when they set about to arouse America to rebellion and final independence. The great majority of men could be regarded as indifferent, ready to stampede and rush along with the successful party; yet, even among the masses, this traditional love of kingship had to be reckoned with and combated. Loyalty was the normal condition, the state that *had* existed, and *did* exist; and it was the Whigs,—the Patriots, as they called themselves,—who must do the converting, the changing of men's opinions to suit a new order of things which the revolutionists believed necessary for their own and their country's welfare.

It is only when we realize this truth that we can see the folly of John Adams' theory of the *creation* of the Loyalist Party. He failed to understand that it was his party that was created and not the Loyalist party. He declared that the British Government excited hopes and fears, avarice and ambition in the breasts of those whose support they desired. They were promised honor, glory, wealth and power in return for their favor. Their antagonism was threatened with disgrace, ruin, poverty and contempt. The menace included even torture and death. For ten years, Adams asserted, "this pious, moral system was pursued with steady and invariable perseverance." In that decade, they "formed and organized, and drilled and disciplined a party favorable to Great Britain." In fact, he concluded, " they seduced and deluded nearly one third of the people of the colonies."[1]

Had Adams spoken only of the influential Americans whose loyalty England tried to retain when the troubled times came, he would have shown a better grasp of the true state of affairs. In respect to them, there was a remarkable monotony of opinion. Many contemporaries of that intolerant decade before the Revolution believed that the British tried "brazing

[1] John Adams, "Works," Vol. X., 193.

England and America together by the golden solder of corruption."[1] In the petty court of some colonial governor the gift of office and contingent station effected the same transformation of political sympathy as in the greater court in London. "A young man is inflamed with the love of his country," wrote an English satirist. "Liberty charms him. He speaks, writes and drinks for her. He searches records, draws remonstrances, fears prerogative. A secretary of the treasury waits on him in the evening. He appears next morning at a ministers' levee. He goes to court, is captivated by the King's affability, moves an address, drops a censure on the liberty of the press, kisses hands for a place, . . . votes against Magna Charta, builds a house in town, lays his farm into pleasure grounds . . . pays nobody, games, is undone, asks a reversion for three lives, is refused, finds the constitution in danger and becomes a patriot once more."[2] Not all of the crown officers in America deserved this cynical sketch, but the type was well represented. The "herd of worthless parasites" was too often sent to America "to fatten on a larger field."

Besides the mere place-men there were the dignified and worthy gentlemen who held office by virtue of a wise selection. These officers good and bad were the backbone of the Tory party in America. Hardly to be distinguished from the

[1] "The Remembrancer," Part III., 46.
[2] *The Spectator*, Sunday, January 19, 1772. Quoted by Trevelyan.

official class were the clergy of the Established Church, who were also dependent for their livings upon the British Government. The officers and clergy received the support of the landowners and the substantial business men, the men who were satisfied with the existing order of things. The aristocracy of culture, of dignified professions and callings, of official rank and hereditary wealth was in a large measure found in the Tory party. The reports that have come down to us of their ceremonious dress reveal the elegance which envy chose to regard as the reward of their servility. The description glows with the words but not the sanction of Enobarbus. One wore broad gold lace about the rim of his hat, and his cloak glittered with laces still broader. He set up a chariot and pair and constantly traveled in it.[1] Green and gold and purple and gold was the daily wear of a certain wealthy Tory merchant. The Governor of Rhode Island would wear no wig unless made in England and of pattern and size worn by the speaker in the House of Commons. Such worthy and unworthy men of high social position were the leaders of the earliest opposition to the rising rebellion; but, it is to be remembered, they only strove to keep things as they were. Supporting them was the natural conservatism of all prosperous men. The men who had abilities, which could not be

[1] Tyler, " Literary History of the American Revolution," I., 358.

recognized under the existing régime, were they who were striving to bring about a change — a revolution.

It is plain that the political action of the well-to-do men would be conservative. Were they officers, they pushed stubbornly ahead in the execution of orders from England; were they merchants, they trusted in King George and let rebellion fry. Now and then the unbridled action of the mob aroused them for a moment. When, in 1765, a crowd surrounded the elegant house of the Massachusetts customs' officer, tore down his fences, broke his windows, and at last forced the doors, destroying his furniture, stealing his money, scattering his books and papers, and drinking the wines in his cellar to drunkenness—then for the moment the Tories shuddered at the power of the enraged democracy.[1] Indeed, a prominent Tory, remarking that his party had been censured for remissness in not having exerted themselves sufficiently in the early period, replied, that the truth of the case was that they saw and shuddered at the gathering storm, but durst not attempt to dispel it lest it should burst on their own heads.[2] They received many intimations that their interference would not be tolerated. Incidents such as that related by James Murray were common. When, one evil day, a

[1] "Letters of James Murray, Loyalist," p. 137.
[2] "Massachusettensis" in *Rivington's Gazette*, December 29, 1774. Copied from *Massachusetts Gazette*.

loyal friend got into trouble, Mr. Murray went into court to go bail for him, and the displeased crowd hissed him. As he was leaving the room, his wig was pulled off, and his " pate clean-shaved by time " was left exposed. While he was led away in dismay, the mob kept "nibbling" at his heels and trying to trip him. With John Gilpin, he might have said that his hat and wig would soon be there, for they were upon the road. Behind him his disheveled wig was borne upon a staff by an insulting mob.[1]

As a result of such terrorizing, it is true that, during the troubled years that preceded 1773, they preserved for the most part an arrogant silence toward the argument of the opposition. Among themselves they dogmatically asserted that the Stamp Act was but a spur to American industry, but such opinions were not for general circulation. They left to Parliament the task of actively combating the colonial theories. They fancied that the British lion was only playing with the colonial mouse and could stop all its antics at will. The Boston Tea Party, and the events which immediately preceded and followed it brought them to a sense of the progress that revolution had made.

That event had not been unannounced by the course of colonial affairs. Boston, under the lead of Samuel Adams, had early taken a decided stand

[1] See "James Murray, Loyalist," p. 161.

against the Townshend measures.[1] Adams' Addresses to the Ministry, his petition to the king, and his circular letter to the legislatures of the other colonies had been adopted by the Massachusetts Assembly, and that Assembly for its pains had been prorogued by Governor Bernard. The circular letters urged that no taxes be levied except by the colonial legislatures. The success of the letters was almost universal. Merchants, the Sons of Liberty, agreed not to import the taxed goods, and the Daughters of Liberty promised that they would wear homespun and would not drink tea. The legislative bodies of America were threatened with suspension, and the Massachusetts Assembly, when it was called together and had refused to rescind, was dissolved by Governor Bernard. Then Gage was ordered to Boston, and ninety-six Massachusetts towns sent delegates to Faneuil Hall to decide how to receive him. Two regiments of his force arrived and were compelled to hire barracks. Then followed the winter of discontent and, in the spring,

[1] In 1767, Townshend, Chancellor of the Exchequer, introduced measures to tax America in the House of Commons. Leading Americans had distinguished between external and internal duties. Townshend resorted to port duties on wine, oil, and fruits, glass, paper, lead colors and tea. The revenue was to be used to pay a fixed salary to royal governors. The crown was to create a civil list and grant salaries and pensions at will. A Board of Revenue Commissioners was appointed for Boston. General writs of assistance were legalized. The New York Assembly was suspended from legislative functions, until it complied with instructions regarding the supplies for the army.

the Boston Massacre, with the resulting removal of the two regiments. Meanwhile all the obnoxious acts were repealed except the tea duty; Bernard had been recalled and Hutchinson made governor. There was nothing now to fight for except a principle. Then it was that the difference between Whig and Tory political philosophy became defined.

Will not posterity be amazed, cried a Tory writer, when they are told that the present distraction took its rise from a three-penny duty on tea? Will they not call it a most unaccountable frenzy and more disgraceful to the annals of America than that of witchcraft?[1] Besides, he urged, there is nothing new in the recent assertion of the taxing power. It is not only impracticable for America to send members to Parliament, but there is no principle lost if we do not.

As we can more plainly see to-day, the principle, "No taxation without representation" was not violated as it was understood and practiced by Englishmen; but as understood and practiced in colonial affairs it was violated. America had so far outstripped England in political evolution, that neither Englishmen nor men recently immigrated from England could understand American political ideals. To the people of England, representative government meant the representation of the *classes* of the community.[2] Representation according to

[1] "Massachusettensis," December 12, 1774.
[2] Channing, "History of the United States, 1765-1865."

population was a new idea born of colonial conditions. When the Americans objected to taxation without representation the English answered that the colonies were represented, because the merchants interested in colonial trade were represented as a class in the House of Commons. When the colonist used the phrase "no taxation without representation," he meant that taxes ought to be levied only by a legislative body in which was seated a person known and voted for by the person taxed. An Englishmen interpreted the phrase, "no taxation except that voted by the House of Commons." The mode of election to that house, and the interests of the persons composing it, were not considered. If a Loyalist understood the American doctrine, he only conceded that reform was necessary in England. He was opposed to nullification, and wished to harmonize, not to disrupt, the empire.

Beyond the question of constitutional law was the question of expediency. The Whig held that the claim of the right to tax was fraught with too much danger to be admitted even if it were constitutional. A Parliament that could lay a tax of three pence on a pound of tea could raise the tax to a guinea. The Tory asked if that political danger really existed. He pointed to the fallacy of contesting the use of power simply because of the possibility of abuse. Parliament was subject to the limitations of conscience and of public opinion. The instincts of the English race would prevent oppression. American interests had many powerful friends in Parliament, and they would defend America from injustice. Chatham, who was not so sure how many contemporaries he could get to join him in defending American doctrines with their blood, asserted that among the dead he could raise up an host innumerable,[1] and he might prophetically have promised as great a host in the generations of Englishmen that were to come.

It was upon this argument of expediency and probability that the American Loyalist placed the stress, and herein lay the chief difference between the English and American supporters of the British Ministry. The English Tory denied all colonial pretensions, while the moderate American Tory granted that things were not as they should be but maintained that the wrong did not justify the bitterness of the opposition.

While the Americans were possessed of ideas such as these, the King had hit upon an ingenious ruse. He would make English tea cheaper in America than foreign tea, and then, though the duty of three pence on a pound could be retained, Americans would buy English tea for mere economy's sake. The East India Company was to be recompensed, and the loss to the British Government was the price of corrupting America. "The British Ministry," said Franklin, "have no idea that any people can act from any other principle but that of interest,

[1] Gordon, "American War," Vol. IV., p. 444.

and they believe that three pence in a pound of tea, of which one does perhaps drink ten pounds in a year is sufficient to overcome all the patriotism of an American."[1] In the autumn of 1773, ships loaded with tea set out for Boston, New York, Philadelphia and Charleston, where agents had been appointed to receive the seductive cargo.

The storm of indignation that greeted the news of this proposed raid on Whig principles aroused the Tories to the necessity of defending their position. Rivington, a printer of whom we shall hear more, gave a page of the New York *Gazette* to the Tory writer who signed himself " Poplicola." This " worthy Latin derivative " tried to show the inhabitants of New York that their grievances were imaginary, trumped up by demagogues, and that there could be no harm in allowing the East India Company to land their teas in America. They might bring tea to Americans, but they could not make them drink. "A Farmer" endeavored in a long argument to show that it would pay the Whigs to yield now when Parliament had given them a hole to crawl out of. He pointed out that there was no profit in carrying the struggle further.[2] Tea was cheaper than before the tax was laid, and the idea was ridiculed that, in buying the tea, America's money would be taken without her consent. No man was obliged to buy, and, when he did buy, he

---

[1] Franklin's "Works," Biglow Ed., V., 147.
[2] *Rivington's Gazette*, December 2, 1773.

consented to pay the duty, and so there could be no duty thereon if no man purchased it. The heated controversy went on in every new issue of the *Gazette*, where both parties had ready access.[1] "An Old Prophet" offered to answer Poplicola if the latter would give his real name. The anonymous Poplicola, however, knew the value of keeping his light under a bushel in those troubled times, and kept his identity a secret in spite of a promise, on the part of the Prophet, not to "give him any hogoo or ungenerous scurrilities." There was in fact good need for giving the assurance, since scurrilous articles *pro* and *con* were making the *Gazette* disgracefully interesting.

The tea commissioners were the first victims of the popular intolerance. A contemporary has recorded for us the sport of hunting a poor tea commissioner, an animal who is "a sort of hermaphrodite in politics," having no title to liberty, property or the freedom of uttering his sentiments like other men.[2] The epithet and its elucidation have a singular fitness, since the commissioners, though regarded as egregious Tories, were roundly abused by their presumed party if they weakened in the discharge of their unpopular duty. There was, however, an easy choice of evils, for the Tories con-

---

[1] James Rivington was at this time honestly trying to conduct an independent paper in New York city, but the Whigs would permit nothing but the most extreme Whig sentiments, and Rivington was in time forced into support of the British government.

[2] *Rivington's Gazette*, June 8, 1774.

fined their abuse to villification, a form of persecution which failed in some cases to satisfy the more ardent Whigs.

In New York, one November evening, a number of persons assembled in School Street, broke the windows and did other damage by throwing large stones into the house of an Agent of the East India Company.[1] As a result of like threats and more formal requests, originating in mass-meeting, the commissioners in New York, Philadelphia and Charleston resigned their commissions. In Boston, alone, the requests to resign met with refusal. As a result Boston became the center of rebellious interest, and Samuel Adams became in Tory eyes the Wat Tyler of America.

After consulting the other towns of the state by means of the efficient committees of correspondence, Boston determined upon uncompromising resistance. The day after the first of the tea ships came into the harbor a broadside appeared with an appeal to "friends, brethren and countrymen." In demagogic phrase it proclaimed: "That worst of all plagues, the detested tea, shipped for this port by the East India Company, is now arrived in this harbor. The hour of destruction or manly opposition to the machinations of tyranny stares you in the face. Every friend to his country, to himself and to posterity, is now called upon to meet at Faneuil Hall at nine o'clock this day (at which

[1] *Rivington's Gazette*, November 25, 1773.

time the bells will ring) to make united and successful resistance to this last, worst and most destructive measure of administration."[1] The paper branded with the name of enemy to his country, to himself and to posterity, every man who was indifferent or opposed to its sentiments. This was the spirit of the time and soon drove all but the most insignificant men into either the Whig or Tory party.

The meeting at Faneuil Hall was adjourned to the Old South Meeting House, where an unanimous vote demanded that the tea be returned to England. That night the tea-ships were guarded, and next day the consignees offered to store the unwelcome cargo if the landing were permitted. The offer was indignantly refused, and a resolution passed forbidding ship-owners bringing tea from Great Britain to Massachusetts while the duty was unrepealed. Any transgressor was to be regarded as an enemy to his country, and his tea should be sent back to the place whence it came. Thus the determined opposition proceeded step by step[2] until at the meeting on December sixteenth, an hour after nightfall, Rotch, the owner of the tea-ships, entered the town meeting with the refusal of the Governor to allow him to pass out of the harbor. Samuel Adams arose and quietly announced:

[1] Sabine, "American Loyalists," p. 342.
[2] The detailed story has no logical place in this book except as it illustrates the forcing of the unsympathetic into the Tory ranks.

"This meeting can do nothing more to save the country." Then the immortal band of Boston Indians did what the meeting had failed to do. Next morning the tea lay like seaweed on Dorchester beach, and the angry loyalists were threatening the terrible wrath of King George.

Yet there was some bravado in their threats, for one of the most zealous of them wrote about this time to an English officer, complaining that for want of support those who had been friends of the government and its servants were now in a much worse state than at any former period.[1] He went on to show that, because Parliament had not taken active measures to coerce the turbulent spirits, the loyalists were giving up their efforts. It is difficult to see that the loyalists had made much effort, but it is certain that they had been wretchedly supported. The ministry, Edmund Burke said, had "never had any kind of system, right or wrong; but only invented some miserable tale for the day, in order meanly to sneak out of difficulties into which they had proudly strutted."[2] The Loyalists therefore hoped against precedent during the months while the Tea Party news traveled to England and the measures of retaliation traveled back.

They had, meanwhile, to hear and read a great deal about the "pestilential herb" and the "detestable plant." Newspaper poets sang of the

[1] Stevens' Facsimiles, No. 2029, MSS. of Lord Dartmouth.
[2] Burke's "Works," II., 14.

"fated plant of India's shore" and urged Freedom's sons to "dash the cup infused with bane." "Pernicious, baleful tea" was shown to be possessed of "all Pandora's ills." No Tory dared offer his neighbor a drink of tea unless he was absolutely sure of the neighbor's political sentiments. Every stranger was feared as a spy, and even the most reckless Tory wanted good proof of the political sympathy of his guest before offering him tea. "Jack Traveller" related that, when he asked for tea, the landlord winked and ordered the maid to bring in some "white coffee." The dish of "white coffee" was, Mr. Traveller informs us, the most delicious tea.[1] Nor was that the only "white coffee" to be found in the colonies in those theoretically tea-less days. Many refused to be deprived of their favorite drink, in spite of the danger of being

"Tarred, feathered and carted for drinking bohea
And by force and oppression compelled to be free."[2]

A philosophic observer of American manners in those days thought that the lack of the advantages for recreation, offered in more settled communities, had caused the Americans to set greater store by the more sensual pleasures of eating and drinking. However logical this reasoning may be, the fact remains that the Tory party secured many a sympathizer from among those who would have been

[1] *Rivington's Gazette*, December 29, 1779.
[2] Moore's "Diary," II., 22.

indifferent had they not been asked to give up the good things of life to maintain a principle they did not understand. Nevertheless, he who "bowed down to the Tea Chest, the God of the Heathen,"[1] went into his closet and shut the door, as we are told in a scriptural parody of the time.

But the Loyalists did not endure all this taunting and repression without an attempt to bring retaliation upon their oppressors. As yet they had no party organization, owing in part to the inefficiency of the crown officers, who could have led the opposition, but who relied too much on English assistance to act effectively in their own behalf. The scriptural parodist represents them as smiting their breasts and crying, "these Whigs fear thee not, O King, neither have they obeyed the voice of our Lord the King, nor worshipped the Tea Chests which thou hast set up, whose length was three cubits, and the breadth thereof one cubit and a half." In long earnest letters to influential men in England the Loyalists, with far more dignity than the caricaturist would have us believe, were urging strenuous action by the British government.

But Lord North and his ministry needed no spur from American friends, for there was no question now whether the time for decisive action had come. "The ministry are checkmated," Lord Chatham said. "They have a move to make on the board

[1] The first Book of the American Chronicles of the Times. Ben Towne, publisher. Philadelphia, 1774.

and yet not a move but they are ruined."[1] When they acted, they did everything that the most violent Tory could have asked of them, and much that the moderate Tories deprecated. Parliament was compelled to pass five acts for the better regulation of American affairs. The Boston Port Bill was the first of these. It closed that port until the town should indemnify the East India Company for the loss of its tea and convince the king that it was truly submissive. The second act, known as the Regulating Act, annulled the charter of Massachusetts and ordered that the council of the colony, hitherto chosen by a convention of the retiring council and the Assembly, were hereafter to be appointed by the Governor on a royal writ of *Mandamus*. The Crown was to pay their salaries and could remove them at will. This council and the Governor could appoint and remove sheriffs, and these sheriffs had the sole right of returning juries. Town meetings could only be held twice a year and solely for the election of town officers. Thus there was a centralization of power in the Governor's hands, and a paternalism established which could be almost French in its efficiency.

The third act provided that any soldier or revenue officer indicted for murder in Massachusetts should be tried in England. The fourth act swept away all legal restrictions upon the quartering of soldiers in any town of Massachusetts. The fifth act sanc-

[1] Gordon, "American War," Vol. I., 42.

tioned the free exercise of the Catholic religion in Canada, which was laudable enough, but it went on to extend the southern boundary of that dominion to the Ohio River, ignoring the claims of Massachusetts, Connecticut, New York and Virginia. A viceroy was to govern this part of North America, and the people were denied the *habeas corpus*, popular meetings and the freedom of the press.[1]

As a sort of penal clause to this legislation, General Gage was made temporary governor of Massachusetts in the place of Hutchinson, and four regiments accompanied him to America to discomfit the refractory people of Boston. Gage was ordered to arrest the leading rebels and send them to England for trial. There was no mistaking the intention of the British ministry in these acts.

The manner in which the news of these measures was received by the members of the Tory party in America elucidates their motives and illustrates the diversity of their characters. When the report reached Boston on the 10th of May, the Tory merchants favored a compromise, and a subscription was started to pay for the tea. On May 18th, Jonathan Amory argued for such a measure, in Town meeting, but the proposition was overwhelmingly defeated. These men, though they deplored the rigor of the ministerial displeasure, argued for submission, because they feared with Chatham, that the

[1] All passed in April, 1774.

first drop of blood " would make a wound of that rancorous, malignant, corroding, festering nature that it would in all probability mortify the whole body." [1] For their caution they were denounced as "dastardly, low-spirited court sycophants." One Whig wrote in amazement: "Yet with horror be it spoken, there are free-born sons of America so lost to all sense of honor, liberty and every noble feeling as to join the cry and to press for submission. O, tell it not in Gath, publish it not in the streets of Ashkalon!" [2]

As for the crown officers, the stalwarts of the Tory party, they found the vengeance of the king not a whit more severe than met their approval. A New York Tory thought that Americans ought to be taught to pursue their true interests, improve their commerce and cultivate their lands and leave the regulation of the state to those competent in the matter.[3] In the face of the Boston Port Bill, Daniel Leonard, an ultra-loyalist, wrote: "If the Egyptian darkness that hovers over the land could be dispersed, people might see George III. as the provident father of all his people." [4] Others like Jonathan Boucher, a clergyman in the Anglican Church, believed sincerely in the divine right of

[1] Gordon, "American War," Vol. I., 445. Gordon's source was doubtless the "Annual Register."
[2] "An Antidote Against and the Reward of Toryism," p. 13, Nath. Whitaker.
[3] "American Archives," series 4, Vol. I., 301.
[4] "Massachusettensis," January 2, 1775.

kings. He asserted that the "families of the earth were subjected to rulers, at first set over them by God,"—" copying after the fair model of heaven itself, wherein there was government even among the angels." To Jonathan Boucher resistance was a sacrilege to which he was little inclined. There was yet another class of whom Dickinson, quoting, said:

> "This word, Rebellion, hath froze them up,
> Like fish in a pond." [1]

These men were peaceful, sober-minded citizens, who perhaps had more than half sympathized with the Whig movement thus far, but the thought of civil tumult and even war had checked their noble rage and brought them to think of things less metaphysical than political principles. The motives and combination of motives, the characters and phases of character might be multiplied indefinitely, for both good and evil motives actuated the Tory as well as the Whig partizans. Many Tories loved America with a sincerity not surpassed by the most high-minded Whigs. Though posterity has not awarded them the name, it may wisely concede to them the character of the patriot.

As for the Whigs, no language was florid enough to express their wrath. Samuel Adams said of the act that "for flagrant injustice and barbarity one might search in vain among the archives of Constantinople to find a match for it." [2] "Impudent

---

[1] These lines head Dickinson's pamphlet entitled, "An Address to the Committee of Correspondence in Barbadoes," etc.
[2] "American Archives," series 4, Vol. I., 332.

THE SONS OF DESPOTISM.

and inflammatory pieces," as the loyalists called them, were spread through every city " by flaming patriots without property or anything else but impudence."[1] From town meetings and from conventions throughout the colonies came words of earnest sympathy. Such an idea, wrote one committee, " as the Port Bill, had hitherto escaped the sagacity of statesmen and even the fancy of poets. The subtlety of Machiavelli's Italian brain had missed it." Another thought, " Future ages will hardly believe that we were descended from British, when they read of our having borne so long and resented so feebly these outrages." It is worse than the treatment of Carthage by the Romans, declared another. In many places the bill was read in the presence of a concourse of people, then sentenced to the flames and executed by the common hangman. The idea of paying for the spilled tea was ridiculed. " If a man draws his sword on me to deprive me of life or liberty and I break his sword ought I to pay for the sword?"[2] From every quarter came resolves to scorn British chains and to resist every effort to fetter American liberty. Extravagant political moralists promised that god-like virtue should "blazon our hemisphere until time shall be no more."[3]

[1] Tory correspondent to a gentleman in England. Force's " American Archives," series 4, Vol. I., 300.

[2] " American Archives," series 4, Vol. I., 389.

[3] See for above resolves and sentiments and for many others, Force's " American Archives," series 4, Vol. I., 331-350.

They began the exercise of this virtue by sending such quantities of provisions into Boston that she at least should suffer no physical want. Unwillingness to give for this purpose was branded as Toryism, and treated accordingly. The loyal clergyman, Jonathan Boucher, declared that the true object of making the contribution was by this means to raise a sum sufficient to purchase arms and ammunition. He declined to preach a sermon recommending the suffering people of Boston to the charity of his parish.[1] As a result he received letters threatening him with the "most dreadful consequences," if he did not desist from preaching. He refused to be intimidated, and for more than six months he preached, so he informs us, with a pair of loaded pistols lying on the cushion. The congregation were given warning that, if any one attempted to drag him from the pulpit as had been threatened, he would feel justified in repelling violence by violence.[2] Other clergyman emulated the opposition if not the indomitable persistence of this

---

[1] "Notes and Queries," 5th series, VI., 82. "Autobiography."

[2] Boucher proved himself as fearless as his word, when some months later two hundred armed men came early to church for the purpose of intimidating the dauntless preacher and listening to a Whig sermon more to their liking. With his sermon in one hand and his loaded pistol in the other he prepared to ascend the pulpit. A friend, to prevent violence, seized him, and he was removed from the church that day, but on the next Sunday returned, preached the sermon that had been prevented and added some comments on the scene at the previous meeting. See "Notes and Queries," 5th series, I., 103–104. "Autobiography."

Virginia parson. Nevertheless, the popular sympathy for Boston remained unabated, and the first of June, when the Port Bill went into effect, was observed as a fast day by many of the congregations of these very clergymen. Party lines were now clearly drawn; personal fealty had to be very great to be heeded rather than the demands of one's party.

It will be well now, before taking up a chapter of incidents in which new motives for active partizanship arose with every footfall of advance, to consider what elements of American society had already become zealous in the support of the King.

Before the coming of the British soldiers, the elements of the active Tory party may be fairly represented in a few well-defined classes. There were the office-holding Tories, whose incomes depended upon the existing régime. Closely linked with these were those gregarious persons whose friends were among the official class. Doubtless many of the Anglican clergy had motives similar to those of the crown officers. With these men drifted the conservative people of all classes, who glided easily in the old channels. Another type of man, who listened and yielded rather to metaphysical considerations than to concrete facts, was the dynastic Tory, the king-worshipper. Others, who were convinced that Parliament had a right to tax, may be defined as legality Tories. Both these types were reinforced by the religious Tory, whose dogma was "fear God and honor the King." Finally there were the factional Tories, whose action was determined by family feuds and old political animosities. The DeLancey party in New York, of which we shall hear more, was forced into opposition because the Livingston party, its ancient enemy, embraced the Whig principles. In Massachusetts, the antipathy of the Otis's to Governor Bernard doubtless aided the formation of revolutionary parties. With the actual outbreak of war came new accessions to the active supporters of the British, as we shall see when the issues arise on the subjects of the Continental Congress, the Declaration of Independence and the French Alliance. It must always be borne in mind, however, that content with the old order of things was the normal state, and that men had rather to be converted to the Whig or Revolutionary views than to the Tory or Loyalist position. The classification only shows what elements of society tended to remain steadfast in the old faith.

CHAPTER II.

THE FIRST EXILES.

THE coming of General Gage and the retirement of Governor Hutchinson became the occasion for the first associated action of the Tory party. In Boston, the Tories had assembled in the coffee houses in numbers respectable enough to give them temporary freedom of speech, but their public declarations had consisted of tavern talk and anonymous letters to the gazettes which the Whigs declared were the work of "ministerial hirelings" to whose "pensioned pen" the "sons of despotism" were reduced.[1] But the Tories, even then, asserted that the press was not a safe medium for *their* arguments, though a Whig writer might appear there "in all the terrible pomp of his own horrid visage." Now, however, loyalty was no longer in terror, and began to assert itself.

The Episcopal ministers and wardens of Boston were the first to assure Hutchinson, the retiring governor, of their gratitude for his generous attention — especially to matters of religion, which fell "more immediately within their province." They manifested a greater solicitude for his "eternity

[1] Force's "American Archives," series 4, Vol. II., p. 8.

of happiness in the life to come" than for the effects of his administration in the days that were past.[1]

On the following day, the Justices of the Peace for the county of Suffolk testified their loyalty to the king and paid their dutiful respects to General Gage. They first flattered him and then flattered themselves that he would be acceptable to the people over whom he was to preside. They wished, but, as events proved, in vain, that the wisdom which is from above might direct him in performing his duty. They recognized that there were public dissensions, but made no partisan comment upon them, and volunteered their assistance in the preservation of peace.[2]

Thirty-three citizens of Marblehead next addressed Hutchinson, reciting the special favors they had enjoyed during his administration. They made some unhappy insinuations regarding their own dispassionate view of his course and closed with the hope that his reception in England would compensate for the insults and indignities suffered in Massachusetts.[3]

Within ten days this address was rebuked by a declaration unanimously voted at a legal meeting of the town of Marblehead. The declaration asserted that the address had been conducted in a secret and clandestine manner and that the movers

[1] Force's "American Archives," series 4, Vol. I., p. 346.
[2] *Ibid.*, series 4, Vol. I., p. 346.
[3] *Ibid.*, series 4, Vol. I., 358.

THE FIRST EXILES.   29

showed a disposition to destroy the harmony of the town in its public affairs, thus planting seeds of dissensions, animosities and discords. In addressing a person who had been censured as an inveterate enemy by both houses of the legislature they had offered an indignity to that body. The address, though "but the fantastical shadow of public respect," would give Hutchinson the opportunity of justifying his own conduct and thus increase the ministerial prejudice against the colony. By innuendo they had called nineteen twentieths of the men of Marblehead passionate and thoughtless men. The Declaration came to the quaint anti-climax that such men ought to be censured by the world " as persons both vain and inattentive."[1] The mildness of this comment affords us a standard by which we may measure the rapid rise in the political temperature. Not a little of this partisan warmth was due to the addresses and protests which we are about to consider.

In Boston, the Tory leaders canvassed up and down King Street and Cornhill, along the docks and wharves, out on Noddles Island, and in the neighboring towns, Cambridge, Roxbury, and Dorchester. As a result, one hundred and twenty-three subscribers were secured to an address which welcomed the coming and sped the departing governor. They deplored the impending calamities of the metropolis, and mildly criticised the measures that

[1] Force's "American Archives," series 4, Vol. I., 359.

threatened it. Referring to the Boston Port Bill and the Regulating Act, they humbly suggested that, "Without meaning to arraign the Justice of the British Parliament, we could humbly wish that this Act had been couched with less Rigour and that the Execution of it had been delayed to a more distant Time, that the People might have had an Alternative, either to have complied with the Conditions therein set forth, or to have submitted to the consequent Evils on Refusal."[1] As the measures stood, choice was precluded, and all must suffer. They conceded that the indemnity to the East India Company was just, and they were willing to pay their share, though they had taken no part in the destruction of the tea. In concluding, they hoped that Governor Hutchinson would represent their case to the ministry as favorably as possible.

On the following day, like sentiments and testimonials of esteem were conveyed to the retiring governor by the barristers and attorneys-at-law of Massachusetts, twenty-four as illustrious names as the colony could afford.[2] Finally, two days before the governor's departure, thirty-one magistrates of Middlesex assured Hutchinson that they had long beheld with an indignant eye those riotous and tumultous proceedings that had destroyed public peace and order. They, too, hoped that the colony might be restored to his Majesty's favor, and they

[1] "Massachusetts Historical Society Proc.," Vol. XII., 43.
[2] Force's "American Archives," series 4, Vol. I., 363.

THE FIRST EXILES.   31

looked upon Governor Hutchinson as an agent to that end.[1] Later, several addresses of nearly the same tenor, of which the most important was that of the merchants of Boston, were presented to General Gage.

The importance of the preceding addresses is out of all proportion to their apparent significance. They are an indispensable genesis to the history of the Tories. For the next seven years the Addressers of Massachusetts or of New York or of some one of the colonies were held up to their countrymen as traitors and enemies to their country. In the arraignments, which soon began, the Tories were convicted not out of their mouths but out of their addresses. The ink was hardly dry upon the parchment before the persecutions began, and, throughout the long years of war, the crime of being an addresser grew in its enormity.

The Tories learned the intolerance of popular faction not only by expressing sympathy for the enemies of the Whig party, but by entering a protest against its measures. In the Committee of Correspondence of Boston there originated a "Solemn League and Covenant" which through the enterprise of Joseph Warren, the chairman, was disseminated through all the towns of Massachusetts. It rehearsed the wrongs of Boston and bound the signers, who, in the presence of God, solemnly and

[1] Force's "American Archives," series 4, Vol. I., 364.

in good faith convenanted and agreed with each other to suspend all commercial intercourse with Great Britain until the hateful acts were repealed. After August 1st, the signers agreed not to trade with those who continued to trade with England, nor would they buy of any contumacious importers who refused to sign an appended oath,[1] in which such trade was forsworn.

The same body of Tory merchants, that had addressed Hutchinson and Gage, now protested against the "Solemn League and Covenant." They had already attempted in a town meeting at Faneuil Hall to have the Committee of Correspondence censured and dismissed, but had been met by an overwhelming negative. They had maintained that the "League and Covenant" had been clandestinely dispersed through the province without the consent or knowledge of the town. The protest was the last resort of the dissentients. Their reasons were that the "League" was "a base, wicked, and illegal Measure." It would distress and ruin many merchants and check industry by stopping the exportation of their oil, potash, flaxseed, lumber and codfish. It would, they concluded, involve rather than extricate the colony from its difficulties.[2] The protest was reinforced two days later by a proclamation of General Gage's in which he denounced the league, forbade all persons to sign it, and com-

---

[1] *Massachusetts Gazette*, June 13, 1774.
[2] *Rivington's Gazette*, July 14, 1774.

manded the provincial magistrates to seize and bring to trial all who published or offered it for signature.¹

The Whigs met the "Protest" and the "Proclamation" with as much vigor as was possible while Gage and his "Pretorian Guard" were in control of Boston. A broadside was printed containing the names of the protestors against the "Solemn League and Covenant" and of the addressers to Governor Hutchinson. The occupations and places of business were given, and stars were placed opposite the names of those who were not natives of America. Tax-collectors, treasurers or their clerks were especially distinguished by one, two or even three exclamation points.² Thus the signers of both the Address and the Protest were subjected to an inspection quite unwelcome to the majority. An unpleasant prominence was given to the fact that out of one hundred and twenty-three Addressers, thirty-one were not natives of America, fourteen were officers of the Crown, and sixty-three were either merchants or traders actuated by a sordid spirit, as the Whigs believed, rather than the "glorious spirit of liberty." As for the forty-six remaining signers, some were shown to be relatives of the Crown officers, and there was a subtle suggestion that those signers who were portrait painters, lapidaries, chaise-makers, jewellers, book-

¹ Force's "American Archives," series 4, Vol. I., 491.
² "Massachusetts Historical Society Proceedings," 1869-70, p. 392.

binders, and "baker to the army," were men whose best custom would come from the wealthy merchants and rich officers who were the adherents of the Crown.

The Proclamation by Gage was wholly disregarded, but, in the matter of a non-importation agreement, the Patriots decided to await the action of a Continental Congress, which had been proposed by the Sons of Liberty of New York, approved by the famous convention at Raleigh tavern in Virginia, and the time and place left to the decision of Massachusetts. Gage had convened the Massachusetts Assembly at Salem, as provided by the Port Bill, and intended to regulate their action by dissolving them at a moment's warning in case they did what he disapproved. But the daring Samuel Adams, who "only shuddered at the sight of hemp,"[1] as the Loyalists conceded, awaited the favorable hour, caused the door to be locked, and put the key in his pocket. Then resolves were introduced appointing five delegates to confer with delegates to be appointed by the other colonies. A Tory member on the pretense of illness was allowed to pass out, and hastened at once to inform Governor Gage. A writ dissolving the assembly was hastily drawn and the secretary dispatched with it to prevent the mischief. He was obliged to read his writ on the wrong side of the keyhole, while,

[1] "Massachusetts Historical Society Proceedings," 2d series, vol. XII., 140.

within, the resolves were passed electing the delegates, and measures were carried for the relief of Boston. In this bold manner the foundation of the Continental Congress was laid and, before September first, twelve of the colonies, through their assemblies or special conventions, had chosen delegates.

Meanwhile, the attempt to inaugurate the new Regulating Acts in Massachusetts, and the employment of leading Tories to fill the offices thereby created,[1] loosed the popular rage against those "ministerial tools." The thirty-six councillors appointed on the King's writ of *mandamus* became at once the object of persecution. The people "seem to be quite awake, and to have awoke in a passion," commented one who watched the events.[2] A contemporary Whig writer speaks of mobs as "the first-born offspring of oppression,"[3] which is as charitable an epithet as the popular action of the time deserves. The house of Timothy Ruggles, one of the councillors, was attacked in the night, and he was ordered to depart. He promised to leave by the time the sun was an hour high, and the delay was permitted. In the morning he found that the mob had improved the time by closely cropping the mane and tail of his horse, and painting its whole body.[4] Israel Williams, though "old

---

[1] See "Letters of James Murray, Loyalist," pp. 137, 138.
[2] "American Archives," series 4, Vol. I., 732.
[3] "American Archives," series 4, Vol. I., 335.
[4] *Rivington's Gazette*, September 8, 1774.

and infirm," was taken from his home at night by a mob, placed in a house with the doors and chimney closed, and smoked for several hours. The poet Trumbull has chronicled the result in the line of "M'Fingal," which tells us that they "smoked old Williams to a Whig." When the mob let him out, he signed a paper promising not to serve on the Mandamus Council.[1] At Taunton, some five hundred inhabitants assembled at the court house, in which was the office of Daniel Leonard, to express their sentiments against his acceptance of a place on the Mandamus Council. Mr. Leonard disappeared, and the crowd dispersed without disorder or violence, but on the following evening certain "Sons of Belial" fired several balls into one of Leonard's chamber windows.[2]

Thomas Oliver, the Lieutenant-Governor of the province, relates, with solicitous detail, the story of his own unwilling resignation. Early in the morning, a number of inhabitants of Charlestown called to inform him that a large body of people from several towns of the country were on their way to interview him. The crowd soon appeared, and Mr. Oliver went out to inquire the meaning of their coming. They replied that they "came peaceably to inquire into their grievances but not with design to hurt any man." He saw that they were landowners of the neighboring towns, and upon being

[1] Sabine, "American Loyalists," p. 708.
[2] *Rivington's Gazette*, September 8, 1774.

asked to speak to them did so. After thanking him for his advice they proceeded on their way. Mr. Oliver then interceded with General Gage to recall some soldiers sent from Boston to restrain the mob. But, in the afternoon, he saw large companies pouring in from different parts, and began to fear that they would become unmanageable. He was about to enter his carriage when a crowd of three or four thousand, one quarter of them armed, came up and surrounded his house. A committee came to him and demanded a resignation of his seat in the Council. He protested, but they insisted upon his signing a paper. Meanwhile, a part of the multitude became enraged at the delay and pressed into the yard swearing vengeance upon the foes of their liberties. They pressed up to his window, and he could hear them swearing they would have his blood if he refused. His family was greatly distressed by the threats, and, moved by their solicitude, he gave way and wrote beneath the recantation: "my house at Cambridge being surrounded by 4000 people, in compliance with their commands I sign my name, " Thomas Oliver." The committee tried to persuade the people to accept this, and Mr. Oliver saw the land-owners, who had come in the morning, using their utmost endeavors to get the paper received. In this they succeeded, but could not save him from some insults by those who were armed.[1] Just as the crowd

[1] Sabine, "American Loyalists," p. 495.

had come to an understanding with Mr. Oliver, the Commissioner of the Customs, Mr. Hallowell, passed through Cambridge in his chaise. The sight of him inflamed the people, and over a hundred horsemen started in pursuit. The affair threatened to rival that of John Gilpin, but the pursuers were finally dissuaded except one, who overtook Mr. Hallowell, and so frightened him that he left his chaise, and on his servant's horse fled to Boston.[1]

In Worcester, there assembled on the common some fifteen hundred men who sent a committee to Timothy Paine, one of the council, to demand satisfaction for accepting the office. He delayed, but finally signed a confession, which he was compelled to read with bared head before the people. The crowd then dispersed in companies, each in the direction of its own town.[2]

The milder methods of social reprobation influenced the resignation of other members of the council. A number of the indignant people of Plymouth left the meeting-house, when George Watson entered on Sunday evening. The venerable head of the old man was bowed for a moment, and then he arose and promised to resign his office.[3] When Deacon Edson, a councillor from Bridgewater, stood up in meeting to read a psalm, the

---
[1] *Rivington's Gazette*, September 15, 1774.
[2] *Ibid.*, 8, 1774.
[3] *Ibid.*, 8, 1774.

congregation refused to sing. He, however, "hardened his heart like Pharaoh," and, this mild social reprehension having failed, he was driven from his home by a mob, and took refuge in Boston.[1]

The Baronet, Sir William Pepperell, was denounced by his neighbors; and the people of his county, in convention, passed a resolution that, as soon as the leases of his land which any of them held had expired, they would withdraw all connection, commerce and dealings with him until he resigned his seat. The same treatment was threatened against any who opposed this measure.[2]

The other provisions of the regulating act met with the same opposition. At Great Barrington, fifteen hundred men assembled at the opening of the courts. They thought that the judges were to proceed under the new regulating act, and, though assured that they were mistaken, they refused to let the court proceed. The judges were ordered to leave the town immediately, and they complied.[3] In the court house at Boston, the justices and barristers took their wonted places, but no one would serve as juror in a court that was regarded as illegal. The men of five towns assembled to warn Colonel Gilbert not to accept the office of high sheriff.[4]

---

[1] *Ibid.*, 8, 1774.
[2] Sabine, "American Loyalists," p. 522.
[3] "American Archives," series 4, Vol. I., 724.
[4] *Rivington's Gazette*, September 8, 1774.

The Attorney General was threatened by a mob of boys and negroes, and some glass was broken in the windows of his residence.[1]

Against all this defiance, Gage issued an impotent proclamation which was not regarded even at Salem under his very eyes. As to that part of his commission which authorized him to arrest and remove the Patriot leaders, he saw the temper of the people and forbore for the present. "Should that be attempted," wrote a correspondent, "it would produce resistance and reprisals, and a flame through all America such as eye hath not seen, nor ear heard, neither hath it entered into the head of the minister or his minions to conceive."[2]

The situation of the Tories, who were not in Boston under Gage's protection,[3] was fast becoming intolerable. The addressers of Mr. Hutchinson, and the protesters against the public measures led "a devil of a life," wrote a Boston Whig. In the country, the people would not grind their corn, and in town they refused to purchase from or sell to them.[4] Every laborer refused them service, either because of the general tacit agreement or by formal convention. The blacksmiths of Worcester County, forty three in number, solemnly covenanted not to "do or perform any blacksmith's work, or business of

[1] *Ibid.*, September 15, 1774.
[2] "The Remembrancer," I., 60.
[3] Gage placed a guard at the door of every Mandamus Councillor, and there was a patrol every night in the streets.
[4] Sabine, "American Loyalists," p. 136.

any kind, for any person or persons commonly known by the name of tories," nor for *mandamus* councillors or addressers, "all of whom should be held in contempt, and those who are connected with them ought to separate from them, laborers to shun their vineyards, merchants, husbandmen and others to withhold their commerce and supplies."[1] The resolution was distributed far and wide on handbills and in the newspapers.

A sanction was given to this social denunciation by a resolve of the first provincial congress of Massachusetts, which had been organized after the Suffolk County resolves[2] had been approved by the Continental Congress. The provincial congress resolved that, whereas the mandamus councillors "by such disgraceful, such detestable conduct" had counteracted the will of the province and the Continental Congress, they must give satisfaction within ten days for the publication of the resolve by publishing in all the Boston papers acknowledgments of their former misconduct and renunciations of their commissions. If they failed, they were to be considered as infamous betrayers of their country.

[1] Thornton, "The Pulpit of the American Revolution," p. 194.
[2] The Suffolk County resolves, September 6, 1774, declared that the king had forfeited the right to their allegiance by violating their charter, that the Regulating Act was null and void and officers appointed under it must resign at once; collectors of taxes were not to pay the money to Gage's treasurer, and the towns were advised to choose their own militia officers; Gage was threatened if he arrested any one for political reasons. This was a virtual declaration of rebellion and the Continental Congress indorsed it.

A committee should cause their names to be published repeatedly and entered on the records of each town as rebels against the state, thus sending "them down to posterity with the infamy they deserve."[1] In this resolution the Whigs put the onus of rebellion upon the Tory, who was naturally surprised at being charged with the very crime against which he had set his face.

At that moment "Massachusettensis," whose letters, John Adams thought, shone like the moon among the lesser stars[2] in the Tory firmament, was arraigning the province for its resistance. He merely hinted at the punishment for rebellion, and insinuated that the idea ought to harrow up their souls.[3] He dwelt upon the hopelessness of the conflict, showing how dearly England valued her colonies and what she would do to keep them. He maintained that a considerable part of the men of property in the province were still firmly attached to the British government. Bodies of men compelling persons to disavow their sentiments, to resign commissions, or to subscribe leagues and covenants, had wrought no change in their sentiments. They were only more firmly attached to government and wished more fervently and prayed more devoutly for its restoration.[4]

[1] "Journals of Each Provincial Congress of Massachusetts," p. 24.
[2] Tyler, "Literary History of the American Revolution," I., 357.
[3] "Massachusettensis" took occasion, however, in a later pamphlet to quote all the English statutes against treason and to give a careful definition for the benefit of his Whig readers.
[4] Pamphlet, "Massachusettensis," December 12, 1774.

There was good reason for the fervency of their wishes and the devoutness of their prayers. After Gage began fortifying Boston neck, the Tories were seen watching the work and viewing the encampment "with the greatest pleasure in their countenances."[1] "Our Duke of Alva," wrote a Whig, "is shut up with his troops and his forlorn Mandamus Councillors in Boston."[2] Numbers of persons of fortune were constantly flocking into the town of Boston as a place of refuge from the vehement resentment of the country people who were daily under arms.[3] Not only councillors, but judges and protesters and addressers had been obliged to fly to the city of refuge.

They reached Boston in no very amiable frame of mind, as their conversation betrayed. Gage was constantly importuned to treat the rebels with greater severity. The refugees, with nothing to do, needed no tempter to find reckless things for their idle tongues to say. One hoped that the rebels would swing for it; another wanted to see the blood streaming from the hearts of the leaders, but would be content to see them become turnspits in the kitchen of some English noble.[4] The aristocratic Tory, Madame Higginson, declared it would be a joy to her to ride through American blood to

---
[1] Frothingham, "Siege of Boston," p. 36.
[2] "The Remembrancer," I., 60.
[3] *Rivington's Gazette*, October 6, 1774.
[4] Trevelyan, "American Revolution," part I., p. 198.

the hubs of her chariot wheels.[1] These partizan amenities were soon noised abroad, and had no small part in creating the terrible breach in the social union which arrayed father against son, and brother against brother.

One night in September of 1774, letters were thrown into the camp of the British soldiers, addressed "to the officers and soldiers of his Majesty's troops at Boston." It anticipated that rebellion would soon cause the King's standard to be raised in Massachusetts, and suggested that the soldiers ought to be acquainted with the authors of the rebellion. The list[2] of the offenders was followed by an exhortation to the soldiers. "The friends of your king and country and of America hope and expect it from you soldiers that the instant rebellion happens, that you will put the above persons immediately to the sword, destroy their houses and plunder their effects. It is just that they should be the first victims to the mischief they have brought upon us."[3]

It is more than probable that this was the work and sentiment of a single individual, and did not represent the wish of any body of Tories; yet it was

---

[1] "New England History and General Register for 1872," p. 431.
[2] The list contained the names of Samuel Adams, James Bowdoin, Dr. T. Young, Dr. B. Church, Cap. J. Bradford, Josiah Quincy, Major N. Barber, Wm. Molineaux, John Hancock, Wm. Cooper, Dr. Chaney, Dr. Cooper, Thos. Cushing, Jos. Greenleaf, and Wm. Denning.
[3] *Rivington's Gazette*, September 8, 1774.

published in the newspapers and added venom to the Whig hatred of the King's friends. These sentimental excesses were not, it must be added, confined to the Tory party.

The impatience of the Loyalists with Gage's inactivity was mild as compared with that of the ministerial party in England. He was called a "lukewarm coward" and his ability more than doubted. The government declared Massachusetts in rebellion, closed all New England ports, and decided to increase the army at Boston to ten thousand men, superseding Gage by Howe. Meanwhile, Gage was sent positive orders to arrest Adams and Hancock, and the London papers promised that the "patriotic noddles of the Boston Saints" should soon decorate Temple Bar.

Gage's endeavor to accomplish the two objects, the destruction of the military stores at Concord, and the capture of Hancock and Adams at Lexington, resulted in the failure of both attempts, in an ignominious retreat into Boston and a loss of two hundred and seventy-three men, to say nothing of so arousing the country that, within a few days, sixteen thousand men were besieging the British army in Boston.

The events of Concord and Lexington sent rebellion irrevocably on its way. It also determined the fate of those Tories who by refraining from violent partizanship had escaped the previous persecutions. Now, even a suspected Tory was regarded as an enemy in the camp, and became intolerable. "We have had much work here of late," wrote a Massachusetts Whig, "a dark plot has been discovered of sending names down to General Gage."[1] It was a poor excuse for persecution, for Gage could not seize or imprison a "name," and he was not in position to seize their persons. The records of the committees of safety show a great activity in reckoning with the Tories. Some were sent to jail and closely confined, others signed a recantation or fled to avoid that humiliation. In the latter case, a hue and cry was sent after them.

Though these fugitives usually tried to reach Boston, yet there were stragglers who made their way to Nantucket where some remained during the war. Others fled to colonies where the fever of revolution was not yet so high as in New England. Nevertheless, their offence seemed to follow them. Samuel Curwen, who sailed for Philadelphia after he had refused to recant for signing an address, was there again solicited to sign a recantation. He became fearful lest, like Cain, he had some discouraging mark upon him or a strong feature of Toryism.[2]

If they escaped at all they had cause to rejoice. Letters soon followed them telling of insults and threats to the friends that remained.[3] Their private

---

[1] "The Remembrancer," I., 98.
[2] Curwen, "Journal and Letters," pp. 26, 27.
[3] "Letters of James Murray, Loyalist," pp. 176–178.

coaches were burned or pulled in pieces, loads of the rich importer's goods were attacked and destroyed or stolen, and his effigy hung up in a conspicuous place in sight of his house, during the day, to be burned or ignominiously treated at night. One had his riding horse, with saddle and bridle tarred and an image on its back, driven through town with an infamous figure pinned on the figure's breast. Others were frightened by finding incendiary letters which intimated terrible tortures for all loyalists.

Even the abandoned property of a Tory was not exempt from attack. A loyal woman wrote that on her estate "every beauty of art or nature, every elegance, which it cost years of care and toil in bringing to perfection, is laid low."[1] Complaints were frequent to the provincial committee of safety of the waste and destruction of the property of those who had left their homes in sundry towns of Massachusetts.[2] Those who staid to care for the property of refugee owners were in constant terror of attack. One wrote that the business of every evening was to see that the fire-arms were loaded and the lights properly placed in the store and house, and that this very care made them the more suspected.

The fear of Tory influence was so great that the post was stopped, the mails were broken open and

---

[1] "Letters of James Murray, Loyalist," p. 246.
[2] "American Archives," series 4, Vol. II., 1352.

their letters taken out. Gage complained that by those means the most "injurious and inflammatory accounts" of Lexington and Concord had been spread throughout the country, because only the Whig stories could circulate.[1]

Still, all this persecution and lawlessness was bloodless, and the wonder is that under the circumstances the people were so self-contained. There was no murderous rioting by mad and uncontrollable mobs, but everything was done, though sometimes roughly, as if with legal sanction. Even the destruction of Tory property was hardly more than happens to abandoned property in times of perfect peace. The preservation of a fair degree of social order seems to have been due to the continued stability of local government which was developed in America as nowhere else in the world, and which now remained when the power of the royal government was destroyed. A Massachusetts gentleman wrote to a friend in London:[2] "The state of this province is a great curiosity. Four hundred thousand people are in a state of nature and yet as still and peaceable as ever they were when government was in full vigor. We have neither legislators, nor magistrates, nor executive officers. We have no officers but the military ones. Of these we have a multitude chosen by the people and exercising them with more authority and spirit than ever

---

[1] "The Remembrancer," I., 101.
[2] Late in January, 1775.

any did who had commissions from a governor."[1] A Tory thought it astonishing that those who were in pursuit of liberty should suffer arbitrary power, "in such an hideous form and squalid hue," to get a footing among them.[2] The only way that Gage could account for their submission to that authority was that it was a tyranny which they had erected themselves.

It gave the Patriots a sense of relief to have made the plunge and to have the strain of apprehension removed. The result of Concord had approached so near a victory that they felt easier on the score of their own abilities. The great Tory pamphleteer had recently prophecied that nothing short of a miracle could gain them a single battle. He had reminded them that the British armies had "already reaped immortal honors in the iron harvest of the field." War was, he warned them, no longer a simple, but an intricate science only to be learned by long years of study.[3] In his last pamphlet he had closed with forebodings as terrible as the fateful vision of some ancient prophet: "May the God of our forefathers direct you in the way that leads to peace and happiness, before your feet stumble on the dark mountains — before the evil days come when you shall say, we have no pleasure in them."[4]

[1] "The Remembrancer," I., 58.
[2] "Massachusettensis," pp. 35, 36.
[3] *Ibid.*, April 3, 1775.
[4] *Ibid.*, April 3, 1775.

There was an earnestness in these solemn words that won attention even from the most violent advocates of revolution.

But it was no time for political precept. Events were moving with too much momentum, and the sword for the moment dominated the pen. The story of Concord was not a month old before the capture of Crown Point and Ticonderoga elated the Whig and withered the Tory hopes. Meanwhile, the second Continental Congress met and, with little delay, adopted the New England army, besieging Boston, as the "Continental Army," and with great wisdom chose Washington as commander-in-chief. He, more certainly than any other military man then fitted to lead, was the man to disappoint the cynical loyalist who thought that a title and a nabob's fortune would bring about a happy catastrophe in that political drama.[1] Before Washington could reach his army, it had scorned the proclamation of Gage, offering free pardon to all rebels who would lay down their arms, and had fought the battle of Bunker Hill.

The Tories in Boston had little part in that battle except giving information and advice, which, had it been heeded, would have saved the British army some of it bravest officers and men. Those with military training had advised that the attack be made in the rear, but were ignored by the English officers, who did not believe that the Americans

[1] "The Remembrancer," Part III., 46.

would fight. Gage, reconnoitering the American position with his glass, asked a Tory, "Who appears to be in command?" The Tory recognized Prescott. "Will he fight?" inquired Gage. "Yes sir," was the reply, "he is an old soldier, and will fight as long as a drop of blood remains in his veins!"[1] He knew his fellow countrymen better than did the blindly confident British.

Curwen, a refugee in England from Whig persecution, was outraged on hearing Englishmen speak of Americans as cowards and poltroons. He confided to his journal that he wanted those "conceited islanders to learn by some knock-down, irrefragable argument that, without regular standing armies, our continent can furnish brave soldiers and judicious, expert commanders."[2] Bunker Hill went a long way to furnish such an argument. There was some American pride in the most confirmed Tory heart as the returning British soldiers confessed that the rebels were not such a disorderly rabble as many supposed. All that night the chaises and chariots, which the loyalists had sent to the waterside to bring home the dead and wounded, filed slowly through the streets of Boston.[3]

At first, the metropolis had been a kind of sanctuary for the Massachusetts Tories. The fugitives had only to reach that and be at rest. Although

---

[1] Frothingham, "Siege of Boston," p. 126.
[2] Curwen, "Journal and Letters," p. 97.
[3] Trevelyan, "American Revolution," p. 337.

they were deprived of some of the comforts and luxuries, they wrote to outside friends, yet their being in a place of safety lessened the want of these conveniences. They wished that their friends, too, were out of reach of the "Tory hunters."[1] "If here, the King will give you provisions and pay you wages," wrote an anxious father to his son,[2] and he added, that at home a Tory would only be robbed by the rebels, who "are more savage and cruel than heathens or any other creatures, and, it is generally thought, than devils." To one who looked upon the outside world as made up of people of this description, Boston was little less than a paradise.

But, even before Bunker Hill, the scarcity of provisions had caused much distress. Gage had permitted people within the city to remove to the country with their valuable effects, and the Provincial Congress had resolved that those in the country who were inclined to enter Boston should be permitted. The removal from the city became so general as to alarm the Tories, who reasoned that none but Whigs would care to leave, and, when they were all gone, the town would be attacked and burnt.[3] Their spirited remonstrance resulted in gradual restrictions upon the freedom of departure. First the removal of merchandise was prohibited, then provisions and

[1] Frothingham, "Siege of Boston."
[2] Sabine, "American Loyalists," p. 322, Thos. Gilbert to his son.
[3] I have constructed this account from original material, chiefly manuscript quoted by Frothingham in his monograph, "The Siege of Boston," see pages 95, 97, 235, 277, 280, 312.

medicine, and finally even passes for persons were refused. Thus, with no provisions coming in and no people going out, the city of Boston was soon subjected to a somewhat lenten diet. Even the commander-in-chief exclaimed, according to the satirist, "Three weeks, ye Gods! nay, three long years it seems since roast beef I have touched, except in dreams."[1] A British officer, son of Lord Derby, vowed that he had not tasted meat twice since his arrival. The Tories, of course, fared no better than these eminent persons. We know in fact that salt pork or peas and an occasional meal of fish was gratefully partaken. An egg was a rarity. The distress in private families was extreme. In September, there was momentary relief upon the arrival of some ships with provisions, but the prophecy of the *Gazette*, that Boston that winter would be "the emporium of America for plenty and pleasure," proved a melancholy failure. In December, there were neither vegetables, flour nor pulse to be spared the inhabitants from the King's stores. "The distress of the troops and inhabitants in Boston is great beyond all possible description," wrote a witness.

The want of fuel was quite as pressing as that of food. The advance of winter could have been measured by the stages of demolition in Charlestown. All that was left, after the bombardment and fire on the day of Bunker Hill, went up the Tory chim-

[1] Trevelyan, "American Revolution," p. 350.

neys or warmed the British soldiers. This wreckage was followed by the garden fences and the doors and rafters of Boston houses. Old North Chapel and the steeples of West Church afforded no small supply, and the Whigs could have forgiven such profanation, but, when the old Liberty Tree was made to yield fourteen cords of wood, the Patriots hoped that the authors of the sacrilege might be warm enough in the hereafter.[1] In spite of all this fire-worship there was much suffering from the cold.

Lack of food and warmth so reduced the physical strength of the besieged that disease found them an easy prey. The mortality varied from ten to thirty each day, and the bells were not tolled for the dead, lest the mournful sound should discourage the living.[2] Amid all these vicissitudes nothing sustained the Loyalist but the pleasing sense of martyrdom to a worthy cause, and confidence in the ultimate triumph of the power of Great Britain.

Inactivity in the midst of such scenes would have been unbearable. As early as the day of Concord and Lexington, two hundred Tory merchants and traders sent their names and offered to arm as

---

[1] A tract entitled "Voyage to Boston" contains the lines referring to a soldier reported to have been killed while cutting down the tree. The Genius of the Shade marked him —

"to dine,
Where unsnuffed lamps burn low at Pluto's shrine."

[2] Marshall, "The Remembrancer," p. 38.

THE FIRST EXILES.   55

volunteers.[1] The offer was accepted, and they were enrolled under General Ruggles, and placed on duty. Later, the general orders of Howe, who had succeeded Gage, allude to three companies, called Loyal American Associators, who were to be distinguished by a white sash around the left arm. Some Irish merchants formed a company of Loyal Irish Volunteers, and a white cockade was their distinctive emblem. A company known as the Royal Fencible Americans was formed which received a gratuity and pay. Not content with the willing organization of the zealous Tories, Howe recommended late in October that the inhabitants associate themselves into companies, which were to be employed solely within the precincts of the town to preserve order and good government. They were to be allowed fuel and provision equal to the allowance of the troops. There was an implied threat that all would do well to obey the recommendation.

Besides this military employment, the inhabitants were busied in cleaning the streets and patrolling them at night. Prominent Tories were employed in taking a careful census of the city; one was appointed sole auctioneer, which kept him busy enough at a time when migration was the main business of society. Another was commissioned

[1] This account of Tory military organization has also been constructed from original material contained in Frothingham's "Siege of Boston," see pages 95, 253, 277, 279, 295.

to receive the goods of people who wished to leave them in trust.

Even amusements were not wanting to the beleagured town. An officer wrote home, "we had a theater, we had balls, and there is actually a subscription set on foot for a masquerade. England seems to have forgotten us, and we endeavored to forget ourselves."[1] Faneuil Hall was converted into a theater, and, one day in December, a Boston paper announced that a new farce was to be presented, called the "Blockade of Boston," to which a Whig paper retorted that they would more likely be presented a tragedy called "The Bombardment of Boston." Nor was that contingency so far removed.

On the night of the fourth of March, Dorchester Heights were fortified by the Americans. "Redoubts were raised," wrote an officer, "as if by the genii belonging to Alladin's wonderful lamp. Adieu balls and masquerades!"

A soldier of fortune might take thus coolly the necessity of evacuation, but "the last trump," as Washington wrote, "could not have struck the Tories with greater consternation." After all the blind faith that they had placed in Great Britain's grandeur and prowess, to see that prop withdrawn, and themselves left at the mercy of their enraged countrymen, was a terrible realization. "One or two have done," commented Washington, "what

[1] "The Remembrancer," Vol. II., 104.

a great number ought to have done long ago, committed suicide." With little commiseration, he added, "By all accounts there never existed a more miserable set of beings, than these wretched creatures now are."[1] There was but one consolation, as one of them expressed it, "neither Hell, Hull nor Halifax, can afford worse shelter than Boston." Acting upon this alliterative sentiment, most of them chose to commit themselves "to the mercy of the waves at a tempestuous season rather than meet their offended countrymen."[2]

When Howe began his hurried embarkation, the refugee inhabitants were permitted to go first. There were few transports, and orders were given to refugees to carry nothing but necessaries.[3] They, however, found means to employ the men belonging to the transports in embarking their merchandise as well; by which means, as a witness relates, several of the vessels were entirely filled with private property. It was an easy matter in the confusion, for "it was not like breaking up camp where every man knows his duty," but like "departing your country with your wives, your servants, and your household furniture."[3] "Nothing can be more diverting than to see the town in its present situation," wrote a Whig, "all is uproar and confusion; carts, trucks, wheelbarrows, handbarrows,

---

[1] Washington, "Letters," March 31, 1776.
[2] Frothingham, "Siege of Boston," p. 312.
[3] "The Remembrancer," Vol. II., 1c8.

coaches, chaises, are driving as if the very devil was after them."[1] The lawless, both soldiers and Tories, took advantage of the turmoil. Large quantities of the public stores were abandoned, while individuals carried away their plunder.

It was in a sad plight that the fleet at last sailed away under the protection of three men-of-war. Abigail Adams, looking out from Penn's Hill, reported it as the largest fleet ever seen in America. Upward of one hundred and seventy sail could be counted; they looked like a forest.[2] The transports were mostly small schooners, and on their top-heavy decks were huddled a wretched throng of soldiers and refugees. In Benjamin Hallowell's cabin "there were thirty-seven persons — men, women and children; servants, masters and mistresses; obliged to pig together on the floor, there being no berths."[3] It was impossible, thought one of them, that more events could concur to render their distress complete, and their ruin almost inevitable. They remembered that March was the most tempestuous month of the year on the American coast, and feared that without a miracle the wretched fleet must be dispersed and lost.[4] In spite of their misgivings, however, the crazy fleet

---

[1] "Memorial History of Boston," Vol. III., 164.
[2] *Ibid.*, Vol. III., 174.
[3] Quoted by Trevelyan, "American Revolution," p. 404
[4] "The Remembrancer," II., 108.

with its nine hundred and more[1] fugitive Loyalists arrived after six days on the Nova Scotia coast.

[1] A list of the refugees reveals that there were thirteen members of the Mandamus Council together with sixty-six members of their families, 37 custom house officers, 95 members of their families. There were 132 families and 92 single men. Fifteen merchants were noted. The significance of these figures will be noted elsewhere.

CHAPTER III.

THE INQUISITION.

However distressing the fortune of the Tories who had sailed away into political exile, at least it gave them freedom of opinion at the expense of physical discomfort. They were no longer subjected to the kind of apprehensions that had been their shame by day and their terror by night. Back in the rebellious colonies, the tide of persecution was still rising. To burn Tory pamphlets at the stake, or to tar and feather and nail them to a whipping post, had for a time contented the "Sons of Licentiousness," as Liberty's sons had come to be termed among the Loyalists. A wag would perhaps warn the author or printer to keep *himself* out of the fire, or remind him that the law of tar and feathers had not been repealed, but the person of the offender was in no immediate danger. To nail up the pulpit of a loyal minister, or to paint out the word *tea* on a Tory sign and burn the confiscated leaves in a public square, were only "foolish freaks of patriotic noddles." But, after the first battle with the British had been fought, the person of the Tory became as intolerable as his opinion.

To become the object of persecution, it was no longer necessary that an address or protest be signed or a pamphlet written or a violent sentiment uttered against the revolutionary movement. If the position or religious creed, or relationship of a person seemed in any way to indicate Tory sympathy, he must clearly and publicly demonstrate his allegiance to the popular cause. "Nothing will go down at present it seems," commented a Tory, "but measures truly inflammatory."[1]

Neglect or failure to meet the demands of the community resulted in a visit from the Sons of Liberty, whose rough horse-play got them denounced as "poor degenerate children," "accursed children to whom is reserved the blackness of darkness forever." "Poor Parson Peters," the author of this invective and one of their victims, escaped easily enough with his clothes and gown torn and a punch bowl broken while the mob was searching his house for firearms. His friends, however, were less reverently abused and two of them tarred and feathered.[2] Tarring and feathering was the favorite vice of the Whig mobs, but was varied in cases by hoisting the victim upon a liberty pole. A New York Tory gravely complained that he was hoisted upon the landlord's sign and there exposed in company with a dead catamount.[3] Another was put in the village pound and had herrings thrown over for

---

[1] *Rivington's Gazette*, November 17, 1774.
[2] Force's "Archives," series 4, Vol. I., 715-718.
[3] Sabine, "American Loyalists," p. 118.

him to eat. Such cases were, however, the whims and vagaries of persecution, while tar and feathers became the accepted antidote for Toryism in all the rebelling colonies.

The persecution of the Tories was not long left to those "mushrooms," as they were derisively called, those "exotics, styled the Sons of Liberty." As early as 1772, committees of correspondence had been organized throughout Massachusetts, and in the following year intercolonial committees were formed in the remaining colonies. These were at first used with great effect to secure unity of action. Adams exclaimed in admiration: "What an engine! France imitated it and produced a revolution."[1] Leonard, with Tory abhorrence, pronounced it the foulest, subtlest and most venomous serpent ever issued from the egg of sedition.[2]

As the activity of the Whigs increased, new committees were created with powers that made them an especial terror to the Tories. The birth of these committees is described by one who leaves us in no doubt as to his sympathies, yet whose picture has a likelihood that carries conviction. "Committees are appointed at county meetings," he writes, "where it is notorious not one fourth of the freeholders attend."[3] "The resolutions are drawn

[1] John Adams, "Letters," X., 197.
[2] "Massachusettensis."
[3] Rivington reports an instance where "three or four furious sons of liberty" took the occasion of a funeral for selecting twelve committee men.

up by some zealous partizan, perhaps by some fiery spirit ambitiously solicitous of forcing himself into public notice." . . . " The orator mounts the rostrum and in some preconceived speech, heightened no doubt with all the aggravations which the fertility of his genius can suggest, exerts all the power of elocution to heat his audience with that blaze of patriotism with which he conceives himself inspired.[1] . . . The threat of tyranny and the terror of slavery are artfully set before them; a measure need only be proposed to be resolved upon — a measure from which a little reflection would have made them retract with horror." The result, wrote another, is that the government of the country is completely committed to those who prevail with their tongues. It is cantoned out into new districts, and subjected to the jurisdiction of these committees, who, not only without any known law, but directly in the teeth of all law whatever, issue citations, sit in judgment, and inflict pains and penalties on all whom they are pleased to consider as delinquents.[2] In reply to the charge of illegality, the Whigs answered, that, as a matter of common sense, the legality of an action depended upon the approval of the majority of the community. They offered their new creed that the people ruled.

When the system of committees was entirely organized, there were committees of safety for the

---

[1] *Rivington's Gazette*, July 28, 1774.
[2] Boucher, "A View of the Revolution," pp. 319-321.

entire province and local committees with a jurisdiction bounded by the existing political divisions. Some were standing committees, and some had merely a passing or occasional existence. In Maryland, the provincial council of safety was the permanent executive committee of the provisional revolutionary government.[1] Sudden emergencies called for special committees, as was that appointed by the New York convention to look out for conspiracies against the people,[2] and that sent by the Connecticut assembly into the Tory section of the state to convene the dangerous persons and put them under guard.[3] There were committees to meet every loyal demonstration. Literally, "legions of senators infested the land." "From garrets, cellars, rushing through the street, the new-born statesmen in committee meet," the Tory[4] poet wrote with a sneer. There were wheels within wheels in this great revolutionary machine. Local committees looked to the state committee for advice, when doubtful cases arose, and received from it such orders as would make action in the state uniform; while both, in cases requiring interprovincial action, looked to the Continental Congress.

In respect to the Tories, the powers given the committees of safety had a great similarity, though

[1] "Archives of Maryland," 1777-1778, Journal and Correspondence of Committee of Safety.
[2] "Public Papers of Geo. Clinton," Vol. I., 360.
[3] "Public Records of the State of Connecticut," Vol. I., 27.
[4] "Loyalist Poetry," p. 2.

some states granted them more arbitrary power than others. The provincial congress of North Carolina conferred upon its committee the power to examine and commit persons accused on oath of practices inimical to America — that is, inimical to the revolutionary party. They were also to restrain persons trying to leave the colonies.[1] The highest executive power, that of pardon, was granted the Virginia committee of safety by the legislature of that state.[2] In time, these committees were made the instruments for enforcing the most arbitrary measures which were directed against the Tory party.

The powers were so absolute and the administration so despotic, that the Tories themselves were soon driven to take up the cry for liberty. "If I must be enslaved let it be by a king at least, and not by a parcel of upstart, lawless committee men," cried one. "If I must be devoured let me be devoured by the jaws of a lion, and not be gnawed to death by rats and vermin!"[3] He went on to picture the "pragmatical committee-men" coming into a house and examining the tea-canisters, and molasses jugs, and the petticoats of the wife and daughters, and, in his wrath, dared them to come to *his* home on such a domineering errand; but he judiciously neglected to give his real name or the whereabouts of his dwelling.

[1] "Col. Recs. of N. C.," Vol. X., 580.
[2] "Henning's Statutes at Large," Vol. IX., 101.
[3] Pamphlet by the "Westchester Farmer," "Free Thoughts," pp. 13–19.

The records kept by the committees of safety prove, beyond the possibility of doubt, the Tory charges that committee rule was despotic and tyrannous; but it was the despotism and tyranny of revolution. The freedom of speech was suppressed, the liberty of the press destroyed, the voice of truth silenced, and throughout the colonies there was established a lawless power,[1] if by that is meant a power not derived from the British government. A state of war existed between conservatism and radicalism, and either might be relied upon to use any weapon, political, diplomatic or physical, that was available and would secure success.

As compared with the committee-men of the French Revolution, these Whig committee-men were not bloody-minded. Alexander Graydon, who witnessed the persecution of the Loyalists, relates the mild treatment of one who shouted "God save great George our king," and remarks that, if "the spirit of seventy-five had in any degree resembled the spirit of Jacobinism to which it has been unjustly compared, this bravado would unquestionably have brought the offender to the lamp-post and set his head upon a pike."[2] The mere written recantation of a Tory usually cancelled the offences of opinion, though refusal brought upon

---

[1] Jos. Galloway, "A Candid Examination, etc.," pp. 1, 2. (Tyler, I., 875.)

[2] "Library of American Literature," Vol. III., 461. (A quotation from Graydon's "Memoires.")

the offender imprisonment or banishment, but very rarely, except in open warfare, the loss of life.

The activity of the committees soon drew upon them the most virulent hatred of the Loyalists. Governor Tryon, the great military leader of the Tories, wrote that, if he were in authority, he would burn every committee-man's house within his reach. He deemed them "the wretched instruments of the continued calamities" of the country, and offered twenty silver dollars for every acting committee-man who should be delivered up to the King's troops.[1] Nor was this the only instance of a bounty offered for these "political wolves." A reward of ten guineas was offered by General Campbell for every committee-man brought into any of the military posts.[2] Tryon thought that they would soon be torn to pieces by their own countrymen whom they had forcibly dragged to take up arms against their lawful sovereign.[1] As soon as Howe gained control of Long Island, Tryon took peculiar pleasure in recommending "that all committees meet as soon as possible for the purpose of revoking all their proceedings under Congress and dissolving their unlawful associations."[3] Those who had been active against the Tories were seized and placed in the prisons in New York. One of them was compelled to wear a coil of rope about his

---

[1] "New York Colonial Documents," Vol. VIII., 736.
[2] *Rivington's Gazette*, February 4, 1779.
[3] Onderdonk's "Revolutionary Incidents of Long Island," Vol. II., 60.

neck with the comfortable assurance that he was to be hung next day.[1]

The position of the "Tory committees," as they came to be known, was rarely enviable. If they persecuted vigorously they gained the bitterest hatred of the opposition, but if they gave a sign of leniency they were at once denounced by the Whigs as "timorous and inactive."[2] Sometimes they were even accused of being controlled by the Tories,[3] as they probably were in the communities where the Whigs were in the minority. In New York, and especially on Long Island, the course of a Whig committee-man never did run smoothly. At Jamaica,[4] ninety-one freeholders, out of one hundred and sixty in the township, signed a declaration that they never gave their consent toward choosing the local committee and utterly disapproved of such tyrannical proceedings. Had it not been for the aid of the neighboring militia, the Long Island committees would have found it impossible to carry out even the more important orders of the provincial and of the Continental Congress.

A discussion of the organization and powers and functions of the revolutionary committees has been

[1] Onderdonk's "Revolutionary Incidents of Long Island," Vol. I., 110.
[2] "Maryland Records; Journal of Committee of Safety," 1775-6, p. 347.
[3] Pamphlet, "Letter of J. Bartlett to Wm. Whipple, of New Hampshire, pp. 9, 67.
[4] Long Island.

necessary, because that political machinery acted directly in the work of controlling the Tory element in the community. The Continental Congress and the various provincial congresses issued general orders and passed comprehensive laws, but the execution was left to the committees, except in cases where armed opposition was to be met, or strenuous measures were to be executed. The various associations were vigorously propagated by the committee system, and that agency, more than any other, overcame the conservative opposition to independence. The story of Loyalist resistance to the associations and to the movement for independence will illustrate the power of the committees.

In October of 1774, the first Continental Congress determined upon an association, as a "speedy, effectual and peaceable measure" for obtaining a redress of their grievances.[1] The "Solemn League and Covenant," which originated in Boston, died in anticipation of this measure; because intercolonial association would be more effective. A sort of commercial declaration of independence with a punitive purpose was adopted. At an early date, throughout the colonies, the importation of all British goods was to cease, as was the importation of certain luxuries from any part of the world. The consumption of East India Company tea was at once forsworn, and the prohibition of all teas was delayed only for a few months. After the follow-

[1] "American Archives," 4th ser., Vol. I., 914, October 20, 1774.

ing September, if Parliament had not yielded, the exportation to Great Britain of any commodity whatever was to be prohibited.

Such measures were sure to be opposed by all thrifty merchants and traders who cared more for the solid advantages of trade than for political ideals. Colden, the Lieutenant Governor of New York, wrote that "the Non-Importation Association affected the smugglers as well as the fair-traders." The smugglers expected large quantities of Dutch tea, and insisted that it be exempt from the effect of the Association.[1] A powerful Tory writer, who signed himself the "Westchester Farmer," called non-importation and non-exportation a "vile, shameful, diabolical device," and demonstrated in a blunt, straightforward way that the farmers must go to the dogs, while the "proud merchants . . . riot in their ill-gotten gains." He pointed out that the distress would fall upon the American farmer long before it would fall upon the people of Great Britain. He asked pertinently, "why revenge ourselves upon them? They have done us no injury." Then, to illustrate how disproportionate the end to be gained was to the means taken to attain it, he demonstrated by ingenious calculation that "in order to pay this monstrous duty on tea which has raised all this confounded combustion in the country, (one has) only to sell

[1] "New York Historical Society," 1877, p. 373.

the produce of a bushel of flaxseed once in thirty-three years.¹

But there were other displeasing features in the "Association." It continued in a puritanical strain to discountenance horse-racing, gaming and plays, and "other expensive diversions and entertainments." None were to go into mourning-dress other than black crape or ribbon on the arm or hat of the gentleman, or a black ribbon and lace for ladies.² By this restriction the religion of some and the sentiments of many were antagonized. Finally, the venders of goods were to take no advantage of the scarcity of the forbidden articles but were to sell at the same rates as had prevailed during the past year. Here again the pocket of the merchant was touched. A false value was given to commodities, since their price was no longer regulated by economic law. A satisfied political sentiment was to be a part of the compensation that a merchant received for his goods.

The association was not to depend for success upon its own merits, but, in every county, city and town, a committee was to be chosen, whose business should be to observe the conduct of all persons touching the association. If a majority of the committee should be convinced that an individual had violated the association, that person's name should be published in the Gazettes. The associa-

---
¹ Quoted by Tyler, "Literary History of the American Revolution," Vol. I., 336-342.
² "American Archives," 4th ser., Vol. I., 915.

tors would break off all dealings with any person or colony that should violate or refuse to accede to the Association. To make sure that all should have a chance to sign it, several thousand copies of these and other resolves were printed and distributed over the colonies.[1] Many people had them elegantly printed, framed and glazed, hoping to perpetuate the resolves to their latest posterity.[2]

North and south, the resolutions were taken up and acted upon with zeal. The committees were organized, the association propagated, and its every resolve punctiliously enforced. Inspectors were chosen who were to watch those who should buy at the stores of non-associators. The moral reforms called for by the association were carried out as rigorously as the economic. Even the horse-races were stopped on the ground that "he only is a determined patriot who willingly sacrifices his pleasures upon the altar of freedom."[3] No tavern keeper could suffer balls or dances in his house if he wished to avoid the censure of the committees.[4] Recalcitrant persons were called before the committees, and, failing to explain their misconduct, were declared subjects of a universal boycott. Those who refused to sign were subjected to signal marks of contempt.[5] Yet, it was the avowed Tory who

[1] "American Archives," 4th series, Vol. I., 969.
[2] *Ibid.*
[3] "North Carolina Colonial Records," Vol. IX., 1091.
[4] *Ibid.*, Vol. IX., 1118.
[5] "New York Colonial Records," Vol. IX., 1102, 1152.

was especially attacked, for, after signing the Association, those whose political tents were indubitably Whig were rarely interfered with by committees. The Tory complained that merchants might advance prices with impunity, if only they were known to favor the revolutionary movement.[1] The effect of these coercive measures upon those who were opposed to the revolutionary principles was to make them feel that they were martyrs to a cause, and thus intensify the spirit of opposition.

Timothy Ruggles, who is described as a scholar, a wit and a misanthrope,[2] and whose political sympathies never were in doubt, at once proposed a counter association. The signers were to defend each other's life, liberty and property, and to support one another in the right to eat, drink, buy, sell, commune and act, what, with whom, and as they pleased, consistent with the laws of God and of the King. They refused to submit to the authority of Congress or committees or other unconstitutional assemblies of men. They would encourage and, if necessary, enforce obedience to the King. If all other means of security failed, they would have recourse to the natural law of retaliation.[3] It is to be remembered that Ruggles was a Mandamus Councillor, and had recently been driven from his home into Boston.

[1] "American Archives," Vol. II., 239.
[2] Sabine, "American Loyalists," p. 586.
[3] "Journals of each Provincial Congress of Massachusetts," p. 68.

As soon as the Tory Association became known, the Provincial Congress ordered the colonial committees to be on the lookout for such combinations, and, if any should be enticed to join, their names were to be published to the world, their persons treated with neglect and their memories transmitted to posterity with ignominy.[1]

Association, as a means of ascertaining political strength, was from this time employed alike by Loyalist and Patriot. But the greater zeal, or preponderance in mere numbers, or, whatever influence soon put all governmental power in the hands of the Patriots, gave to them also the mastery of the associating activity. A Patriot might sign an association before all the world. A Loyalist found it to his interest to sign in secret.

Ruggles' association became the model of similar associations formed elsewhere. Col. Thomas Gilbert, at the suggestion of General Gage, organized a band of three hundred Loyalists in Massachusetts; whereupon, the Whig assembly denounced him as "an inveterate enemy to his country, to reason, to justice and the common rights of mankind," and Gilbert's "banditti" were to be "cut off from the benefit of commerce with, or countenance of, any friend of virtue, America, or the human race."[2] Wherever the Loyalists attempted to organize, they were set upon with the same verbal fury, and the

[1] "Journals of each Provincial Congress of Massachusetts," p. 69.
[2] Sabine, "Loyalists," p. 322.

individual members exposed to the uncurbed rage of the mob.

In some parts of America, however, the numbers of the Loyalists gave them license. In Ulster County, New York, they defiantly erected the royal standard upon a mast seventy-five feet high. Inscribed upon it were sentiments testifying their unshaken loyalty and incorruptible fidelity to the best of kings. They emblazoned their attachment to the parent state and the British constitution. They abhorred the republican government, and "detested treasonable associations, seditious meetings and execrable mobs." At the hazard of their lives, they volunteered to maintain the just rights and constitutional liberties of free-born Englishmen, and to defend that "most excellent sovereign, George the Third."[1] In various loyal centers, from one end of America to the other, this courage and confidence in the strength of loyalty could be found. When Georgia's Sons of Liberty called for a meeting of deputies to accede to the Continental Association, five hundred men from three parishes protested. They dissented to any proceedings tending to express disloyalty to their "most gracious sovereign."[2]

Besides the Continental Association, whose chief object was retaliation by commercial restriction, there began, early in 1775, the organization, in the

[1] Sabine, "American Loyalists," p. 331.
[2] *Rivington's Gazette*, December 29, 1774.

several colonies, of associations of men pledged to promote opposition by arms to England's aggression.[1] In these associations the spirit of war appears for the first time. Their object was quite distinct from the associations whose object was commercial, but peaceful, retaliation. The people now bound themselves to defend their rights with their blood and treasure. The papers, on which men now placed themselves on record, were practically militia-rolls—promises to serve in a war for their liberties. These associations, too, were propagated by committees who presented the document for signature to all the inhabitants of the town or district, and rendered an account of all who declined to sign.[2] Indifference and neutrality were no longer tenable positions.

The Continental Congress early gave its approval to this action of the committees. It saw clearly that democracy must fight its battles, and that the people's aid must be actively solicited. June 26, 1775, the state of North Carolina was taken into consideration, and Congress resolved that, since the enemies of the liberties of America are pursuing measures to divide the good people of the colony of North Carolina and to defeat the American Association, . . . it be recommended to all in that colony, who wish well to the liberties of

---

[1] A good example of the type may be found in the "Archives of Maryland," Vol. XI., 66.

[2] "The Remembrancer," Vol. II., part I., 15.

America, to associate for the defense of American liberty." There was, at this time, more respect for Congress than at a later period, and the recommendation increased the proselyting zeal.

The drawing up of this defensive association was usually the work of a committee. Well-worded and effective documents were often adopted by all the committees in a county or section, though in different colonies they varied in expression as widely as the minds of men vary. The general tenor, however, was that the subscribers, inhabitants of such a county or town, feeling themselves bound by the most sacred of all obligations, the duty of good citizenship toward an injured country, associated as a band in her defence against every foe. They invoked the ties of religion and honor to hold them faithful. The measures of Congress and their provincial assemblies should be executed. They saw the dangers of anarchy in the dissolution of the powers of government, and they gave to their committees the preservation of peace and good order. The obligation of their bond held until there should be a full reconciliation. The document closed with the bald statement of their political intolerance: "We will hold all those persons inimical to the liberties of the colonies who shall refuse to subscribe this association." It was the proclamation of a civil war.

The defensive association was no passive instrument to be laid upon a table, where he who pleased might sign. Like the Koran, it was to be propagated with the sword. The letters and records of the time contain many tales of the aggressive methods of committee-men. "Being duly sworn upon the Holy Evangelists of Almighty God," as the quaint phrase ran, the indignant victims of party rage told the British officers their grievances.

The ordinary experience will better serve the purpose of conservative illustration than the more extreme cases. Three men took a North Carolina planter into custody and carried him by force "before several persons who called themselves committee-men." He was confined two days and two nights. They read over several papers, and endeavored to persuade him to join with them. He did not concur with their measures, and refused to answer their questions. He was discharged, and on his way home stopped at a house to sleep. After dark, five unknown men seized him, and in a violent manner carried him into the woods. They said that they intended to treat him as an enemy to the country, and ordered him to strip. He removed his coat, and they began to tie him. After much threatening, however, he was released. But, go where he would, there was no peace, for every man's hand was against him. One taunted him that Lord North was a Catholic, and another informed him that the king's crown tottered upon his shoulders. In desperation he fled for refuge to the governor's ship in Charleston harbor.

Insult and threat met a non-associator at every turn. One day he was, perhaps, set upon a cake of ice to cool his loyalty,[1] and then was informed that a certain famous liberty-man had sworn to be his butcher. Next he was told that he might expect a "san benito" of tar and feathers, and even an "Auto Da Fe." The committees sent Patriot newspapers and other propaganda to the wavering or obstinate, but seldom failed to follow this system of conversion with a personal interview if the literature failed. When the political sentiment of a whole community was in doubt, special committees, or in some cases clergymen of Whig views, were appointed to confer with the inhabitants upon the subject of American freedom.

Committee control of the Tory opposition was only possible where the dominant party was Whig. More drastic measures were taken where a loyal city or community was to be coerced. Governor Martin, from his safe retreat in Fort Johnson, North Carolina, wrote the Earl of Dartmouth that at Wilmington "there was a noble and honest dormant spirit nurtured" among the Scotch merchants, but a certain Colonel Ashe appeared there at the head of a body of between four and five hundred men, menacing the people with military execution if they did not immediately subscribe an association dictated by the committee. When this bumptious Colonel was asked his authority for such arbitrary

[1] Moore's "Diary," Vol. I., 359.

proceedings, he only pointed to the men he had assembled. "They were obliged to sign," the Governor added bitterly, "what their consciences revolted at and abhorred."

Governor Martin had issued an impotent proclamation against these "sundry ill-disposed persons" who industriously propagated "false, seditious and scandalous reports" derogatory to the king and court. Upon the pretense of apprehensions of intestine insurrection, he asserted, they got the people to subscribe papers promising to form armed companies and submit to committees. The "incendiaries" resorted to the deceit and artifice of urging the people to support his Majesty against the evil designs of Parliament. They threatened unwilling individuals with tarring and feathering, and menaced even with death. Their "deluded followers" were promised the lands and properties of the recalcitrants.[1] People were obliged, the governor said, to frequent meetings in arms, by the usurped authority of committees. To all this his obedient Tory council said amen, and testified that the governor had done all in his power to preserve order.[2]

In reply to the governor, the Whig committee at Wilmington denied that force had been used to propagate the association, and denounced the governor as an enemy to the happiness of the colony and the

---

[1] "Colonial Records of North Carolina," Vol. X., 16, 17.
[2] *Ibid.*, Vol. X., 38.

freedom of America.[1] Whether the committee intended that force should be used we can not know, but it is sure that something very akin to it ensured the success of the association. Nor were the arts of the demagogue wanting to the committee-men, for their rhetoric left an impression upon the minds of the people that the British ministers were "like so many master-devils in the infernal regions, sending out their servant furies to torment wherever . . . their infernal vengeance should fall."[2]

The very desperation of the Whig cause made it successful. If they were to do anything, they must organize, and be on the alert, as they were, even to carrying arms to meeting on the Sabbath.[3] The Tories were too prone to wait the chastening hand of Great Britain. Where they could overcome their fatal tendency to rely upon the British government, however, they formed associations of their own or protested against the Whig combinations. The extant records of the Whig committees show that they often seized the Tory leaders and investigated their proceedings.

A North Carolina Tory leader encouraged his friends with the assurance that fifty thousand Russians had been hired by the King to subdue America. To aid these hypothetical myrmidons he tried to organize a company of militia. He was seized by

---

[1] "Colonial Records of North Carolina," Vol. X., June 20, 1775.
[2] *Ibid.*, Vol. X., 123.
[3] "American Archives," series 4, Vol. II., 1419.

the nearest committee, and, after examination, was censured as a seditious incendiary who was as destitute of property and influence as he was of principle. The friends of liberty were to avoid all intercourse with him, because he had traitorously endeavored to make himself conspicuous in favor of tyranny and oppression.[1]

Similar abortive attempts are recorded in the journals of other colonial committees. The Maryland Council of Safety displayed little activity in controlling Tory sentiment during the first year of the struggle; but, in November of 1775, when the Maryland Loyalists attempted to associate and give aid to Lord Dunmore, who was making every endeavor to save Virginia for the King, they were aroused to an active investigation of the attempted organization.

An examination of the state of affairs in that province reveals the fact that they began none too soon their tardy preventative measures. Hugh Kelly, of Maryland, testified and produced proof, before the British Commission for inquiring into the Loyalists' claims, that he had associated one thousand nine hundred men capable of bearing arms. He said that, "in 1775, when the Rebels were associating," he instituted a secret mode of organizing the friends of the British government. He "circulated writings to be signed by the people."

[1] "Records of North Carolina," Vol. X., July 7, 1775. Proceedings of the Committee at Wilmington.

But the necessity of doing all this in the dark, the fear of the established power, and the vigor of the Whig persecution rendered these efforts ineffectual. In the biting satire of a parodist, "thus dread of want makes rebels of us all; and thus the native hue of Loyalty is sicklied over with a pale cast of *trimming.*"

The depositions of the witnesses examined by the Maryland Council reveal the secret methods of association to which the Loyalists were obliged to resort.[1] The leader visited the man-of-war, whither Lord Dunmore had betaken himself, and arranged for some powder and shot to be sent ashore and divided among certain faithful Tories who were to be assembled. He then returned home and quietly called upon those friends of the King in whom he could trust. They were called from their houses by a silent beck or a significant touch on the arm, and, while walking in the recesses of the forest, the plot was unfolded. Imprecations were heaped upon the members of Congress, and the opinion passed that there would be no peace until their heads were off. If the friend joined heartily in these sentiments, he was at once admitted to full confidence. A paper was signed and an oath of secrecy administered. The signers were soon called to meet for instruction in military exercise. Here the association was read

---

[1] "Maryland Archives," Vol. XII., 369-383.

in the presence of all, when, as the story runs, they pulled off their hats and hurrahed for the king. One who said amen and hurrahed, but neglected to pull off his hat, was suspected as a spy. He was threatened with a broadaxe, and was warned that he would be brained if he signed the Continental association. Some seventy subscribers agreed not to go to Boston nor to let others go, and, if summoned by the committee, would aid each other in resisting the summons. Fifty armed men were selected to guard the home of the leader against the committee. When the summons came, he refused to obey.

But this Tory opposition was not merely negative, for this band had a plan to capture the members of the Worcester County Committee while asleep in their beds, and hurry them away to Lord Dunmore. This plot failed, but some doubtful Whigs were allured from home in quest of salt, and then seized, placed upon a tender under the hatches, and taken on board the man-of-war. They were there urged to enlist under Lord Dunmore, and promised a guinea and a crown in addition to their pay.[1] This offer failed in most cases to attract them. The whole enterprise failed, in fact, and the leader was seized and brought to trial.

The loyal associations did not always meet annihilation at the comparatively gentle hands of the civil authorities. Their fate was often that of a Sussex, N. J., association, whose destruction was

[1] "Archives of Maryland," Vol. XII., 369-383.

reported in "Holt's Journal." "This morning about four hundred of the militia assembled at Newton, and from thence proceeded in good order and regularity, in quest of Tories, a considerable number of whom had entered into a combination and agreement not to comply with any Congress measures. We hear about forty are taken, most of whom have recanted, signed the association and profess themselves true sons of liberty, being fully convinced of their error."

In this way, all the early attempts of the Loyalists, not supported by the British army, came to naught, either from lack of intercolonial organization, or on account of a fatal delay, which gave the Whigs strength to overcome the tardy efforts. In some of the colonies, indeed, not even an effort seems to have been made to organize the conservative forces. The Tory leader, Joseph Galloway, who was acquainted with the situation in Pennsylvania, if any one was, testified during his examination before the House of Commons that he never heard of associations to oppose the Whigs in any part of Pennsylvania.[1] This statement, added to the fact that Pennsylvania was one of the states that contained the largest number of Loyalists, goes to show that the Tory party lacked vigorous leaders, and that the members often had not the courage of their convictions. Under the fostering

[1] Galloway's "Examination," *Rivington's Gazette*, November 16, 1779.

care of the British army of occupation they organized a formidable association at Boston, and later, under similar circumstances, we shall find active loyal organizations at Newport, Philadelphia and New York City.

CHAPTER IV.

THE DOWNFALL OF THE OLD FAITH.

THE policy of the Tories, if they may be said to have had any policy, seems always to have been a negative one. Instead of taking part in the colonial politics, they withdrew, in many cases, and looked frowningly on while rebellion advanced by leaps and bounds. The more influential disdained to enter into controversy with the "noisy, blustering and bellowing patriots."[1] By such conduct they failed, except in one or two colonies, to make their influence felt against the assembling of delegates to the Continental Congress. The arch-Tory of them all, Galloway, who spoke the truth when he knew it, or when it was not obscured from him by passion, testified upon oath, that in the election of delegates very small proportions of the people turned out to vote. Only the more violent, he asserted, took part in the elections which determined the appointment of the delegates. "In one place two men met, and one appointed the other, delegate to Congress." In many districts a decimal part and in some not an hundredth part of the

[1] "American Archives," series 4, Vol. II., 240.

voters was present.[1] Governor Martin, of North Carolina, wrote Dartmouth that ten of the thirty-four counties[2] of that state sent no representatives to the convention called for the purpose of appointing delegates to the second Continental Congress. In some of the represented districts, committees of ten or twelve men took it upon themselves to name the representatives. In others they were not chosen by a twentieth part of the people, "notwithstanding every act of persuasion was employed by the demagogues upon the occasion." In Georgia, the Loyalist influence was so strong that only five out of twelve parishes sent deputies to a provincial congress, which met for the purpose of appointing delegates to the Continental Congress. Notwithstanding the fact that they represented a minority in the province, they elected delegates who, from fear or modesty, refused to serve, and sent a letter of explanation to Congress.[3] Likewise, in New York, the Loyalists were more active, and, in some districts upon Long Island, the records show heavy majorities against sending representatives to a provincial congress which was to appoint the delegates to the Continental Congress.[4] In spite of majorities

[1] *Rivington's Gazette*, November 6, 1778, Report of Galloway's "Examination."
[2] "Records of North Carolina," Vol. IX., 1042. (The records of the convention show that eight of the forty-four districts failed to send delegates.)
[3] "American Archives," series 4, Vol. II., 279. (Only the parish of St. John was represented finally.)
[4] "Revolutionary Incidents of Long Island," Onderdonk, pp. 16, 22-28, 39, 40.

against the measure, delegates were sent by small bodies of patriots who relied upon outside support.[1] Lieutenant Governor Colden asserted that in Queens County not six persons had met for the purpose of choosing delegates for Congress.[2] In New York city, a desperate attempt was made to arouse the conservative forces against the new Congress. "A Citizen" exhorted all friends of government to let neither indolence nor any other consideration deter them from stopping the mischief that was coming swiftly upon them. They were urged not to suffer "this maddest freak of rampant republicanism to take place — the appointment of a Provincial Congress." "Crush this accursed cockatrice whilst it is in embryo," he cried, "if you permit it to grow up to maturity it will sting you to death."[3] Neither the commercial interests of New York, which gave the Loyalists strength, nor the unusual efforts against the Whig policy prevented the provincial congress or the appointing of delegates to the Continental Congress. The New York members, however, felt the restraint which minority representatives cannot evade.

In failing to prevent the Continental Congress, the Tories had lost their last political opportunity. When Democracy and Union had once created a regulating body like Congress, they were sure to be led far afield by their creation. The audacity of the

[1] "Revolutionary Incidents of Long Island," Onderdonk, p. 26.
[2] *Ibid.*, Onderdonk, p. 16.
[3] "American Archives," series 4, Vol. II., 46.

second Continental Congress will ever be a matter of wonder. Without unity in instruction, with no power to form a government, without jurisdiction over an acre of territory, with no authority to administer government in an acre if they had it, with no money, no laws and no means to execute them, they entered upon the task of regulating a society in the state of revolution. Had the Congress declared to the colonists, wrote a Tory, "that they were the children of the sun, sent by their beneficent parent to instruct and reclaim them," as Manco Capac and Mama Ocollo declared to the Peruvians, they would have claimed nothing fabulous in the minds of the Whigs.[1] The patriots thought every man in a " state of reprobation beyond the power of heavenly mercy to forgive, who was not willing to meet death rather than concede a tittle of the Congress' Creed."[2] There was something more than jingle in the song of the Jamaica minute men,

> "We have some noble Congressmen
> Elected for our nurses,
> And every jolly farmer will
> Assist 'em with their purses." [3]

The elected Congress, which by mere virtue of existence was enabled to direct a rebellion against British authority, became the head and front of the

[1] *Rivington's Gazette*, June 30, 1779.
[2] "North Carolina Colonial Records," IX., 1280. (Wm. Hooper, a member of the Continental Congress, to Samuel Johnson.)
[3] "Revolutionary Incidents of Long Island," Onderdonk, p. 37.

Whig offense. Nothing was left to the Tories but impotent vilification and denunciation. Every Congressman was a "lean and grinning Cassius" and an "independent incendiary."[1] The "Westchester Farmer" described Congress as a law-making body unknown to the law or to the constitution of the country; its members had no real claim to represent the government or the people of their several provinces; in many cases their election was a sham, in all cases invalid; the doctrines they had put forth were unsound, misleading, dangerous, from beginning to end; the measures they had undertaken to force upon the people were without authority, were tyrannical and would bring on unspeakable calamity.[2] The Tories liked to think that this baleful conduct of Congress was due to its irresponsibility, and that it consisted of obscure, pettifogging attorneys, bankrupt shop-keepers and outlawed smugglers.[3] Political significance was given to the scriptural promise that the lowly shall be exalted. The mushroom growth of political fortunes was thus satirized by a rhyming Loyalist:

> "Down at night a bricklayer or carpenter lies,
> Next sun a Lycurgus, a Solon doth rise."[4]

[1] "American Archives," series 4, Vol. II., 240.
[2] Quoted by Tyler, "Literary History of American Revolution," I., 343.
[3] *Rivington's Gazette*, May 23, 1778.
[4] Moore's "Diary," II., 22.

This sudden appearance of democracy as the dominant class gave the Tory aristocrats a political shock which went on vibrating through all the loyal literature of the time.

Success in the organization of the committees and the associations and two successive congresses had given the revolutionary party courage for the final measure, a formal declaration of their independence. Mere political momentum tended to bring about a successful issue. The opposition would, it is true, gain some adherents from the timid ones, who feared that they had gone too far; but, on the other hand, the idea of independence flattered the people, as the great Tory pamphleteer confessed, while the Tory plan supposed a degree of subordination which was rather a humiliating idea.[1] The existing unsettled condition was feared even by the most ardent Whigs. Every measure for opposing the Tories and Great Britain became, of necessity, a kind of evasion of the actual state of affairs, because they were pretending allegiance while acting independently. John Adams complained that all the powers of government were left in the hands of assemblies, conventions and committees, which composed a scene of much confusion and injustice. He dreaded the continuance of this, as tending to injure the morals of the people, and to destroy their habit of order and attachment to regular government.[2]

[1] *Rivington's Gazette*, December 29, 1774, "Massachusettensis."
[2] J. Adams, "Works," Vol. III., 34.

In 1768, Samuel Adams probably stood alone in the belief that America must become independent. Many of the leading patriots had not come that far on the rebellious road, as late as 1775. Washington was not sure that the war was to be one of independence even when he took command at Cambridge. Jefferson denied that armies had been raised with the desire of separation from England. Resistance to arbitrary misgovernment and disaffection to Great Britain were entirely different matters. Loyalists had, indeed, warned the colonists against gilding over the resolves against Parliament with professions of loyalty to the king. "The golden leaf is too thin to conceal the treason," sneered Massachusettensis.[1] But the Whigs were more sincere than the Tories would believe. Franklin would willingly have pledged his private fortune to compensate the East India Company for their loss at the Boston Tea Party. In fact the responsible statesmen of America were slow to advocate the doctrine of independence, until obscure song writers and newspaper humorists had for many months set the idea buzzing in the minds of discontented men.[2]

In July of 1775, Massachusetts formed the first government in which the king's authority was dis-

---

[1] Tyler, "Literary History of American Revolution," I., 257.

[2] It is not in the province of this work to tell the full history of the gradual and reluctant consent of the colonies to a declaration of independence. The opposition of the Loyalists is alone the proper theme. Only a rapid summary of the other facts is fitting in this place.

allowed.[1] A proclamation, enjoining all to obey the new government, closed with an invocation, "God save the people," instead of the "God save the king" which alone a Loyalist could recognize. Meanwhile, in Congress, Samuel Adams urged that to declare the colonies independent would simply be to recognize a fact. Dickinson, of Pennsylvania, opposed, urging that Congress must have instructions from each colony. This view prevailed, and Richard Penn, an undoubted Tory, was sent with a petition to their "Most gracious sovereign" George III. This the king refused to receive, declared the colonies in rebellion, and called on his loyal subjects to aid in their subjection. He then tried to hire twenty thousand Russian troops, but the Empress Catharine refused him. Some petty German princes, however, supplied his demand for mercenary troops, and this success dealt one of the heaviest blows to the hopes of the king's friends in America. They made sorry work trying to picture George III. as a "benign Augustus," when confronted with this seeming proof that he was an "implacable Nero." Nor did Parliament give them any aid, for it supported the action of the king and declared that Americans had forfeited their lives and fortunes to the justice of the state. The kind-hearted Dartmouth was succeeded by the truculent Lord Germain. Every measure tended to strengthen the

---

[1] The facts in this account, except where special reference is given, are taken from Fiske's "American Revolution."

hands of the Whig and render the Tory more impotent than ever. In October of 1775, the British burned Falmouth, leaving its people without cover at the mercy of a Maine winter. That outrage and the news of the German "myrmidons" reached Congress at the same time. Tory counsels were brushed aside. New Hampshire, Virginia and South Carolina were advised to frame their own governments.[1] South Carolina was to seize British vessels found in its waters. Congressional committees were organized to correspond with foreign powers.

Only a short time before, a delegate had said with horror, that he had heard of persons in America who wished to break off with Great Britain, and "a proposal had been made to apply to France and Spain." He threatened to inform his constituents, and added, "I apprehend the man who should propose it would be torn to pieces like De Witt."[2] There appeared, soon after this, Paine's "Common Sense" to reinforce the logic of the hiring of the mercenaries. And, as if the over-matched Loyalists had not odds enough in argument already, Parliament again came to the aid of those who wanted reasons for independence. It passed an act

[1] See "Journals of Congress," Vol. I., 215, 219. It is to be noticed that Congress recognized the necessity of enlisting the *democracy* in its cause, for they recommended a *full* and *free* representation of the people—a method of election unknown in any of the colonies before.

[2] J. Adams, "Works," Vol. II., 458.

to close American ports, and authorized the confiscation of American ships, and the impressment of American seamen. Congress retorted by throwing open American ports to all nations, and recommended the disarmament of all Tories who refused to aid in the common defense. Still they continued "to hobble along under a fatal attachment to Great Britain."

North Carolina, where the King had looked with confidence for adherents, took the first decisive action for independence. The very loyalty of the back country forced the issue at an early date. In May of 1775, the royal governor received addresses signed by 1,500 men from the central and western counties of the state.[1] The Scotch Highlanders, who had settled the uplands of North Carolina and Georgia, were not in sympathy with the revolutionary movement. After negotiating with Governor Martin, and learning that Sir Henry Clinton with 2,000 troops and Sir Peter Parker with seven regiments and ten ships of war were coming to the aid of the loyal subjects, Donald McDonald, a leader among the Highlanders, issued a manifesto. He reassured the faithful and invited them to repair to His Majesty's Royal standard erected at Cross Creek. "Those," he continued, "who have been under the unhappy necessity of submitting to the mandates of Congress and Committees — those lawless, usurped and arbitrary tribunals — will have an

[1] "North Carolina Records," Vol. IX., 1256.

opportunity to restore peace and tranquility to this distracted land — to open again the glorious streams of commerce — to partake of the blessings inseparable from a regular administration of justice and to be again reinstated in the favorable opinion of their sovereign."[1] The efforts of McDonald and some twenty-five others with local influence, who were commissioned by Governor Martin,[2] succeeded in raising some 1,600 men. This little army of Loyalists started for the coast; but, at Moore's Creek bridge, were met and defeated by Richard Caswell with about one thousand minute men and militia. The moral effect was immense. Within ten days an army of 10,000 militia stood ready to repulse Clinton, and Tory influence was temporarily eliminated from the field of politics. A provincial congress was assembled, which at once instructed the North Carolina delegates to concur in a declaration of independence and in measures for making foreign alliances.

The situation in Georgia was unfavorable to revolution. In addition to the fact that the colony was annually receiving pecuniary aid from the British Parliament,[3] the inhabitants were in constant danger from the attacks of the Creek Indians, and felt that their hands were full. The Tory party, under the leadership of the prudent Governor Wright, had prevented the sending of any delegate to the first

[1] "North Carolina Records," Vol. X., 429.
[2] *Ibid.*, Vol. X., 441.
[3] *Rivington's Gazette*, October 13, 1774.

congress, and but one, locally chosen, was sent to the second. Then, the British made the mistake of sending a threatening squadron to Savannah. The insult ruined the work of Wright; the Whigs seized the governor and such of the crown officers as had not fled, and at once, in February of 1776, assembled a provincial congress. This body instructed its delegates to "concur in all measures calculated for the common good."

South Carolina had been in a condition resembling its northern neighbor. Whigs predominated along the seaboard, but the farmers and herdsmen of the interior had Tory sympathies. Campbell, the royal governor, made the most of this, and sent his agents, not only to arouse the Tories of the western counties, but to enlist the aid of the Indians. The latter attempt came to little, except to make England hated the more. After Campbell's escape to a British man-of-war, control of the colony fell for the time into Whig hands. They, under the lead of Rutledge, repulsed the British attack on Charleston, enforcing the logic of Washington's victory at Boston. After framing a new government, they instructed their delegates in practically the same phrase as Georgia.

In Virginia there had been a very even balance of forces, but the action of the governor gradually estranged the loyal people of the colony. He first threatened, and then freed by proclamation all the negroes and indented servants who should enlist to reduce the colony to subjection. No heed was paid to the proclamation. In November of 1775, he had built a fort where, with the aid of some loyal Scottish merchants, he hoped to defend Norfolk. The Patriots defeated the loyal band, and forced Lord Dunmore and the Scottish merchants of Norfolk to take refuge on board ships in the harbor. There, with their families, they were huddled in cheerless cabins, without food or warmth.[1] Hoping to relieve their wants, Lord Dunmore sent a flag of truce to Norfolk and asked for fresh provisions, which were refused. Then, acting upon the royal instructions in regard to a town in actual rebellion, Lord Dunmore ordered the town to be burnt. This was done in such a relentless manner that Virginia now had as good a reason as Massachusetts for wishing independence. In the following May, a convention favorable to independence instructed Virginia's delegates to that end, and voted to establish a new government for the commonwealth.

In the same month, Rhode Island omitted the king's name from the public documents, and, as to the relations with England, concurred with the measures of Congress.[2] Massachusetts took occasion, during the May town-meeting, to vote the support of the colony to a declaration of independence by Congress. The future status of the avowed

---

[1] Bancroft, "United States," Vol. IV., 320.
[2] "Rhode Island Colonial Records," Vol. VII., 522–526.

Tory was significantly stated in the instructions sent to the Massachusetts delegates by the Boston town-meeting. "For prayers of peace (the king) has tendered the sword; for liberty, chains; for safety, death. *Loyalty to him is now treason to our country.*" Here was the keynote to the whole future treatment of the Tory by the Whig. The Tory was no longer regarded as a political opponent to be coerced, but as a traitor deserving retributive justice.

Meanwhile, in Congress, a resolution[1] was adopted which, with its preamble, practically settled the whole matter. The preamble declared that the American people could no longer conscientiously take oath to support any government under the crown of Great Britain. All such governments should be totally suppressed. The resolution then recommended that all colonies form independent governments for themselves. Nearly a month passed before another step was taken, and then Richard Henry Lee offered his resolution for declaring the United Colonies free and independent States. John Adams seconded the motion. It was resisted by the most powerful representatives of New York and Pennsylvania, on the ground that the middle colonies were not ready for such a measure. Finally, to maintain harmony, a postponement of the question for three weeks was voted.

[1] "Journals of Congress," May, 15, 1776; Preamble, May 10, Resolve.

During these weeks of grace, the work of conversion went on rapidly. Connecticut, like Rhode Island, had no need of a new government, and had only to omit the King's name from her public documents. This and the instruction of her delegates for independence was done in the middle of the month of June. On the following day, New Hampshire declared for independence and established a new government. In New Jersey there was a strong loyal party supporting the Tory governor, Franklin.[1] Under his influence the assembly had, only recently, instructed the delegates against independence and had resolved to send a petition to the King. A committee sent by Congress coerced the Assembly, which yielded, and was at once prorogued by the governor. The revolutionary faction now gained control, arrested Governor Franklin and sent him to Connecticut for safe-keeping.[2] Within a week, the Whigs organized a new government and instructed their delegates for independence.

Meanwhile, in Pennsylvania, Maryland and New York, the political campaign became daily more active and more uncertain in its result. John Adams asserted, many years later, that "New York and Pennsylvania were so nearly divided—if indeed their propensity was not against independence—that, if New England on the one side and Virginia on the other had not kept them in awe, they would

---

[1] Son of Benjamin Franklin.
[2] June 16, 1776.

have joined the British."[1] Timothy Pickering called Pennsylvania "the enemy's country,"[2] and the philosopher, Curwen, thought that the Quakers and Dutchmen had too great regard for ease and property to sacrifice either on the altar of an unknown goddess of rather doubtful divinity.[3] In that colony there is no doubt that the proprietary government was able to wield a powerful opposition. They were reinforced by the Quakers who wished to avoid war on any terms. In convention[4] they denounced the putting down of kings and governments, asserting that such action was God's prerogative and not men's. They proclaimed an abhorrence of measures tending to independence. This gentle and peaceable disapproval, enforced by the conservatism of the Pennsylvania Germans, delayed favorable action by that colony, until the mass meeting at the state house, in the middle of May, denounced the act of the assembly which had instructed its delegates in Congress to oppose independence. This event simply meant that the party favorable to independence, failing to control the legally elected assembly, had now resorted to an extra-legal means to defeat the evident wish of the legal majority.[5]

[1] John Adams, "Works," Vol. X., 63.
[2] It is to be remembered, however, both were New England men.
[3] Curwen's "Journal," p. 26.
[4] Fiske, "American Revolution," Vol. I., 186.
[5] However, as Mr. Lincoln has shown in his "Revolutionary Movement in Pennsylvania," this majority was only of the limited number to whom the suffrage had been jealously restricted. Now the people at large were appealed to.

Then, while the Tories were cowed by a reign of terror, the Whigs called a convention to which delegates were elected favorable to independence. Late in June this convention falteringly pledged the colony to that measure.

The popularity of Robert Eden, the Governor of Maryland,[1] and the immunity from British insult which that colony had enjoyed, gave the Tory party great strength. Nothing but the active campaign carried on by Samuel Chase and Charles Carroll in every county won that colony to the side of independence. When that decision became evident, Eden, alone of all the royal governors, departed in peace, and the Maryland delegates were instructed to agree to independence. Twelve colonies[2] now stood pledged to separation from Great Britain.

New York, the stronghold of Toryism in America, could not be brought into line. As a commercial state, with only one seaport, it had every reason to hesitate. The British army was on its way to attack and seize the port, and the probability was very small of a successful defense by Washington's "rotten regiments of rag fair," as the Tories called his provincials. The course of events there will receive attention in the following chapter. Here it is sufficient to note that the twelve colonies

[1] "Maryland Archives," Journals and Correspondence of Committee of Safety, 1775-6, pp. 334, 338, 355, 357.
[2] Delaware had acquiesced June 14, 1776.

agreed unanimously on July 2, to a declaration of their independence of Great Britain, and on July 9th their resolution was formally adopted by New York.

With the final decision of this momentous question the position of the Tory in America was wholly changed. He was no longer a mere political opponent of the Whig. Little as he had been tolerated during the great political struggle for supremacy, and scornfully as his arguments and cautions and threats had been treated, he was at least recognized as an opponent with possible rights. Henceforth every Tory was an enemy in camp, a suspected traitor and a wretch to be charged with all the ills of the state. He was accused of enjoying the protection of the new state without giving it support in return.

From the Tory's own point of view, also, his position was changed. He no longer argued against the measures of the Whigs, with a hope of preventing, but became a fault-finder, a prophet of evil, and a railer against independence. As the Tories grew more and more hopeless the nature of their assertions grew more reckless. One solemnly assured the readers of *Rivington's Gazette* that, " If an archangel had planned the connection between Great Britain and her colonies, he could not have fixed it upon a more lasting and beneficial foundation." [1] Another was confident that, if America

---
[1] *Rivington's Gazette*, June 12, 1782.

should get her independence, "that unfortunate land would be a scene of bloody discord and desolation for ages." Internecine war would continue until a few provinces or one sect should conquer all the rest.[1] Then "the dream of independency must vanish like the baseless fabric of a vision." England, the Tory believed, was as necessary to America's safety and honor as a parent to his children in an infant state.[2]

The language of the Declaration was ridiculed by witty writers who especially attacked the phrase concerning the natural freedom and equality of men. One told in humorous rhyme of the rival suitors of the maiden liberty :

> "After John Presbyter
> Will Democrat came next,
> Who swore all men were even
> And seemed to be quite vext,
> That there's a king in heaven.
> Will curst the hilly country 'round'
> Because it made unequal ground."

The horses in the Continental army were very truthfully described :

> "With bellies full of liberty,
> But void of oats and hay." [3]

As the misery and ruin extended in the struggling colonies, a loyal writer sneeringly observed that

---

[1] *Rivington's Gazette*, July 17, 1779.
[2] Curwen's "Journal," p. 334.
[3] "Loyalist Poetry," pp. 65–78.

Americans " advanced rapidly in independence. At the beginning of the contest they were independent of principle, independent of credit and independent of all gratitude to the mother country. . . . Since which time thousands have been independent of cash, clothing, law, liberty, domestic comfort and every social enjoyment."[1]

The Whigs, themselves, did not get an unalloyed pleasure in contemplation of the new state of independence. "We tremble," wrote a Whig to an English friend, "at the thought of separation from Great Britain. All our glory and happiness have been derived from you. But we are in danger of being shipwrecked upon your rocks. To avoid these we are willing to be tossed without a compass or a guide for a while upon an ocean of blood."[2] "We were," admitted another, "formed by England's laws and religion. We were clothed with her manufactures and protected by her fleets and armies. Her Kings are the umpires of our disputes and the center of our Union. In a word, the island of Britain is the fortress in which we are sheltered from the machinations of all the Powers of Europe."[3]

The Tories believed all this and more. They were honestly aghast that men could be so mad as to cast away all these blessed fruits of union and fly to an independence that they knew not of. In

[1] *Rivington's Gazette*, May 1, 1782.
[2] "The Remembrancer," Vol. I., 56.
[3] "American Archives," series 4, Vol. I., 335.

fact, many conservative men were drawn into the Tory ranks when the tremendous fact of the Declaration came upon them with all its relentless significance.

The extravagant demonstrations of joy on the part of the mob caused revulsion in the minds of many sensible men. After the Proclamation of Independence, in Boston, the King's arms and every other sign with any resemblance of it, "whether Lion and Crown, Pestle and Mortar and Crown, Heart and Crown, etc., together with every sign that belonged to a Tory was taken down," and of the latter a general conflagration was made in King's Street.[1] In New York, the soldiers pulled down the leaden statue of George III. on the Bowling Green. Such disregard of that very common conservatism, which is more annoyed by the destruction of material things than of intangible principles, lost the Whigs many easy-going citizens who had, up to this time, gone about their daily work unmoved by the prevailing discussion.

[1] "The Remembrancer," Vol. III., 25.

CHAPTER V.

THE OVERTHROW OF THE LOYAL STRONGHOLD.

THE reason why New York was the last state to agree to the Declaration of Independence might be suggested by certain generalizations, without resort to special inquiry. It bordered on Canada and was influenced by loyalty there. Its commercial interests were such as to make England's powerful protection desirable. But a closer investigation of its history during the years that preceded the Revolution reveals other reasons why over half the refugees from the thirteen colonies, of whom we have any record, were citizens of New York.[1]

The Stamp Act caused "a universal tumult," and even existing party lines were for the moment obliterated. The governor found himself supported only by his personal friends, obsequiously reinforced by the royal officers and the Episcopal clergy. But, as the action of the extremists in the opposition to England grew more reckless, all the conservatives

[1] Flick, "Loyalism in New York," p. 180. As Professor Flick has gone more carefully into the history of the loyalists in New York than a general writer on the subject of the loyalists can do, I shall draw largely on his material in this chapter, where it is supported by the results of my own studies.

began to draw to the loyal side. Soon, all supporters of the British measures merged into the old Episcopal or DeLancey party, and all opposition became identified with the Presbyterians or the Livingston party. The old political feud between the leading families does not immediately concern us, but the religious element, prominent among the causes of the Revolution, deserves a digression.

In New York and in New England, too, the division of parties along religious lines was very plain. In New England, the people became convinced that their religion as well as their liberty was in danger.[1] An evident design, on the part of the ministry, to send a bishop to America aroused resolute opposition. The opponents argued that, if Parliament could create dioceses and appoint bishops, they could collect tithes and crush heresy. The advocates, on the other hand, claimed that the Anglican church in America had a right to complete its own organization by the introduction of bishops, and that an episcopate was no menace to the religious or civil liberties of the colonies. A state church was assumed to be an essential part of the body politic. The Episcopal and Congregational churches were therefore pitted against each other in New England; and, as the Episcopalians received support from Great Britain, they, as a sect, came to be regarded as opposed to colonial interests. But, it is not to

[1] "Publications of the Colonial Society of Massachusetts," Vol. III., 42.

be ignored that the Episcopalians and the men whom we should expect to be supporters of the King and Parliament, the crown officers, were identical. As a result the political antipathies were only intensified by the religious differences.

The demagogues were quick to see this danger which threatened the Whig cause. They accused the Episcopal clergy of writing home "amazing falsehoods," and eagerly seized upon intercepted letters to publish these evidences of what they chose to call treason. Much capital was made of Samuel Peters' letter which anticipated the coming of the British soldiers to Boston, and gloated over the fact that "so soon as they come hanging work will go on." He comforted the Episcopalians with the assurance that the blood sprinkled on the side-posts would preserve the faithful.[1] Another letter of his especially concerned the non-Anglican clergy of Connecticut. The Episcopal church, there, he said, must soon fall a victim "to the rage of the Puritan mobility, if the old serpent, that dragon is not bound." Calling attention to the support given the Whig party by the Puritan clergy, he wrote, "spiritual iniquity rides in high places, with halberts, pistols and swords," and he pictured the preachers and magistrates, on their "pious sabbath day" . . . leaving their pulpits "for gun and drum" and setting off for Boston "cursing the King and

---

[1] "Journals of Each Provincial Congress of Massachusetts," pp. 21, 22.

Lord North, General Gage, the bishops and their curates, and the Church of England." He, himself, had had his windows broken, his clothes, and even his holy gown, rent for urging the church people not to take up arms. The mob had cried, down with the church and "the rags of popery." "The Lord deliver us from anarchy," prayed the good man, after declaring in despair "rebellion is obvious, and treason is common, and robbery is the daily devotion!" It may be readily conceived that such epistolary amenities when read before the Massachusetts provincial congress, did not grace the cause of the Anglican clergy.

At the beginning of the war, the Anglican church had three hundred parishes in America. In the South, it was the religion of the wealthy and cultured. It was the church of the representatives of royalty in the courts of the provincial governors, and of those who sought political prominence in the colonial assemblies. Judges and lawyers and the collectors of the ports were almost sure to grace Episcopal pews. Yet the rivalry between the Church of England and other denominations was identified very little with politics in the southern states.[1] In South Carolina, only five out of twenty Episcopal ministers were Loyalists; although

[1] Chevalier de Fleury, an observing Frenchman, said, however, "The Quakers, Methodists, Anglicans and other sects which have a sort of affinity with monarchy are intestine but paralytic enemies." See Stevens' Facsimiles No. 1616.

every man, who took the holy orders, had taken a solemn oath of allegiance to the crown. Virginia was a stronghold of the Episcopacy; yet many of the church's adherents were in full harmony with the patriotic spirit.[1] Except those persons who had an economic reason in addition to the religious motive, as for example the dependents upon the British "society for the propagation of the Gospel," few men living south of New York seem to have had their politics influenced by their religion.

In New York, the division on religious lines was plainly seen and commented upon at the time. The Sons of Liberty were denounced by their enemies as a "Presbyterian junto." Not, as one writer said, that there were no Church of England men among them, for "there were, to their eternal shame be it spoken!" But they were smugglers of tea, or merchants overloaded with dry goods who saw profit in non-importation measures. The chief instruments in all these flaming measures, however, were those "turbulent, anti-monarchical" Presbyterians. If the English government wished to look for real loyalty, said the writer, it must look in the hearts of the genuine professors of the English Church.[2] During the late violent times, he asserted, "the Presbyterian pulpits groaned with the most wicked, malicious and inflammatory harangues

[1] W. S. Perry, "American Episcopal Church," Vol. I., Ch. XXIV. Maryland was perhaps an exception. See "Md. Arch.," 1777-78, "Journal of Council of Safety," p. 175.
[2] "American Archives," series 4, Vol. I., 301.

... spiriting their godly hearers to the most violent opposition to government." He closed with a sanctimonious picture of the Church of England people, during all this agitation, "without any public oratory to spur them on" doing from their own "truly loyal principles, in which care is taken to educate them," everything to stop the rapid progress of sedition. He forgot in his partizan zeal that, for a Tory, "public oratory" was not a judicious way of expressing political views. A coterie of writers, all of whom were Episcopalians, were writing strenuous Tory articles for publication in pamphlets or the gazettes.[1]

As a result of the introduction of a religious controversy into the larger political conflict, it came to pass, in New York and Connecticut, that altar was arrayed against altar. Where the British were in control, the Presbyterian churches were insulted; and the patriots, except when restrained by motives of policy, were ready for any vandalism against the Episcopal churches and rectories. After the British were in control of Long Island, some young Tories sawed off the steeple of the Presbyterian church, and they attempted the same clownish sacrilege at Jamaica. The British took out the pews and used the house of worship as a guard house; while the

[1] These writers, who were usually masked under a nom-de-plume, were Myles Cooper, President of King's College, Dr. Samuel Seabury, Rev. T. B. Chandler, Isaac Wilkins, Rev. Chas. Inglis and Rev. John Vardill.

pulpit pillar was made to serve as a hitching post.[1] When the British soldiers burned a certain Presbyterian church, a Whig editor, who chronicled the event, asked with a rhetorical flourish, "because we refuse to worship your idol king, will you prevent us worshiping the King of Kings?"[2] He forgot that, not far away, a troop of American cavalry was quartered in the Episcopal rectory, the pews of the church being used for firewood, and the church itself utilized as a hospital.[3]

Sneering allusions were constantly made in Tory literature to Presbyterian deacons struggling unsuccessfully with the flesh and the devil;[4] and the Puritan mob facetiously recognized the religious views of its Tory victims by branding them with the sign of the cross.[5] The satirical Tory writers loved to describe individual Whigs, saying of one that "formality and a Presbyterian face were his ornaments"; another was "a great Puritan, but without religion." A third was a "deserter from the church of England," and a surly humdrum son of liberty.[6] The Puritans, as a sect, were reproached as "those hypocritical fanatics who brought the best of princes to the block"; their chief devotion lay in "odd perverse antipathies," and, now, their

[1] Onderdonk's "Revolutionary Incidents of Long Island," p. 132.
[2] Moore's "Diary of the American Revolution," II., 192.
[3] M. C. Tyler, "Literary History of the American Revolution," Vol. I., 354.
[4] Moore's "Diary of the Revolution," Vol. II., 204.
[5] "Narrative of Walter Bates," Kingston, etc., p. 5.
[6] "Massachusetts Historical Soc. Proc.," series 2, Vol. XII., 140.

absurd hatred of royalty had introduced all this misery into a once happy country.[1] There are many assertions in contemporary literature that the Revolution was a religious war; but these are the views of men with limited understandings who saw in the struggle only the phase in which they were interested. Religious differences no doubt greatly embittered the conflict, and in many cases determined the sympathy of individuals who had no other interest at stake.

In returning from a long digression, which has had for its object a summary examination of the whole subject of the part played by religious faction in the Revolution, we have to recall that, in New York, the Presbyterians were the adherents of the Livingstons, and the Episcopalians, the followers of the De Lanceys. The two families and their adherents appeared upon opposite sides of the successive controversies which preceded the outbreak of war. Upon the question of non-importation, in 1770, the Livingston party came out squarely for a boycott of all English goods.[2] The Tories, however, canvassed the town and defeated the measure by a decisive majority. The non-consumption was confined to tea alone.

Party rancor appeared again when the attempt was made to collect the tea tax. The Tory or Anglican party had control of the three branches

[1] *Rivington's Gazette*, January 31, 1778.
[2] Flick, "Loyalism in New York," p. 21.

of the government; and though the party embraced Liberals enough to enable the Whigs to get a committee of correspondence appointed, yet the other action of the legislature was very conservative. The dispute was, however, on the question of the *form* which opposition should take; for all except the ultra-Tories were opposed to the Parliamentary exactions. Liberal Tories strove only to prevent rash action. This wing of the Tory party was really in control, and, after the Boston Port Bill, succeeded, at the mass meeting in the city, in getting a majority of the moderate committee-men, in the committee of fifty-one chosen to deal with the problems of the moment.

The moderates won again when the election of the delegates to the Continental Congress became the political issue. In seven agricultural counties no interest was shown in the election. Three others carelessly authorized the city delegates to act for them.[1] One loyal town in Westchester County even entered a protest. They were, they declared, happy subjects of King George, and they hoped to remain so. Seabury, the great Tory pamphleteer, doubted whether one hundredth part of the people acted in the matter. Yet, the moderate loyalists were not opposed to the Congress, for it took the dispute out of the hands of the rabble, and rebellion might be avoided by its prudence.

[1] Flick, "Loyalism in New York."

When this first Continental Congress adjourned, however, many of the moderate Tories disapproved of its "dangerous and extravagant measures." They believed that it had basely betrayed the interests of all the colonies. The question was agitated whether New York was bound by the acts of Congress. Non-consumption and non-intercourse were not relished by the agricultural interests of the colony. Farmers, who were in no wise injured by the tea tax, did suffer by non-intercourse and war. Congress was in favor only in the mercantile centers, New York and Albany. The moderate business men were rebuked by the Sons of Liberty because they did not go far enough. Liberal Loyalists were, in consequence, forced to join the ultra-Loyalists, repudiate Congress and refuse to sign the association. To retrieve the error they had made in permitting the state to be represented in Congress, they now endeavored to get control of the local legislative body, and, through it, to carry out their conservative plan.

Having hit upon no effective plan of organization, like the Whig committees of correspondence, the Tories began, as we have seen them do in Massachusetts, signing papers protesting against the Whig resolutions and activities. This harmless and ineffectual method of checking the rebellious tide was especially in vogue on Long Island, where a large proportion of the freemen signed. The easy-going Dutch of King's County, however, simply ignored the whole matter.[1] Several counties repudiated the action of Congress outright. They did not relish the idea of foreign dictation as they regarded its recommendations. An adroit appeal had been made to the colonial self-love, and attention called to the fact that "laws made at Philadelphia" had been imposed upon them "by most imperious menaces."

For a time the Tory power seemed to dominate. The moderates controlled the New York assembly, and all radical measures were voted down. The lower house refused to consider the recommendations of Congress, or even select delegates for the next Congress. The Whig committee of inspection and observation then proposed to elect members; and, in a mass meeting, they defeated the Tory efforts to prevent the election. Undismayed, the "King's friends" vigorously opposed the sending of delegates to the convention held for the purpose of choosing New York's representatives at the coming Continental Congress. Several counties protested against the sending of delegates by a minority of their freeholders; and one county[2] opposed by a solid majority, while another unanimously refused to send representatives.[3] Indifference in other parts of the state, however, defeated the loyal attempt to prevent the success of the convention. When

---

[1] Flick, "Loyalism in New York."
[2] Dutchess County—Flick, *ibid*.
[3] Staten Island.

this provincial convention met, it assumed legislative powers, and approved the acts of Congress which the more loyal assembly had frowned upon.

This provincial convention was given confidence by the fact that the excitement after the Lexington affray had, for the time, placed the mob in power. "New York has been converted almost instantly as St. Paul was of old,"[1] wrote a jubilant Whig, "a Tory dares not open his mouth." Tory leaders became silent, and those whose unpleasant sentiments had been recorded were forced to recant or flee. Governor Tryon lamented that the colony was in a state of anarchy and confusion. Like the frogs in the fable, cried the Tories, the people had rejected the government of one king, Log, and were now obliged to submit to the tyranny of an hundred king storks. The committee, which the Tories thought was in their control, censured obnoxious loyalists, arrested and imprisoned the violators of the association, and finally surrendered its powers to the Provincial Congress.[2]

This revolutionary body, upheld by the second Continental Congress, now took measures to make sure of its supremacy. It threatened with an interdict the county of Richmond, which had failed to send a representative; and the county yielded to the extent of sending two delegates. The Continental Congress then stepped in and outlawed Queens County for a

[1] "North Carolina Colonial Records," Vol. IX., 1247.
[2] See Flick, "Loyalism in New York," p. 44 *et seq.*

similar neglect, cutting off all its trade and ordering the inhabitants to be disarmed and the leaders imprisoned. Even New York city was whipped into more submissive compliance with the will of the Provincial Congress. Its undesirable deputies were rejected, and the local committee ordered to choose more subservient ones.[1] Seeing the drift of events the Tory governor, Tryon, took refuge on a British warship, and performed the duties of his impotent office from that safe retreat.

Yet, in spite of the terror which it inspired in the minds of the ultra-loyalists, the Provincial Congress was in control of a majority by no means in favor of separation from Great Britain. It was ready to coerce the Tories who did not march in step with its own rebellious advance; but it fully intended to halt short of a declaration of independence. It was not at all convinced, as the ultra-Whigs asserted, that "our bleeding country beckons us to shut up the temple of Janus."[2] The majority regarded all its measures against the Tories as intended only to prevent them aiding the British army, in enforcing the "cruel and oppressive acts of Parliament against the liberties of America." The Congressional conscience was quieted by specious phrases concerning the "immutable laws of self-defense and preservation" which justified every reasonable measure to counteract Tory disaffection.

[1] Flick, "Loyalism in New York," p. 49 *et seq.*
[2] "Moore's Diary," Vol. II., 36.

In August of 1775, the Provincial Congress resolved to give an appearance of legality to the persecution of the Tories. Any person, ran their resolution, found guilty of supplying the "ministerial" forces with information, should be punished by the city or county committee which made the discovery. For furnishing supplies the offender forfeited twice their value, and was disarmed and imprisoned.[1] Other offenses of similar nature were given judicious attention, and the penalty always reached the offender's property and especially his arms.

A month later, the Committee of Safety went a step further. The edict went forth that the arms of all "non-associators," whether otherwise offensive or not, should be seized.[2] The work was at once begun in the region about the city and on Long Island. It was a curious collection of weapons, as we may see from the lists that were made appraising the values, that they might be returned or paid for after the war. A silver-hilted sword, a cutlass and a paunch-belt and canteen were taken from one delinquent. Another gave up a pair of brass barreled pistols, a cartouch-belt and a small blunderbuss. A third parted with a "morning sword," a pair of holster pistols and a "Halbert Hanger."[3] The rich variety in the armament of our

[1] Flick, "Loyalism in New York," p. 60.
[2] Flick, *Ibid.*, p. 62.
[3] "Calendar of New York Historical MSS." Vol. I., 259.

forefathers must have been lavishly displayed in the committee rooms, where these treasures were received. A rough and ready description of the persons disarmed sometimes accompanied the appraisement. "A silversmith who was rid upon a rail lately" was the unique label attached to the name of one of the victims. The clerical work was done by the members of the committees, who were aided in the execution of the more difficult part of the task by the persuasive presence of the local militia. This work of disarmment went on for a month, and then was disapproved by the Provincial Congress; but not before bitter animosity was aroused against the revolutionary government.

The scruples of the Provincial Congress were not, however, shared by the Continental Congress; for, early in the spring of 1776,[1] the recommendation was made to all the colonies, that all persons who were non-associators or "notoriously disaffected to the cause of America" should be disarmed. This measure would render harmless the internal foes, and help to arm the patriot forces. Again the work was begun by the committees in New York. Whole districts whose sentiments were loyal were compelled either by the militia, or by detachments of the continental army, to give up their weapons, and "in the presence of Almighty God" swear that their fire-arms, side-arms, powder

[1] March 14, 1776. See "Journals of Congress," Vol. II., 88, also 6.

and lead had all been given up, and that they had hidden none and destroyed none. Gratuitous phrases about "ministerial tyranny" were thrown into the wording of the oath, which made it none the easier for a Tory to "swallow."[1]

Two months later, it became evident that the Provincial Congress was coming to the views of the continental body. Exasperated by the conduct of the Queens County loyalists, it adopted a resolution to disarm them by military force. Some had, it was reported, declared Whigs to be worse than infidels, and had sworn to oppose Congress in seeking independence, even if they were "quartered or cut into inch pieces." One had assured a member of Congress that the devil would have him soon and carry him off for his impudence. Another had saved a friend from a mob by warning him and bribing a boatman to take the endangered man on board the British ship.[2] Such incorrigible men were to be sent into the neighboring states on parole,[3] or, if they refused, they were to be imprisoned. A special committee became necessary to execute this resolution, and, before the midsummer was reached, its task became so great that a larger committee was appointed with increased powers.

During all these months, the Tories were harried by the Whig militia. If the soldiers found a man

[1] "New York Calendar of Historical MSS.," Vol. I., 217.
[2] *Ibid.*, Vol. I., 328.
[3] For original references see Flick, "Loyalism in New York," p. 66.

in the swamps or woods, or with a gun charged, or in possession of powder, or who was confused when asked about Tory schemes, or who slandered Washington or denied the authority of Congress, they seized him and hurried him away to be tried by the committee.[1] The swamps of Long Island were said by the Whig officers to be regular "nests of those obnoxious vermin."

As for the Tories, their confidence in the final triumph of the British arms gave them courage. They had heard with sad forebodings of the forced evacuation of Boston by the "American Anthony," as Howe was called; yet now they were promised that the British forces were soon coming to New York. They meant to seize the city, and then by getting control of the Hudson they would sever the colonies and conquer the divisions at their leisure. The Tory governor, from his secure station afloat and out of reach of committeemen,[2] encouraged them not to yield their arms; and the ship *Asia* hovered off shore ready to supply the needy with the means of defense. So the hard-pressed Tories concealed their valuable arms and gave up the poor ones with daring dissimulation. Some-

---

[1] Onderdonk, "Long Island," Vol. I., 73. One victim had "more guns than he ought" and another "threw suspicious looking writing in the fire."

[2] Washington, after urging the seizure of the principal loyalists, who, he said, were so well known that there could be little danger of making a mistake, added "happy should I be if the Governor should be one of them." See Washington's "Writings," Vol. III., 273.

times, they retaliated by stealing the patriot arms, and in sundry places grew audacious enough to parade and fire their muskets in pure bravado.[1] Nevertheless they were constantly pressing upon Governor Tryon their distressed condition, and he reported that they suffered " from Committees, Congresses and Minutemen . . . a species of tyranny and despotism scarcely to be equalled in History." They are, he wrote, without arms or ammunition even for the harmless purpose of self-defense. " They incessantly wait upon me with the strongest assurances that they look up to their king for protection."[2]

This activity against the Tories had already received the sanction of men high in the colonial estimation. As early as November of 1775, Washington had ordered the seizure of all unfriendly government officers who were in the vicinity of the scene of war. To the Governor of Rhode Island he addressed the rhetorical question, whether it would not be "prudent to seize on those Tories, who have been, are, and that we know will be active against us? Why should persons, who are preying on the vitals of the country, be suffered to stalk at large, whilst we know that they will do us every mischief in their power." When "Sachem Schuyler," as he was dubbed by the Tories, marched

[1] Onderdonk's "Revolutionary Incidents in Long Island," p. 70 et seq.
[2] "New York Colonial MSS.," Vol. VIII., 662.

to the very heart of the Loyal district in the Mohawk Valley, disarmed Sir John Johnson and his loyal Highlanders, and placed the leader under heavy bonds to keep out of the king's service, Washington wrote hearty approval and congratulation. "I hope," he added, "that General Lee will execute a work of the same kind on Long Island. It is high time to begin with our internal foes when we are threatened with such severity of chastisement from our kind parent without."[1]

Charles Lee, who at this time posed before the credulous colonists as a military genius, and whose sententious piety glowed most brightly when his zeal was most hypocritical, declared, when he was beginning his work on Long Island, "I should be responsible to God, my own conscience and the Continental Congress, . . . in suffering at so dangerous a crisis, a knot of professed foes to American liberty to remain any longer within our bosom."[2]

As soon as Washington felt sure of the safety of Boston, he had moved his army to New York, which promised to be the new scene of conflict. As soon as he arrived, he remonstrated vigorously with the colonial committee of safety for permitting the intercourse between the inhabitants of New York and the British on board their ships. "To tell you, gentlemen, that the advantages of an intercourse of this kind are altogether on the side of

[1] Washington, "Writings," Sparks' ed., Vol. III., 263.
[2] Onderdonk, "Revolutionary Incidents of Long Island," p. 52.

the enemy, whilst we derive not the smallest benefit," [1] is obvious. "Even the enemy themselves must despise us for suffering it to be continued." He closed his appeal by showing that not only supplies, but information, were thus conveyed to the enemy. The committee agreed with his position, and increased their efforts to prevent the traffic.

The few months, between the time of the arrival of Washington in New York and the coming of the British under General Howe, were months of terror for the Loyalists. Though some attempts were made to protect them, yet they inevitably suffered at the rough hands of those who were commissioned to limit their power to aid the British. Their lot was rendered all the more wretched because of the discovery, late in June, of a plot against the life of Washington. Leading Tories were implicated, and thus discredit was thrown upon the party. The plot, or at least the discovery, was a great misfortune for the Tories. They had been gaining adherents among those who wanted to go no further until they learned what the "conciliatory policy" might be, which had been heralded as the benevolent mission of Lord Howe. Now, the patriots became bolder, and, though they failed to get the New York delegates instructed for independence before its adoption on July 2d, yet they needed but a week more of agitation, before the

[1] Washington's "Writings," Sparks' ed., Vol. III., 357.

Declaration was formally adopted by the Provincial Congress.

For the Loyalists, there now came the darkest hour before the dawn — melancholy dawn as it was. When Lord Howe came and landed on Staten Island with his olive branch, it was discovered that the King's benevolence extended only to granting pardon to all who would desist from rebellion and aid in restoring peace. Such a proposition, at this stage of the war, could only be greeted with jeers; and the Tory party received another set-back. But for a time their misfortunes were ended. The American party was defeated at the battle of Long Island; the British took possession of New York city, and, at last, the Tory had a haven of refuge in America. The tables were now turned. The Whigs of Long Island were disarmed and compelled to take an oath of allegiance.[1] The Tories expressed their exultation in fulsome addresses to Lord Howe, full of joy that they had been "restored to the King's most gracious protection." From the day of the occupation of New York by the British army, until the last British soldier left it, in 1783, the persecuted Tories had a sanctuary. From every colony they came by boat, on foot, in carriage or on horse, ready to thank God when they had passed the British lines, and had left behind them the din of persecution.

[1] "New York Colonial MSS.," Vol. VIII., 693, 696, 697, 750, 753. Nearly 3,000 took the oath directed by Tryon.

CHAPTER VI.

THE POLITICAL SHIBBOLETH.

AFTER the loss of New York and the dark six months of almost continual defeat for the patriot forces, there was a lull in the aggressions upon the Loyalists. The Whigs did not know what day might bring total destruction upon their cause, and they did not care to invite retaliation if the Tories should come once more into power. But, when the holidays came with the stirring victories at Trenton and Princeton, the hearts of the Whigs beat high with courage, and they attacked their internal enemies anew. Washington himself began the work with a proclamation. He commanded all persons who had accepted Lord Howe's recent offer of protection, either to retire within the British lines or take the oath of allegiance to the United States. This simple method of distinguishing friend from foe had already been used in a tentative way, but now the work received a new impetus.

The simplest and earliest method of discrimination was, as we have seen, the Association,[1] a docu-

---

[1] Association implied the voluntary assumption of an obligation to give military service in defense of a principle, and, therefore, met with

ment circulated by committees and signed by those who approved its sentiments. Now, the various state legislatures enacted the "test" laws, the purpose of which was to compel a declaration of principles from those who were indifferent or who were secret enemies of the revolution. Political friends must be distinguished from political foes. The facetious proposition of a Whig, that all the Tory houses be painted black, would hardly suffice. The legislators strove to prevent a neutral attitude. They sought to create a moral ground for adherence to the patriot cause. However unwillingly the oath of allegiance was taken, it became at once a factor in determining the action of the person taking the oath. For those who had taken a previous oath to Great Britain it was hoped that abjuration would furnish a sort of moral balm to relieve the conscientious scruples against the Patriot cause. The main purpose, however, of the machinery of discrimination was the separation of the political chaff from the political wheat.

In the several colonies, the oath demanded by the "test acts" varied in expression, but contained the same general pledges. Oaths were frequently couched in the most vigorous phraseology. Gen-

opposition from men who were peaceably inclined. Men, who were willing to give moral support, would not engage their lives. The legislators now saw the need of an oath of allegiance that would foster the idea of responsibility to the country. The "test laws" were enacted to accomplish this end, as well as to perfect a system of discrimination between Whig and Tory.

eral Lee imposed one in which the juror "as he hoped for ease, honor and comfort in this world and happiness in the world to come, most earnestly, devoutly and religiously swore . . . by the tremendous and almighty God," to aid the American cause and fight the British.[1] But in the diluted form, as administered by the civil authorities, it did not thunder so much in the index. The juror simply testified and declared before the Everliving God and the world that the war of the colonies against Great Britain was just and necessary. He promised not to aid and abet the forces of Great Britain. All plots and conspiracies against his colony he would betray. He renounced all allegiance and obedience to George III., and promised faith and true allegiance to the state in which he resided.[2] In the test acts passed before the Declaration of Independence, the oath of abjuration and allegiance was omitted.

No benevolent despot with a desire for unity or regularity of action existed in the colonies. As a result there was no well preserved order in the evolution of the test acts. With some exceptions, however, the earliest test acts were demands for an oath of allegiance from Government officers. Pro-

---

[1] Congress disapproved of Lee's test oath, and Lee wrote to Hancock that he was sorry that this had brought down such "a thundering stygma" on his head, and vowed that he hazarded so irregular a measure only for public safety. See "New York Historical Society Papers," Lee Papers, Vol. I., 360.

[2] For examples see "Laws of Pennsylvania," June 13, 1777, also "Public Records of the State of Connecticut," Vol. I., 4.

fessional men were next brought to the political touchstone. Finally, the inquisition was extended to all free, white, male citizens above the age of sixteen.[1]

There were various limitations of the class of persons to be subjected to the test. Rhode Island, New Jersey, South Carolina and New York obliged all who were suspected of being inimical, to take the oath.[2] Those who had levied war against the United States, or who had taken an oath to Great Britain, were offered pardon, in Connecticut, Delaware, Virginia and North Carolina, on condition of swearing allegiance. Travelers were made a special subject of inquiry in several states. Spies were abroad in various guises, and in order to detect them every traveler was obliged to carry a certificate that he had taken the test oath. The Carolinas compelled all, who had held commissions under the British government before the war, to swear their affection for America. This was supposed to extract the sanctity of the previous oath to which the person had subscribed on taking office under the British crown. It was, also, a way of probing the consciences of people who came naturally under suspicion. In North Carolina, all who had traded "immediately to Great Britain or Ireland within

[1] Pennsylvania and Maryland made age limit 18 years, Delaware 21. In New York the order of attack was reversed.

[2] See for these facts and the sources for facts in general, contained in this chapter, the table of the test laws in the appendix. As facts and generalizations may be verified there I shall omit footnotes.

ten years last past" were asked to take the "test," on the supposition that such persons were likely to be in sympathy with the British. While the King's army was in Philadelphia, the Pennsylvania Assembly passed a law making all who traveled out of Philadelphia or the county of their residence liable to be tendered the oath. Men who were living peaceably with the hated Briton were thought to be in need of this spiritual prop.

Several states made certain exemptions from the comprehensive sweep of the law. Policy usually dictated these exceptions, though in several cases they were necessary in order to get the laws passed at all. In Delaware and Maryland, officers and soldiers in the pay of the United States were assumed to have given enough assurance of their fealty to the new government. Pennsylvania did, at first, exempt delegates in Congress and merchants and marines coming to her ports; but later repented the exception and covered their cases fully. Quakers, Mennonites and Dunkers, because of their religion, were generally allowed an affirmation instead of an oath.

Even the *privilege* of taking an oath was denied to some who had outraged the Patriot sensibilities by overt acts of hostility. In Massachusetts, refugees to Boston, those who had agreed to aid the enemy, and the members of the Mandamus Council, were denied the privilege of the oath and, as a consequence, the rights of citizenship. In other instances all persons, "now in open enmity," were denied the comfort of the oath, though, as a rule, the conciliatory policy prevailed, and the opportunity was open to all who repented.

To the sympathizer with the American cause, the oath of fidelity was only a slight annoyance. He received a visit from a member of the local committee of correspondence, or, perhaps, had to attend a session of court himself, where the law dictated that the oath was to be taken. The discomfort lay only in the extra exertion. Even the indifferent persons were likely to take it in the spirit of the poet, whose philosophy was better than his verse.

> "When penal laws were passed by vote
> I thought the test a grievance,
> Yet sooner than I'd lose a groat,
> I swore the state allegiance." [1]

But, for the Loyalist, it was the beginning of persecution by the state. If he attended the town meeting of the eastern states, the law was read and all were urged to take the oath. The minister announced the new test from the pulpit. From the steps of every Virginia or North Carolina courthouse the sheriff read the law at the gathering of the people. At every muster of militia in South Carolina the captain proclaimed the act and made sure of its execution. Throughout the length and

[1] "Loyalist Poetry," p. 65.

breadth of the land, the newspapers notified the people that the winnowing process was to be completed. In the little state of Rhode Island, even the members of the upper and lower houses of the legislature were pressed into service, and obliged, personally, to tender the oath to all "suspects."

In most of the colonies, the Justice of the Peace administered the political shibboleth. Sometimes, he wrote the oath on parchment, announced a place where he could be found, and the signers became their own recorders. In other states, the signing was done in the courts of record.[1] Careful registers of the "jurors" were kept, and a certificate was given them which read : " I do hereby certify that —— hath voluntarily taken and subscribed the oath or affirmation of allegiance and fidelity, as directed."[2] Without such a certificate no traveler was safe from arrest ; no suspected British sympathizer was safe from annoyance and persecution.

In Massachusetts, if a member of the Council or House, a selectman, a military or civil officer, or a member of a committee of correspondence suspected any citizen, he reported the "suspect" to the justice of the peace. The latter summoned the

[1] Commissioners were sometimes appointed in various districts of the state, and they announced days when they would meet the public.

[2] Where the offering of the oath was considered as an act of grace a goodly fee was exacted. In Delaware, the refugee who took advantage of the act of pardon paid the justice of the peace five shillings for administering the oath, and the Governor took 30 shillings more for a certificate.

proscribed man, gave him two hours to decide whether he would sign or not, and then, upon refusal, cast him into jail. All the fees and cost of maintenance in jail came out of the estate of the delinquent. An analogous process was followed in other states, differing only in the agents employed and the time allowed for decision. The militia was often employed to execute the test laws or proclamations. Ignorant and brutal men were too often employed upon this business. Isaac Sears wrote General Lee that he "tendered the oath to four of the grate Tories which they swallowed as hard as if it was a four pound shot, that they were trying to git down." Again, he had "ben able to ketch but five Torries, and they of the first rank, which swallowed the oath." He could not "ketch many without hosses to rid after them."[1]

Every test act mentioned some date, several months in advance, after which all who had not taken the oath would be treated as if they had refused it. In some cases, the person refusing the oath was bound over to the next term of court to be tried for his offence; but, in general, the offence was established by the refusal, and the penalties followed. Political, legal, and civil disabilities were invariable results of refusal, unless the offender could get sureties heavily bonded. Disarming, imprisonment, special taxation and confiscation of property were penalties suffered in various states.

[1] Onderdonk, "Revolutionary Incidents of Long Island."

Banishment, temporary or permanent, was reserved usually for those, who, having fled to the British lines, refused the offer of pardon which was to be granted on condition of taking an oath.

In the midst of alarms and civil war, it is natural that these test acts were not always administered in the correct and equitable way that the legislators may have wished. Over-zealous agents of committees often hurried the non-jurors, quite ignominiously, before a justice of the peace, and, as the loyalists expressed it, "forced the oath down their throats." In some cases, the justice was paid a stated fee for every oath administered; and the fee had an effect like that of offering a bounty on wolves' heads. The justices hunted for them, coaxed and threatened them and almost herded them.

Personal spite had, no doubt, only too great an influence in deciding the action of certain officials. One of many hundreds of credible stories will serve for an illustration. John Dunn, under oath "on the Holy Evangelists," relates the enmity existing between him and a certain patriot, who had missed being elected a delegate because of Dunn's efforts. Shortly after, Dunn was at home recovering from a fit of sickness, when a number of armed men entered his house. They seized him and forced him away to one Louis Coffee's house. Soon, another Loyalist was conducted to the same place. A patriot attorney-at-law arrived upon the scene, and when he was asked why they were restrained and by what authority, replied that it was the desire of some gentlemen to the southward to examine them with regard to their political sentiments. After some delay, two men, who were first sworn to secrecy and fidelity, led the prisoners away. Upon reaching the house, where the guards said that the prisoners were to meet their inquisitors, there was a long delay. Some friends of the prisoners offered to go surety for their appearance before the committeemen, but all to no purpose. Then a messenger was sent off, and returned soon with thirty or forty armed men. This guard escorted the victims to the court-house. But, instead of being met by the committeemen, they were carried off next day, by a guard of sixty horsemen, to another state, and thrown into jail. There they remained nine months without even a trial. Dunn attributed all this to the "pernicious and wicked designs of the man whose ambitions he had foiled."

The best testimony of the difficulty of carrying out the test acts lies in the statute books themselves. In nearly every case, the test act was followed by frequent laws "for the relief of non-jurors," or extending the limit of time for taking the oath. Eight or ten extensions of the time were not uncommon. Then there were laws excusing those who had been sick or absent, and prolonging the time limit for their benefit. These rapid legislative somersaults did not escape the Loyalist's wit. The epithet of a "heated body with a hot head" was applied not without point to the executive council of Pennsylvania. A very small proportion of the people of that state signed the oath submitted to them.[1]

Individuals conjured up the most motley array of excuses. One had been out of the country during the time in which the oath was to be taken; another had been sick, and a third had been unable to read the proclamation of the law. Where the local committees were unable to pardon them, a special act of the legislature gave the relief. Many undoubted patriots refused the oath. They urged that it was an indignity, after the sacrifices they had made for the cause. Soldiers and Continental officers, especially manifested their indignation, and a revision of the law often recognized the justice of their protest. Loyalists with many personal friends succeeded in certain localities in getting so many to refuse to sign, as to destroy the force of the law. Each pleaded that others did not sign, why should he?[2] Thus the Loyalist at heart evaded a declaration of his principles.

The laws enacted to reinforce the test laws threatened with heavy fines the inspector of election, sheriff or justice of peace who failed to do his duty in making the test acts effective. Yet the best intentions were futile, when directed at the enforcing of a law which offered so fair an opportunity

[1] See "Pennsylvania Archives," Vol. III., 6 *et seq.*
[2] "Records of the Colony of Rhode Island," Vol. III., 595.

for cunning evasion. At every attempt to enforce the law, thousands fled to avoid taking the oath of fidelity to a state whose very existence they did not acknowledge. Many swore their allegiance recklessly, taking refuge in the philosophy of the comforting couplet—

> "The imposer of the oath 'tis breaks it;
> Not he who for convenience takes it." [1]

As a parodist of the time expressed it: "The dread of something after flight . . . puzzles the will; and makes ten thousands rather sign and eat, than fly — to starve on loyalty."

The folly of the test laws was pointed out even by the most rampant Whigs. In a tirade against Tories, a newspaper scribbler expressed a common criticism. The Tories ought to be banished, but, he complained, "they have taken oaths and are under the protection of the laws. Some of these miscreants, 'tis true, have put on a sham repentance and have dared to call the Almighty to witness their perjuries, they take the oaths one day, and break them the next. Do they not tell you, to your faces, that no faith is to be kept with the rebels . . . ? Are men who act on principles like these to be trusted?" There is much proof that the reputed Tory was no more tolerated, socially, after he had taken the oath than before.

[1] "American Archives," series 4, Vol. I., 720.

With every change in the fortunes of war, the fortunes of the test acts wavered. At the time of the successful defence of Charleston, South Carolina, we learn that "the Tories flocked to sign the tests," but when "the Sun of Liberty was almost obscured" the oath administering business of the justice of the peace was very dull.

Besides the civil action, the military commanders on either side issued proclamations, as we have seen, urging or demanding an oath. Sir William Howe, while in New Jersey, offered pardon to all such of the inhabitants as would come in and take the oath of allegiance to the crown, with a promise to protect them in their persons and property. This was followed, to quote the *New York Gazette*, by a proclamation of the "Lord Protector, Mr. George Washington." He said that, in some instances, the British had *compelled* men to take an oath of allegiance to the King.[1] In retaliation, he commanded every person, having subscribed such a declaration, to deliver up his certificate at the quarters of some Continental army officer and take the oath to the United States. He, however, permitted those who preferred the protection of Great Britain to retire with their families within the British lines. The loyal critic of this proclamation said that he could not read it without pity and astonishment. That Mr. Washington, who *once* was esteemed a

---

[1] This was very true. See the proofs in Onderdonk, "Revolutionary Incidents of Long Island," Vol. I., 132–252.

gentleman should be so contaminated by the vice of his associates as to lose all regard to the common forms of morality was not to have been expected. The critic thought that the Proclamation might be styled a proclamation for the encouragement of perjury. It commanded an oath that destroyed an oath. "Such impious disregard, such a flagrant violation of all that is serious and sacred among men, has rarely been seen in any age, country or profession." But, naturally, he "who can call the gentle Government of Britain 'tyranny' can become the most insolent and outrageous tyrant himself."

Criticisms of the test laws and their makers are common and severe in all loyalist literature. James Allen, of Pennsylvania, one of the mildest of loyalists, wrote in his diary,[1] "Our Assembly have at length in their wisdom, prepared a test act obliging all to vow allegiance to the state and abjure the King; the penalty is, being in effect outlawed. . . . But it is little regarded, like the rest of their laws. They are, indeed, a wretched set. This convulsion has, indeed, brought all the dregs to the top."[2]

Peter Van Schaak, a moderate Loyalist, who was thoroughly in sympathy with American political institutions, but who, by the extreme measures of the Whigs, was forced into exile, arraigned the test laws in a very calm and thoughtful paper. He argued that the tendering of an oath in a matter

---

[1] July 2, 1777.
[2] *Pennsylvania Magazine*, Vol. IX., 285.

of opinion, under the penalty of banishment or confiscation, was a severe attack on the weakness of human nature. Duty to God and affection to an innocent family were brought into conflict. In such a struggle even a good man might sink under the weight of trial. He had understood that an oath, repugnant to a duty previously existing, could not be obligatory. As to the expediency of offering such an oath, he gravely doubted it. He thought that it actually did harm, because it is sometimes dangerous to probe a wound too deeply. Men who would do no harm if undisturbed would become implacable enemies, if brought to bay by such a measure. "Had you," he continued, addressing the Whigs, "at the beginning of the war, permitted every one differing in sentiment from you, to take the other side, or at least to have removed out of the State, with their property . . . it would have been a conduct magnanimous and just. But, now, after restraining those persons from removing ; punishing them, if, in the attempt, they were apprehended ; selling their estates if they escaped ; compelling them to the duties of subjects under heavy penalties ;[1] deriving aid from them in the prosecution of the war . . . now to compel them to take an oath" is an act of severity. It was said that a choice was now given them. Yes, "the galley

[1] Referring to the compulsory militia service.

slave too has a choice, for he has full liberty to prefer the oar or the lash." [1]

In the preambles, the legislators justified the test laws. From their point of view a new state had been established. Everyone had had time to determine whether he would be an American or British subject. In all states, protection and allegiance are, and ought to be, reciprocal, and those who will not bear the latter are not entitled to the benefits of the former. As a war measure, the sympathizers with Great Britain must be treated as enemies of the state. It is impossible to be certain of an individual's neutrality, and men cannot be sheltered under a government which they are trying to subvert. Men have, they argued, affected to maintain a neutrality, but there is reason to suspect that it was in many cases dictated by a poverty of spirit and an undue attachment to property. Others advocated the American cause until it became serious. Then "ungratefully and insidiously . . . by artful misrepresentations and subtle dissemination . . . of fears . . . they seduced certain weak-minded persons." The internal enemy in the guise of a neutral was felt to be quite as dangerous as an out-and-out traitor. We can hardly deny that each, Loyalist and Patriot, from his own point of view was right. The Loyalist might urge with all honesty that the test laws were due to political bigotry,

[1] See the whole argument p. 112 *et seq.*, "Life of Peter Van Schaak."

because for him no new state existed, and Whig and Tory were only political parties. For the Patriot the *political* struggle was over, and a new state, created by the Whig, had the sovereign right to take the measures necessary for its preservation. The military necessity of measures like these is made quite evident, when we consider the activity of the Tories, as we shall in the next chapter.

CHAPTER VII.

TRYING TO PRESERVE THE UNION.

THE arrival of Howe, as we have seen, and the occupation of New York was an occasion of great joy for the Loyalists. Some of them immediately joined the British army; but the great majority merely settled down contentedly under the kindly protection of the British arms, and contemplated with satisfaction the prospect of immediate "peace and union with the parent state." In spite of the series of successes that attended the British arms, however, the hour of complete triumph seemed discouragingly deferred.

This inactive mass of men constantly grew in size and in hopeless dependence upon the charity of the British. Those who reached New York, after escaping the persecutions of the Whigs, brought with them little more than their clothes and a small sum of money. As the months passed and the war seemed no nearer an end, these destitute refugees, men of every social rank, grew more and more importunate. The influential men often succeeded in getting some dignified employment within the British military system; but there was a far larger class

TRYING TO PRESERVE THE UNION.   147

who found themselves in the direst need. Of these, many would gladly have taken up arms and a soldier's life, but were deterred by the lack of encouragement. The British clung stubbornly to the idea that these provincials could not fight, and only encouraged their services in the regular army, where they might be trained by British officers. It took several years to recognize their value as provincial militia. The expectation that the hour of complete victory was imminent acted also to prevent the early enlistment of the Loyalists, because there was no wish to embitter their relations with the "rebels" with whom they would soon return to live.

The plight of these men soon drew the attention of the British authorities, and plans for their employment were matured. Large numbers were made of service as sappers for the army. As soon as the Whigs outside of New York learned of this undignified employment, their satirical writers seized upon the theme, and embellished it for sympathetic readers. One of the bitterest gibes was that of a Whig poet who summed up the whole situation with malicious courtesy :[1]

> "Come, gentlemen Tories, firm, loyal and true,
> Here are axes and shovels and something to do!
> For the sake of our king,
> Come labor and sing."

[1] "Historical View of the American Revolution," by G. W. Greene, p. 430.

The poet suggests that the King will remember the suffering Tory, and though there is, it is true, some work to be done, yet it shall be paid for at twelve coppers a day. He urges them to throw off their jerkins and build the ramparts and walls, and pull down old houses. All day they must work at fortifications, and at night they may steal their food from the rebels. The forts must be built, the writer comments, even though Tories are slain; but they must not have long faces, for the events of the year will alter their circumstances and, anyway, after they are dead their names shall be read,

"As who for their monarch both labored and bled,
And ventured their necks for their beef and their bread."

Thus, with mock encouragement, they were urged to scour up their mortars and work for their king, for, if they failed to save New York, they would probably be hung.[1]

The subject lent itself to ridicule, yet it was, of course, creditable to the Loyalists that they, as a rule, preferred any labor rather than becoming mere objects of charity. They never showed a lack of courage in doing what they were permitted to do. They were ready to go as spies into the country held by the patriots, and were frequently sent to sow sedition or to proselyte among their

[1] For more sober testimony as to this employment of the Loyalist, see "Valentine's Manual of the Corporation of the City of New York," 1863, p. 653, and *Rivington's Gazette*, June 3, 1780, and "Clinton Papers," Vol. I., 629.

old friends and neighbors. Washington repeatedly complained of the "diabolical and insidious arts and schemes carried on by the Tories to raise distrust, dissensions and divisions among us." He even recommended that the granting of traveling-permits cease entirely, because it settled "a channel of correspondence with the disaffected."[1] The extent of their services in this direction even drew the attention of Congress. Every state was advised to seize all suspected emissaries and abettors of General Howe, who were dispersed through the United States, "under various pretenses of amusement and business, whereby they are enabled to spread disaffection, intimidate the people by false news, and depreciate the currency of the United States."[2] A patriot merchant, however, put a different interpretation on the danger of allowing freedom to Tory travelers. He declared that in the guise of pedlars they escaped registration in the militia rolls. They escaped taxes, sold at exorbitant prices, and were, the writer declared, "the harpies of trade," "caterpillars allowed to hang on the branches of commerce."

Not only the Tories who actually went out from the British lines, but the large number of secret Tories still living among the Whigs in the neighboring states, were of great service to the British.

---

[1] Washington's "Writings," Sparks' ed., Vol. III., 396.
[2] "Journals of Congress," Vol. III., December 20, 1777. Philadelphia, 1800.

Every facility of the surrounding country was at the beck of British gold. Powder was stolen from the American magazines; the stores of salt were broken open and robbed; the millers smuggled flour to the British when they had none for Washington's "starvelings," and horses were sent in droves to the British lines where the prices fairly compensated the risk.[1] New Jersey, Delaware, Connecticut and Rhode Island found it necessary to threaten the most terrible penalties against those who piloted the British vessels or gave them information,[2] or sold them provisions.[3] A proclamation to this effect by Gov. Livingston, of New Jersey, was ridiculed by the Tory press in New York. It was all very well, they sneered, for this Whig despot, this "knight of the most honorable order of starvation," to talk of the traitorous practice of selling provisions to the enemy for solid coin, "the mammon of unrighteousness"; but a "boundless aversion to rag-money" was quite natural.[4] The newspaper wit went straight to the heart of the problem. It mattered not so much to these shrewd Yankee farmers whether their political principles

---

[1] Stevens' "Facsimiles," p. 2068.

[2] Congress appointed a Special Committee to look into this evil. "Journal of Congress," Vol. IV., June 17, 1778.

[3] "Colonial Records of Connecticut," Vol. XV., 179. "Session Laws of Delaware, May 20, 1778." "Public Records of Connecticut," Vol. I., 528. "Records of Rhode Island," Vol. VII., 388.

[4] *Rivington's Gazette*, October 14, 1778.

were satisfied, if, only, their purses did not suffer. It is hardly a fair measure of the political sympathy of a colony to ascertain the amount of aid given by its people to the British. The aid given them measured rather the difference between British gold and American paper money, and the opportunity to exchange commodities for the former.

One of the greatest services done the British cause by the Tories was their effort to depreciate the Continental currency. They aided the perfectly natural tendency not only by refusing, when they dared, to accept it, but by counterfeiting it or circulating the counterfeits made within the British lines. Advertisements appeared from time to time in the Tory newspapers, announcing that persons going out into the colonies might receive large sums of Continental paper money by merely paying the price of the paper and printing. Besides circulating the counterfeits, the Tories took every opportunity of ridiculing the " pasteboard dollars "[1] and threatening all who accepted them. It was regarded as a huge joke when a Connecticut parson was seized and compelled to chew up the paper money which he had on his person. Rivington, the Tory printer, gave many columns of his paper to the discussion of the financial straits of the Americans; and these columns were delectable reading for the Loyalists who were anxiously awaiting the downfall of "congressional tyranny." Yet, in spite of

[1] Moore's " Diary of the American Revolution," Vol. I., 414.

all the efforts of the Tories to hurt the American money, they could hardly do as much damage as the insane laws recommended by Congress, which, as a Tory declared, " would have depreciated the gold of Ophir." [1]

The most effective service given the British by the Tories was the active proselyting, carried on throughout the war, among the great class of half-hearted Americans who were ready to go into the arms of either combatant that seemed for the moment the probable victor. They were Tory emissaries who carried, among the people of New Jersey and other neighboring States, the broadsides proclaiming Lord Howe's offer of pardon to those who would take an oath of allegiance. They promulgated Lord North's belated repeal of all the obnoxious laws [2] which had been the immediate cause of the revolution. The almost contemporaneous treaty with France, which, to those wholly in sympathy with the Revolution, seemed the most desirable of all consummations, was regarded with horror by the Tories; and they tried to communicate their views to the wavering and uncertain people in the states.

The French alliance was, in fact, a terrible blow to the Tory hopes, and was quite as much of a shock to their ideas of international affinities. Can the "tiger and the ox feed at one stall, or the lion

[1] *Rivington's Gazette*, May 23, 1781.
[2] February 17, 1778.

and the lamb lie down together?"[1] They asserted their utter inability to understand the exultation of Congress and its friends over such an alliance. It seemed like the madness of the poor Trojans who pulled down their walls and dragged in the wooden horse. The French alliance would bring the Americans just such speedy and inevitable ruin.[2] There were dark hints about secret clauses of the treaty, in which Congress had ceded part of America to France. At one time it was positively asserted that Rhode Island, with Narragansett and sundry islands, had been ceded to America's new "guardian of liberty, Louis the King."[3] A significant story gained credence that, when Gerard, the French minister, landed, he received a piece of turf, symbolic that he was given possession of the land.[4] The meeting of Gerard with Congress was satirized in prose and rhyme.[5]

[1] Moore's "Diary," Vol. II., 145.
[2] *Rivington's Gazette*, July 13, 1782.
[3] *Rivington's Gazette*, August 23, 1782.
[4] *Rivington's Gazette*, July 29, 1778.
[5] One of the best productions was the well-known,

"'From Lewis, Monsieur Gerard came,
To Congress in this town, sir.
They bowed to him, and he to them
And then they all sat down, sir.
Degar, said Monsieur, one grand *coup*
You shall bientot, behold, sir.
This was believed as gospel true,
And Jonathan felt bold, sir," etc.
See *Rivington's Gazette*, October 3, 1778.

The most vulnerable point of attack on the French alliance was the fact that the ally was Catholic. The Tories declared that Congress adopted all sorts of Romish mummery. Loyal newspapers printed the most absurd canards announcing that the French king was preparing a fleet which should come to America and convert his new subjects. Some of the vessels were laden with tons of holy water and casks of consecrated oil. A thousand chests of reliques, beads and crucifixes were ready, and a vast number of crape shifts, hair shirts, cowls and scourges. Another vessel contained many thousand consecrated wafers, crucifixes, rosaries and mass books as well as bales of indulgences. To provide for the conversion of heretics of whom America had many, the good king had not forgotten the necessary equipment of wheels, hooks, pincers, shackles and fire brands. To instruct the Americans in the use of these pious instruments, there was ready an army of priests, confessors and mendicants. Finally it had been reliably reported that Dr. Franklin had been decorated with the order of the holy cross of Jerusalem.[1]

[1] *Rivington's Gazette*, October 7, 1778, and January 29, 1780. A popular verse draws the same picture.

> "The French alliance now came forth,
> The Papists flocked in shoals, sir,
>   Friseurs, Marquis, Valets of Birth
> And priests to save our souls, sir."
>   "Loyalist Poetry," p. 65.

All that was detested in the French character or political institutions was prophetically promised for America. Hordes of French dancing masters, fiddlers and friseurs were reported coming from Brest to instruct the Puritans in French manners. Portable soups, garlic and dried frogs were being prepared for importation.[1] The contract for a Bastille in New York had already been granted, and America would soon enjoy the blessings of French government and the felicity of popery.[2] The infamy of such an alliance, cried a Tory writer, could not be matched, and to think that it was done just as England was again offering the balm of peace to her ungrateful children![3]

The whole unlucky career of the French fleet was watched by the Tories with great pleasure. The French admiral, it was declared, had "not even Pantagruel's luck, who conquered two old women and a duck."[4] Lafayette and his fellow countrymen were described as "the frog-eating gentry now capering through your provinces," and the marquis was represented amusing himself before the glass or taking snuff, and always bowing thirteen times—the exact number of the United States—when the "renowned Don Quixotto, drawcansiro de Fayetto" was saluted by the Lieutenant-General of France, George Washington.

[1] *Rivington's Gazette*, October 18, 1778.
[2] *Ibid.*, October 7, 1778.
[3] *Ibid.*, October 10, 1778.
[4] *Ibid.*, November 6, 1779.

After the Declaration of Independence, nothing so amazed the loyalists as the French treaty. They could not see why Americans chose "instead of England, a faithful and loving mother — even though at times a severe one," — to have " France, a treacherous and cruel stepmother." They made all the political capital possible out of this, as they chose to regard it, fatal step of Congress. Rivington published every preamble of Whig laws, every proclamation and every letter, which approved of the alliance with France. Such quotations were regarded as terrible testimony against the Whig cause. Of all the errors made by the Whigs this was regarded as the keystone. The wretched financiering, the oppressive laws, the despotic powers given Washington in respect to all who refused to take the Continental currency, and even the occasional success of the British arms were but minor arguments compared with the sinfulness of this wicked alliance.[1]

The varying fortunes of the war greatly influenced the strength of both parties. After the 4th of July, 1776, nothing so hurt the Whig party, temporarily, as the loss of New York, and nothing so weakened the Tory spirits as Burgoyne's defeat. Yet the

[1] The following appeared in *Rivington's Gazette*, October 20, 1779 : " Since Dr. Franklin has ceded Canada and Florida to the French and Spaniards, it is to be hoped that he will give New England to the pretender and make the Pope Archbishop of North America and that the whole continent in the end may go to the devil."

Tories met every vicissitude with renewed endeavors to win over their erring friends in the colonies. They never wearied of the argument that in Washington's camp the soldier had 13 kings and no bread, and that it was better to serve one king and have plenty of bread. Their efforts in disseminating the proclamations of the British commanders, promising pardon and employment to the deserters from the Whig armies, and the numerous arguments with which they fortified these inducements provoked the greatest wrath of the American leaders.[1]

Joseph Galloway, when the British were in possession of Philadelphia, was assigned the task of enrolling and ascertaining the character of the people who came into the city. He testified that 2,300 deserters came into his office.[2] At this time the Patriots were humorously quoted as crying in alarm, "our men now depreciate as fast as our money." A member of Congress asserted that officers in the American army even stimulated their men to desertion that they might find an excuse to follow them. Regimental surgeons, he declared,

[1] Lord Howe's proclamation (December, 1776), his proclamation at Elkton in the following year, General Prevost's proclamation after subduing Georgia, and Sir Henry Clinton's proclamation requiring all people of South Carolina to take an active part in the reëstablishment of the royal government were the principal proclamations; but there were many others and all were assiduously disseminated by the Loyalists.

[2] Of these one half were Irish, one fourth English and Scotch, and the rest Americans. Howe's proclamation offered passage to Ireland to deserters.

took bribes to certify sickness and thus exempt the soldiers from duty.[1] The successes of Howe have, wrote this congressman, given a strange spring to Toryism. "Men who have hitherto lurked in silence and neutrality seem willing to take sides in opposition to the liberties of their country."

It is just that great mass of the Americans, which was always ready to move toward the point of least resistance, that has been least regarded by those who have sought a theory of the American Revolution. That mass has never been a flattering object for the contemplation of either the Whig or Tory sympathizer. As a result, one student has pronounced the Revolution the work of "an unscrupulous and desperate minority"; while another declared it was "the settled conviction of the people that the priceless treasure of self-government could be preserved by no other means."[2] A study of the political struggle between the Whig and the Tory seems to show that, at both extremes of political thought, there was a small body of positive and determined men, while between them lay the wavering neutral masses ready to move unresistingly in the direction given by the success of either Whig or Tory. Leagued with the positive Tory minority was the British Government, while the Whig minority began the struggle with the aid of the great natural advantages of a field vast and

[1] "North Carolina Records," Vol. X., 818.
[2] Fiske, "American Revolution," Vol. I., 196.

far removed from the resources of the enemy. Then the aid of alliances turned the tide steadily and irresistibly toward Whig victory, and, as the trend of events became evident to the mass of neutral Americans, they also joined the favorable flood and assured the ultimate success.

The deserter, then, was not necessarily a rascal. In many cases no doubt he might be induced by the "difference between doubloons and rags" to quit an unprofitable service for one more beneficial, but many a deserter had a more laudable motive. He might be only a thoughtless fellow who had been carried into rebellion by the enthusiasm of men with positive convictions. Then some terrible calamity to the American cause, some real suffering and privation, or a proclamation containing a terrible threat or a fearful reminder that he was a traitor, brought him to a realization of the true situation. A revulsion of feeling brought back all his natural conservatism, and he made the best of his earliest opportunity to join the cause to which his conscience bound him. The Tories understood the nature of this neutral body of men, far better than the British, and constantly urged the British commanders to send skeleton regiments into the neutral districts with arms to be distributed among the loyal men who would at once flock to the king's standard. Joseph Galloway, the most active of all the Loyalists, pled earnestly for such an experiment. He asserted that "the people in every quarter of the provinces of Pennsylvania, New Jersey, the Delaware counties and Maryland are daily petitioning to be supported with a few of the King's troops and offering . . . to take up arms in behalf of government to seize and disarm their . . . oppressors."[1] The influential men in those parts were making incessant offers, he declared, "to raise the loyal in their several districts and form them into a militia," to defend the country, "provided they are duly and properly authorized to do so and are furnished with arms."[2] Galloway offered to furnish lists of those gentlemen, but his advice, as well as most other counsel offered the British by the Tories, was not heeded.

Leading Loyalists, like Joseph Galloway and Governor Tryon, did not aid the British merely by giving advice.[3] They busied themselves tirelessly with schemes and plots to overthrow the patriot

---

[1] Stevens' "Facsimiles," No. 2090, dated March 4, 1778.

[2] Stevens' "Facsimiles," No. 2097, dated June 17, 1778. He listed the counties as follows:
Pennsylvania: Philadelphia, Bucks, Chester, Lancaster, York.
Delaware: Newcastle, Kent, Sussex.
Maryland: Kent, Queen Ann's, Dorset, Somerset, Caroline, Talbot.
New Jersey: Burlington, Gloucester, Salem, Cumberland, Hunterdon, Monmouth.
Virginia: Accomack, Northampton.
N. B.—Several of the counties would raise 1,000 men, none under 500, so that we may safely count upon 500 on an average in each, making in the whole 10,000 men.

[3] See Stevens' "Facsimiles" No. 438 for interesting light on the subject of the Tory advice to the British.

cause. The plot against Washington's life had been traced to Tryon's instigation, and he was suspected of another which had no less an object than the capture of the entire New York provincial convention.[1] Galloway, not to be outdone by his famous rival, planned to seize and bring into the British camp the "rebel Governor Livingston," and his whole council and assembly sitting at Trenton.[2] He was not permitted to execute this plan, and turned his attention to another scheme, which had no less an object than the capture of the Continental Congress. Again he failed to get proper support, and then confined his efforts to directing the movements of certain refugee foragers who captured quantities of cloth and provisions intended for Washington's "armed tatterdemalions" at Valley Forge. These services to the British cause seem, many of them, petty and valueless, but in the sum total they were most annoying to the Whigs. The Tories made every effort to render the state of war as odious as possible, and, to this end, many turned renegade and robbed and destroyed in so secret and mysterious a manner as to make life in their vicinity a state of terror. They made the mails unsafe, and, more than once, valuable letters[3] were stolen and published by Rivington for the edification of the Tories in New York.[4] They har-

[1] "Clinton's Papers," Vol. I., 716.
[2] "Galloway's Examination," p. 62.
[3] "Journals of Congress," Vol. IV., June 17, 1778.
[4] *Rivington's Gazette*, July and August, 1781.

bored the British soldiers in their houses and guided them through dangerous passes. It even became necessary to enact laws with severe penalties to prevent them buying the clothing and accoutrements of the soldiers in the Continental army.[1] A strange state of affairs is indicated, however, by the necessity of such a law. It quite excused the cynic who advertised a book entitled "Genuine Patriotism or a disinterested love of our country" and described its contents as "Fables for the amusement of children."

Of all the ways which the Tories had of making themselves obnoxious to the Whigs, none was so disquieting as the ever-imminent danger of a Tory insurrection. Every attempt to enforce an unpopular law, or any real or rumored approach of the British forces was enough to make every secret Tory alert and eager to overthrow his Whig oppressors. The latter were only too well aware of the unstable nature of their tyrannical power, and their apprehensions were a source of very real sufferings. We shall see, further on, the measures they took to remedy this ill. It is sufficient, at present, to note the effect of this always present danger in lessening the efficient fighting power of the patriots. Upon several occasions the local militia might have greatly aided the continental army,[2] but the threatening attitude of

[1] "Laws of New Jersey," p. 147, dated June 17, 1780.
[2] For one instance see "Clinton Papers," Vol. II., 193.

their Tory neighbors compelled them to remain at home to protect their own property.

In the light of these facts, it is not strange that the Whigs began very early to disarm the Tories, and that they increased their zeal in this work as the war progressed, or when the threatened approach of the British augmented their fear of Tory coalition. The wisdom of the action from a political standpoint was questioned, but its military effect was undoubted. The Loyalists were unable to aid the British, in a military way, until armed and incorporated in the royal armies. Their uprisings were rendered ineffective, while their confidence in themselves and the weight of their opinions with others was greatly reduced.

The work was begun merely as an expedient in certain places by local committees, but soon won the approval of the military commanders and, finally, the endorsement of the Continental Congress, which in turn quickly received the legal support of the state legislatures. The agents employed were civil officers, in cases where no opposition was met, but there was no hesitation in the employment of the militia, or even of detachments of the regular army, where any resistance was expected. Lists of the disarmed persons were made out, partly to save the unfortunate from being fined for appearing at muster without arms; in other cases, that the law might be enforced, which imposed a fine of double the value on all arms concealed.[1] So thoroughly was this work done that, in some instances, the insurgent Tories were armed only with clubs.[2] The subject of Tory military organization, however, and the aid thus given the British is the theme for a subsequent chapter.

[1] See the table of Test Laws in the Appendix in the columns of "penalties."
[2] Galloway's "Examination in the House of Commons."

CHAPTER VIII.

UNDER THE STANDARD OF THE KING.

THE lack of initiative in the Loyalists has been suggested as one of the reasons why they failed in the political contest with the Whigs. Again, when they might have been a tremendous force in the military contest, they waited for proper commissions from the king. The very conservatism, which made them the opponents of the Whigs, rendered their opposition weak and ineffectual. Before the British gained control of New York, there had been sporadic efforts to enlist and arm the Tories, but the Whig activity in organizing their own forces had so far outstripped these weak attempts that they came to nothing. When too late to be effective, there began a period when active military men obtained commissions and went about organizing companies of exiled or outlawed Tories to become a part of the British army. A regiment composed of Scotch refugees and old soldiers, raised by Allan McLean and Guy Johnson in New York,[1] in the spring of 1775, was hurried out of the colonies into Canada.

[1] Flick, "Loyalism in New York," p. 101.

One, Duncan Campbell, enlisted some New York Loyalists to aid Gage when he was cooped up in Boston. But these bodies, like that which was defeated at Moore's Creek in North Carolina,[1] were merely auxiliary forces, brought into being and encouraged by the expectation of aid from the British armies.

Early in 1776, fugitive Loyalists were organized by Sir John Johnson, and these companies hung on the Canadian frontier, waiting the opportunity of vengeance which came for the first time with Burgoyne's campaign. Then St. Leger, with Johnson's "Loyal Greens" and Butler's "Tory Rangers," descended from Niagara and fought the terrible battle of Oriskany. After this murderous engagement, horrible even amid the dreadful scenes of war, came the sortie from Fort Stanwix by which the patriots routed the Tory forces, and St. Leger was sent flying back over the Canadian line. But Johnson and Butler with their Loyal bands had simply fled to return again and become the terror of the New York frontier. In less than a year, the "Rangers" and the "Greens" with their Indian allies returned and swept through the valley of the Wyoming, leaving such a scene of desolation, that the name of the valley suggests the horror of massacre to this day. In the Cherry Valley, Butler

---

[1] Galloway's "Examination in the House of Commons," p. 27. He also speaks of 2,000 men who rose in arms in the peninsula between the Chesapeake and the Delaware.

and Brandt, his Indian ally, repeated the terrors of the Wyoming expedition, and at last aroused Congress to send General Greene to the rescue of the frontier. At the battle of Newtown, the Tory forces, some 1,500 men, were defeated and a check given them for a time, but they returned and created a reign of terror in the Mohawk Valley until the end of the war.

This brief sketch of Tory aggression is fearfully suggestive of the work they might have done, had they earlier abandoned the idea of leaving their fate to the success of British arms. The only defense that can be made for that procrastination was made, late in 1779, by Rivington, the Tory editor of the famous loyal *Gazette*. He defended the Tories against the insinuation that they were not willing to aid. It was absurd, he wrote, to expect a people, however well affected, to rise without arms and without any encouragement or commission to do so. The British had already been obliged to abandon the Loyalists of New Jersey to the resentment of the Americans, and several uprisings in Maryland, Delaware, North Carolina and New Jersey,[1] unsupported by the British, had been suppressed and punished. The Loyalists had learned a lesson. The British general should have invited their aid, if he wished it.[2]

[1] Another was suppressed in Virginia, see "Laws of Virginia," Vol. X., 195.
[2] *Rivington's Gazette*, November 10, 1779.

Such a defence, of course, could only apply to the period after the British had come to New York. Rivington's views were supported by the Commissioners who had been sent to America by the king. They thought that insufficient means had been used "toward engaging, employing and retaining the well-disposed inhabitants,"[1] and they highly approved of a recent resolution of Parliament to give half pay to the provincial officers having enlisted a certain number of men. It would, they felt sure, "draw off multitudes of good recruits from the land service of the Rebel Congress."

When Lord Howe came to New York, he had expected great aid from the Loyalists, and, in spite of the common aversion to joining the regular army, he had by offers of bounties and the pay of regulars increased his force by thousands.[2] Tryon, the exiled Governor of New York, was made Major General of the provincial forces, and he, with able men commissioned under him, began the work of recruiting.[3] Their success was only moderate until the announcement, early in 1779, that provincial officers on service with regular troops should take rank as juniors of the rank to which they belonged. If wounded they should receive the same gratuity as officers of the regular army.[4] This concession,

[1] Stevens' "Facsimiles" No. 1269, dated March 8, 1779.
[2] Flick, "Loyalism in New York," p. 104.
[3] Oliver de Lancey, Major Robert Rogers, Colonel Fanning and Colonel Simcoe were the most successful Tory officers.
[4] *Rivington's Gazette*, May 19, 1779.

added to a movement that had already begun among the Tories in New York, gave a great spur to the organization of loyal troops.

Early in 1778, Rivington began to publish letters written by Loyalists urging their fellow refugees to form companies of militia which would be at liberty to choose their own officers. Many had held back previously because they did not care to enlist under officers in whose choosing they had no voice. Now the agitators urged initiative action by the loyalists. One writer was greatly surprised that, for months past, the Loyalists had rested contented in a state of indolence and languid inactivity without embodying in volunteer companies to take up arms against their "cruel and inveterate enemies, the rebels," by whom they had been "plundered, insulted and persecuted in a most barbarous and brutal manner."[1] Some time later, "Scotus Americanus" recited the wrongs of the Tories and urged them to convene and devise a means of co-operating with the British. "What hinders it, but that a handful of men may overset this rebellion, which has been brought about by a handful of men?" Those, he declared, who had neither spirit to defend rebellion nor to oppose it, can not be of much use to any party, and are a sort of monster in politics.[2] Some had doubted the ultimate success of the war, and hesitated to fight because

[1] *Rivington's Gazette*, April 11, 1778.
[2] *Ibid.*, December 16, 1778.

of the penalties that the successful Whigs would impose, but had not the king said that he would not agree to American Independence until the Tower of London was taken sword in hand?

Aroused by repeated appeals, the large number of refugees, then gathered in New York, began to call meetings to consider the project of an organized body of militia. Those who had not already been lured into the companies, formed by the active men who had received commissions for that purpose, now entered the more promising bodies in which they might choose their own leaders.

They had long been used to seeing the gazettes filled with the most enticing propositions to join the enterprising adventures of commissioned officers. "All aspiring heroes," ran the advertisements, were now given a chance to distinguish themselves. They could " coöperate in relieving themselves from the miseries of anarchy and tyranny." Every true friend of America ought to step forth.[1] "Any spirited young man," announced an officer of dragoons, would be immediately mounted on an elegant horse and furnished with clothing worth £40. He could then take part in the "finishing stroke of this unnatural rebellion."[2] Again the reader was informed that "none but the Brave deserve the Fair," and, as a corollary, all aspiring young

[1] *Pennsylvania Evening Post*, October 14, 1777; *Rivington's Gazette*, May 2, 1778.
[2] Subordinates should receive 50 acre grants of land and six guineas, officers should have 200 acres.

men, whose hearts panted for military glory, and who wished to serve their king and country, might join a new enterprise against the dominions of the "Golden Spaniard." The advertiser was now waiting to lead them on to the field of victory and to splendid fortunes.[1] In spite of the El Dorado presented by a Florida campaign, however, many had preferred the safety of the British protection in New York.

The new inducement offered by the militia organization was that the officers were, to a man, Americans, "who felt very sensibly for the sufferings of their loyal brethren." With infinite pleasure they now offered all refugees an asylum in the loyal band where they might live in harmony with their friends. The militia companies thus organized were supplied with clothing, by subscription or by the proceeds of a lottery. Residents in the territory controlled by the British armies raised large sums of money, or, as in the case of some Quakers, made clothing, for the provincial corps. This provision for the comfort of the militia was, in itself, a great inducement for many to join the organization; for they had nothing, themselves, and the charity provided for the idle was very scant.

When these volunteer companies first appeared, the Tory editor thought that every loyal heart must have been delighted with the view.[2] It was

[1] *Rivington's Gazette*, January 6, 1781.
[2] *Ibid.*, November 22, 1777.

all the more pleasing, he said, because none had been required to take arms "not even the most apostate amongst those who have taken the benefit of the proclamation and come to the city for protection." The organization was reviewed and very blandly complimented, one pleasant morning in July. As the volunteer companies, dressed in their uniforms, paraded in the fields, they were addressed "in the politest manner" by the British Major General, and were promised that he would acquaint the king with their loyalty and military ardor.[1] It was said with pride, and believed, that the whole number of Loyalists mustered on one of these occasions exceeded Washington's Continental army. In January of 1780, the strength of the Loyal militia in New York was estimated at 5,855 men.[2] It gave Rivington great satisfaction, that, besides the regular army, so respectable a body had united to contribute its aid for the "suppression of this unnatural rebellion."

Still, the complaint was made some months later that many thousands of refugees and Loyalists[3] were not yet enlisted in his Majesty's service. It was hoped that those not employed in any department under the king would serve as volunteers, and

---

[1] *Rivington's Gazette*, July 29, 1778.
[2] *Ibid.*, January 29, 1780. See for detail of companies, etc.
[3] A distinction was drawn between those who early fled to the British army and those who only came in under the stress of persecution and encouraged by the British proclamations.

defend the city, if the army went into the country.[1] In an hour of danger, in the winter of 1779-80, when the intense cold had frozen the bay and shut out the British ships, many of the refugees, not in the militia, offered to embody to resist a threatened attack. Some 900 armed at their own expense, and others were supplied from the king's stores.[2] Yet, so many still held back that General Robertson felt justified, in June of 1782, in declaring that, thereafter, all persons were to perform military duty, except "ministers of God's word," and his Majesty's councillors. All persons, who, from age and infirmity, were unable to act, might employ substitutes, as might also "gentlemen of the learned professions." Those who refused were to be removed to the guardhouse. No person deserved protection in a place to the defence of which he refused to contribute. Those who were enrolled under this order were, however, of no avail; for the end of the war and the day of final defeat was even then upon them.

When the loyal militia had been organized, there fell to its unfortunate lot the performance of those acts of war which especially aroused the hatred of the patriots. The small expeditions to burn and pillage towns and to annoy the Whig farmers were left to them. The great campaigns were recognized as legitimate warfare, and those who took part

[1] *Rivington's Gazette*, June 3, 1780.
[2] *Ibid.*, June 28, 1780.

were regarded as honorable enemies; but the men who harassed and worried the country by petty attacks came to be hated in a most virulent way.[1] Add to this the fact that, on the frontiers, they frequently acted in conjunction with the Indians,[2] and we may understand why a Tory was "a devil in human shape,"[3] in the eyes of the patriots.

The regulations that governed their operations provided that they should plunder only "rebels," and that they should be entitled to what they seized. They were to practice no excesses or barbarities contrary to the recognized laws of war. Any prisoners seized by them were to be kept apart and exchanged for captured Loyalists.[4] They were, therefore, licensed to prey upon the country for their subsistence.[5] This sort of warfare soon led to outrages and retaliation, and much embittered the Whig and Tory relations.

Leaving the British lines for a few hours, they would dash into the enemy's country, up the Hudson, into "indigo Connecticut" or over to New Jersey, and drive off horses and cattle, kidnap the Whig owners, and, in some cases, leave a village in ruin and desolation. Every farmer lived in fear of

[1] See Gov. Livingston's summary of their deeds, Sabine, "Loyalists," p. 21.
[2] See "Pennsylvania Archives," Vol. III., 192, "New York Colonial Documents," Vol. VIII., 159, etc.
[3] "Clinton Papers," Vol. I., 746.
[4] "Documents Relating to the Colonial History of New York," Vol. VIII., 770.
[5] *Rivington's Gazette*, June 5, 1779.

the Tories "lurking in the woods," and measured his loss not only by the amount of which he was robbed, but by the harvests which he dared not gather, and which lay rotting in the fields. Committee-men and members of the state legislatures were kept in terror by the occasional capture of one of their number and horrible stories of his fate. Jails were emptied and burned, and many Tories thus liberated. The effect or imagined effect of this sort of warfare was described by Rivington in the most florid newspaper rhetoric. He loved to represent the Whigs, "those pickaroon gentry," being chased headlong cross country by loyal rangers; and, if these bands had killed and captured half as many on each little foray as Rivington claimed, there would not have been a patriot man, woman or child left in the devastated country.[1] In defending the marauding

[1] *Rivington's Gazette*, July 7, 1779. Lieut. Col. Tarleton attacked a party of "rebel Nags" (near Bedford). [The Tories compelled the "rebels" to quit their "Jades" and killed 22—got 17 prisoners—burned several houses.] "Amongst the prisoners is one of the Vantassals . . . of a pedigree partly Indian, partly Batavian; this despicable caitiff has of late amused himself with cruelly flagellating numbers of inoffensive women, whom he had suspected of frequenting the N. Y. Markets; 4 of this handy varlet's brothers . . . are held as hostages for 4 men of the Provincial corps who had been made prisoners . . . tried and destined to the cord by their new Republican legislature, . . . the fate of the Vantassal fraternity will depend immediately upon that of the Loyal Provincials. When once the gallows of castigation shall be erected on the side of loyalty, a period to the public and wanton murder of the king's friends will assuredly follow. One Hunt, formerly a breeches maker of this city, but of late a vender of the confiscated estates of Loyal Refugees, an orator, a messenger employed by Congress, etc.,

expeditions, however, he made a very good point when he noted that, "The Rebels in their accounts of these excursions, speak of the Refugees as Thieves, Robbers and Murderers, while they represent their people when concerned in the same kind of transactions as brave Warriors, Heroes and Demigods."[1]

For the purpose of making this mode of attack more dangerous, the New Jersey Legislature denounced these "felonious outrages," and ordered the governor to issue a proclamation for apprehending these associated persons as men guilty of murder.[2] Thereafter, Rivington asserted, "scarcely a rebel newspaper" did not contain an account of some Loyalist hanged. "By way of blind," they represented him as guilty of theft, or of acting as a spy. "They wanted rebel foragers," he cried indignantly, "exchanged as prisoners of war, but Refugees in the same work were treated and executed as traitors."

About this time, the Loyalists began openly to declare their intention of entering on a course of retaliation. The confiscation of their estates had

was also taken and can sympathize at leisure, *en provost* with his mongrel friend Vantassal on the disastrous condition of their paper piastres, the dwindling number of Mr. Washington's scal'd miserables, and the chap-fallen countenances" (of the delegates of the Continental Congress).

[1] *Rivington's Gazette*, June 5, 1779.
[2] "Acts of New Jersey" (1775-83), p. 83. Congress also acted in the matter of abductions. See "Journals of Congress," Vol. IV., February 27, 1778.

begun under the Whig direction, and their persons had been proscribed. Now, "actuated by the eldest law of nature," they believed themselves justified in making retaliations and reprisals. They, therefore, declared themselves the avowed enemies of the rebels, and would at once begin hostilities. They did not propose to involve the innocent with the guilty, and, if, in any expedition, the property of some peaceful loyal subject should by mistake be injured, the Loyalists would make good the damage.[1]

The Loyal Associated Refugees living under the British protection at Newport, R. I., came to a like decision. They were sorry that the "hardened obstinacy" of the Whigs had forced the Tories to arm against them for justifiable revenge. They had wished America to be reclaimed rather than subdued. Now that such a consummation was impossible, they would make war — but only on the guilty.[2] This would enable "the much-injured Loyalists" to "do themselves justice upon their rebellious countrymen."

Supported in such resolutions by Governor Tryon, the Loyalists of New York set out upon the expedition which laid Fairfield and Norwalk in ashes and burned the ships in New Haven harbor, as well as a part of the town, before the yeomanry in the vicinity drove the marauders away. Tryon said

[1] *Rivington's Gazette*, February 13, 1779.
[2] *Ibid.*, July 14, 1779.

that the refugees possessed a zeal which, with their intimate knowledge of the country, rendered them very useful on such expeditions.[1]

Their effectiveness in such warfare was greatly augmented by a kind of enterprise which has, so far, been unnoticed, but the beginning of which somewhat antedates this attack on New Haven. Privateering had been discouraged by the British government as long as there was any hope of conciliating the colonists; but, when that hope was gone, ready sanction was given to any means of making war a greater curse.

Early in 1779, the gazettes announced that some of the principal loyal ladies of New York proposed to subscribe money for fitting out a privateer to be called the "Fair American." The obsequious editors remarked that there was no doubt that this privateer would be "extremely well manned with gallant youths." The whimsical Rivington thought that the rebels ought to be ashamed to have aroused the indignation of the fair sex, "whose natural characteristics are gentleness and benevolence."[2]

[1] *Rivington's Gazette*, July 20, 1779.
[2] *Ibid.*, January 6, 1779. A few days later, January 16, a rhymster attempted to immortalize the theme. The essential lines —if there are such—are as follows:

> "Hail, Lovely Fair! who grace that safe retreat
> Where Britain's friends in cordial union meet.
> . . . . . .
> Since your sweet bosoms loyal ardors feel
> . . . .

The British government had been importuned by Tryon, for some time, to issue letters of marque and reprisal. It now yielded[1] to the pressure, and, in a short time, the refugees were being allured by every device to enlist in these enterprises. Broadsides urged them to call at the tavern "Sign of St. Andrew," the store ship "Leviathan," or other rendezvous, and learn the advantages of this or that "superb and elegant ship." All "gentlemen sailors or able bodied landsmen" were wanted. The most ample encouragement would be given refugees; solely that those brave men who had suffered in the cause of their country might have a chance to repair their losses at the expense of their perfidious enemies. There was some rivalry between those ships which only proposed to ravage the coasts and those intending long voyages. A recruiting officer for one of the latter declared, with a sneer, that "seamen of spirit" would prefer rich

> Assured be that every honest man
>   Will idolize the Fair American.
> Brave loyal Tars, with Hearts of Oak will vie,
>   For you to fight, to conquer, live or die;
>   . . . . .
> With equal haste the French and Rebels beat,
>   As if they rushed your lovely lips to meet.
>   . . . . .
> Thus when Rebellion, to her native Hell,
>   With Diaboliads, is confined to dwell:
> Your gallant youths, will claim no higher prize
>   Than New York nymphs in chaste endearing ties.
>   . . . . .

[1] "New York Colonial MSS.," Vol. VIII., 740-764.

French prizes "to piddling along shore in boats."[1] Even the nature of the armament was described for the conviction of the reader. One mounted sixteen six-pounders, cohorns and swivels, with hand grenades, fire arrows and every necessary implement of war. Another, appealing to a different constituency, was well stocked with wholesome provisions and a sufficient stock of "the Creature, which warms, cherishes, and stimulates the heart of the seaman in cold weather." The "never exhausted floating wealth of the Spaniard, the Frenchman, and remnant of the Rebel, points out an ample field upon which the seaman may reap a golden harvest."[2]

The near-shore fleet of small boats could not present such Pactolian temptations, but they, too, hinted that profit and honor were "inseparably blended." Every member of that "determined band of Loyalists" should receive five pounds advance and three pounds per month and one share in all property taken.

The service was evidently popular, for the commanders of the British fleet began to complain that the manning of the privateers was done at their expense. They demanded that the practice cease, and threatened to impress all of a crew found to have a single British seaman. Finally they actually began

[1] *Rivington's Gazette*, April 7, 1779, and July 25, 1779.
[2] *Ibid.*, November 27, 1779. Recruits were to receive three pounds above the King's bounty, a suit of clothes, and fifty acres of good land in New York. See July 25, 1779.

taking man for man out of the privateers and merchant vessels.[1] Nevertheless, the work of the privateers was heartily approved by the British government. Lord Germain was greatly pleased "to find the spirit of annoying the commerce of the King's Enemies" had increased among the Loyalists, and that their efforts had been attended with private benefit as well as public advantage.[2]

The direction of the whole enterprise was later entrusted to a board of directors, consisting of the principal loyalists from each American province. The officers who commanded the associated refugees were approved by this board, and commissioned by the British commander-in-chief. The latter furnished the shipping, as well as the arms and rations, and provided for the care of sick and wounded in the King's hospital. Captures made without the aid of the British regulars were shared by the refugees concerned.[3] Their sailors were not to be impressed, and their prisoners were to be exchanged only for Loyalists. As concerned the object of their undertaking, the board "appealed to God who is the searcher of all hearts" to witness that they had no wish to prolong the horrors of war, but hoped to "emancipate the country from Republican tyranny."

[1] *Rivington's Gazette*, October 9, 1779.
[2] "New York Colonial MSS.," Vol. VIII., 764.
[3] See the Proclamation of Dec. 28, 1780, in *Rivington's Gazette*, Dec. 30, 1780, where the names of the members of the board are given.

From a station at Lloyd's Neck, which was assigned to them,[1] the fleet of associated Loyalists made repeated attacks upon the whole New England coast. So many of these marauding ventures went forth under the cover of night that "owls and ghosts, and thieves and Tories" came to be closely associated in Whig minds. Many of these attacks were of a most petty nature, and resulted only in captures of sheep, poultry, cattle, wood, corn, and an occasional Whig who had tried to resist their predatory attempts. Annoying as it was, it lacked dignity, and the Whig newspapers explained that the British at New York, "heartily fatigued with having so many importunate hungry Tories hanging upon them, have come to a kind of compromise with these wretches. They are now to prowl for their own living and maintain their families by plunder and robbery."[2] A natural result of this method of attack was to invite retaliation by the Whigs and to help evolve that hatred of the Tory which persisted long after the other wounds of the war were healed.

The real service rendered the British by the Tories was not through these associated bands but by the thousands of individuals who enlisted in the regular army. New York alone furnished about 15,000 men to the British army and navy, and over

[1] Onderdonck's "Revolutionary Incidents of Long Island," p. 220 et seq.
[2] Moore's "Diary of the Revolution," Vol. II., 152.

8,000 loyalist militia.¹ All of the other colonies furnished about as many more, so that we may safely state that 50,000 soldiers, either regular or militia, were drawn into the service of Great Britain from her American sympathizers.

It is not in the province of this work to tell again the story of those campaigns in which the Loyalists played a subordinate or even a principal part. Those campaigns have been described too often and too well to require a repetition. It will suffice simply to recall those events, that the summary may remind us of the important rôle played by the Tory volunteer in the Revolution.

In addition to the work of Butler and Johnson on the New York frontier, it is not to be forgotten that Tories formed no inconsiderable part in the invading force of Burgoyne. Even when they failed actually to join his army, their known presence in large numbers among the inhabitants of the region prevented the Whig militia from joining the American forces.² The British forces were greatly aided also, in the matter of supplies, by the Tory inhabitants. Even after the surrender, many of the soldiers were aided to escape by sympathizing friends among the Americans.³

---

[1] Flick, " Loyalism in New York," p. 112. This fairly agrees with my own estimate, made from various inexact sources, such as the newspaper estimates and general statements made in proclamations, etc.

[2] Clinton's " Papers," Vol. II., p. 193.

[3] Galloway's Examination, published by the '76 Society, p. 23.

All of the frontier warfare seems to have been carried on by Tory bands in league with the Indians. The southern frontier, in 1776–77, was ravaged by Tory guerrillas and Indians, and it was chiefly the Tories who were relied upon to aid the few British regulars in preserving British control of the Northwest. When George Rogers Clark attacked Vincennes, he defeated some 500 Tories, regulars and Indians, and he found them in other posts in the disputed country.

In South Carolina and Georgia, there were, throughout the war, small bands of Tories carrying on a bitter internecine war with the Whigs. After the capture of Savannah by the British, and when the timid inhabitants of Georgia had all sworn their allegiance to save their property, an attempt was made by the Whigs of the neighboring states to regain the lost territory. When North Carolina sent 2,000 Whigs for this purpose, some 700 Tories started to counteract this force. As the latter were marching across South Carolina, they were defeated by Col. Pickens; and those who were taken prisoners were tried by a civil court and five of them hanged. The Tory commandant, at Augusta, at once retaliated by hanging some of his Whig prisoners. That was sufficient to begin a long series of reprisals and greatly embitter the party strife in the South.

Not only did large numbers of Tory soldiers go with the British forces for the invasion of the South, but many refugees and deserters joined them after their first success. By October, 1779, nearly two thirds of the British troops in Savannah were Tories.[1] Early in the year, General Prevost had proclaimed that the laws in force in 1775 were restored until a loyal legislature could be convened.[2] Wright, the royal governor, was reinstated. The inhabitants had been urged to come under the royal standard, and the intimation given them that only by supporting the British cause with arms could they be protected.[3] This pressure forced many into the ranks; and it was this garrison chiefly which defeated the French admiral's attempt (in conjunction with the Americans under General Lincoln) to capture Savannah, in September and October of that year.

When, in the next year, Sir Henry Clinton captured Charleston, his force contained a large body of Tories,[4] and, in the internecine warfare which followed, small bands of Tories kept up a continual struggle with the Patriot leaders, Sumter, Pickens and Marion.

At this juncture began the famous career of Tarleton and his Tory "Legion," which he had raised in New York. In the wild warfare with the

[1] "Stevens' Facsimiles," No. 2016.
[2] *Rivington's Gazette*, March 27, 1779.
[3] *Ibid.*, February 4, 1779.
[4] McCrady, "South Carolina in the Revolution," pp. 446, 448, 510. A list of Tory regiments from the North which fought in South Carolina is here given.

partisan commanders, Sumter and Marion, no British force came so bravely off, for a time, as did Tarleton and his Loyal Cavalry. When the battle of Camden was fought, it was Tarleton's cavalry and Rawdon's Volunteers of Ireland, raised in Pennsylvania, that carried the day. Nearly 2,400 refugees took part in that terrible defeat of Gates,[1] and the Tories in New York took special delight in accounts of this battle, because they felt that it was their victory. They taunted Gates in prose and rhyme; and mock advertisements were hung up offering millions reward for a whole army, horse, foot and dragoons, strayed or stolen from the subscriber, near Camden, South Carolina. The owner, Horatio Gates, suspected that Cornwallis had stolen them.[2]

This triumph of Tory arms was quickly followed by an engagement in which Tarleton defeated Sumter and took some 300 prisoners. The Loyalists' exultation was only marred by the defeat of some 500 of their number[3] by Colonel Williams, one of the Whig leaders.

The proclamation of Clinton, requiring all people of South Carolina to take an active part in the reestablishment of the royal government, had resulted rather in antagonizing the indifferent people than in winning them to the Loyal side. When the detachments were sent into the country to force the

---

[1] *Rivington's Gazette*, September 20, 1780.
[2] *Ibid.*, September 16, 1780.
[3] There were some British in the force.

inhabitants to take the oath of allegiance, the work was unwisely left too much in Tory hands. These men often had old scores to settle, and their rough methods led to bloodshed and fierce reprisals. Now, when even the indifferent had been aroused and forced into action, Cornwallis, before starting for the conquest of North Carolina, detached Colonel Ferguson, next to Tarleton the best of his partisan officers, to enter the highlands of South Carolina, enlist all the Tories he could find, and rejoin the British army at Charlotte. As Ferguson with a thousand Tories and a few British infantry penetrated the hills of the back country, he was surrounded by constantly growing bands of frontiersmen; and, after endeavoring to escape, made a stand on the top of King's Mountain. From that position, with a characteristic Tory sentiment, he challenged "all the rebels outside of hell" to dislodge him; and it seemed as if most of them were there when the attack began from behind every tree on the mountain side. No human heart could stand the steady, ruthless advance of those Indian hunters, and, when at last Ferguson himself was killed, the white flag was raised and over 700 Tories surrendered as prisoners of war, while the rest of the detachment lay dead or wounded on the field.

Hardly had this terrible blow to Tory hopes become known, when Tarleton, on whose career all loyal eyes were turned, received a defeat of no great moment from Sumter's guerrillas. Two months later, however, at the battle of the Cowpens, Tarleton's Tory force was entirely destroyed by Daniel Morgan.

Meanwhile the terrible tragedy of Benedict Arnold's treason had been enacted, and Arnold, in New York, attempted to assume the part of a loyal American whose past, and not his present, was in error. With the approval of the British commander he issued a proclamation to the "officers and soldiers of the Continental Army."[1] All who had the real interest of their country at heart, and who were determined to be no longer the tools and dupes of Congress were invited to join a corps of cavalry and infantry. They should have rank in the King's service proportioned to their former rank, and should be paid as the British troops were paid. This chosen band of Americans he wished to lead to the attainment of peace. He believed that all would be glad to escape from the neglect, contempt and corruption of Congress. He asked rhetorically whether they knew that "the eye which guides this pen lately saw your mean and profligate Congress at mass for the soul of a Roman Catholic in Purgatory." When he had organized a regiment of some 1,600 men, chiefly New York loyalists, he was sent by Clinton to Virginia. After a career of plundering and burning in that state, he was recalled, and Tarleton, who had escaped when his force was destroyed at the Cowpens, became again

[1] *Rivington's Gazette*, November 1, 1780.

the center of Tory interest. He made some brilliant raids of which the most famous was his attempt to capture Thomas Jefferson at Monticello, which failed only because the intended victim was forewarned and fled from his home. Thus to the last act of the war, Tories were active as members of provincial corps in the British army.

When the surrender at Yorktown was made, Cornwallis wished to provide for the safety of the large number of Loyalists in his army by a clause in the articles of capitulation, stating that Loyalists should not be punished on account of having joined the British army.[1] To this Washington refused assent, on the ground that this was a matter of civil character. The difficulty was disposed of, however, by permitting a British ship to depart for New York with the news of surrender and such troops as Cornwallis might choose to send with it. In this vessel were huddled the forlorn Loyalists, glad, even in this plight, to regain their friends and to escape the fury of their enraged countrymen.

[1] Lossing's "Field Book of the Revolution," Vol. II., 317.

CHAPTER IX.

UNDER THE BAN OF THE LAW.

THE chapters on the activity of the Tories help us to a better appreciation of the Whig hatred of his political opponent. The average Patriot seemed unable to view the Loyalist in any other light than as a traitor. They finally came to make no distinction between Benedict Arnold and a Tory who had consistently opposed the Revolution from its very inception. As the war advanced and one outrage after another was attributed to natural Tory depravity, the Whigs forgot that these men had been their respected neighbors, and believed them to be born with a natural ferocity like the savage. The common idea, of the menace to the community which a Tory had become, is admirably summed up in an exhortation addressed to the inhabitants of Philadelphia in 1779.[1]

"Rouse, America! your danger is great,— great from a quarter where you least expect it. The Tories, the Tories will yet be the ruin of you! 'Tis high time they were separated from among you. They are now busy engaged in undermining your liberties. They have a thousand ways of doing it, and they make use of them all. Who were the

[1] Moore's "Diary," Vol. II., 166.

occasion of this war? The Tories! Who persuaded the tyrant of Britain to prosecute it in a manner before unknown to civilized nations, and shocking even to barbarians? The Tories! Who prevailed on the savages of the wilderness to join the standard of the enemy? The Tories! Who have assisted the Indians in taking the scalp from the aged matron, the blooming fair one, the helpless infant and the dying hero? The Tories! Who advised and who assisted in burning your towns, ravaging your country and violating the chastity of your women? The Tories! Who are the occasion that thousands of you now mourn the loss of your dearest connections? The Tories! Who have always counteracted the endeavors of Congress to secure the liberties of this country? The Tories! Who refused their money when as good as specie though stamped with the image of his most sacred Majesty? The Tories! Who continue to refuse it? The Tories! Who do all in their power to depreciate it? The Tories! Who propagate lies among us to discourage the Whigs? The Tories! Who corrupt the minds of the good people of these States by every species of insidious counsel? The Tories! Who hold a traitorous correspondence with the enemy? The Tories! Who daily send them intelligence? The Tories! Who take the oaths of allegiance to the States one day and break them the next? The Tories! Who prevent your battalions from being filled? The Tories! Who dissuade men from entering the army? The Tories! Who persuade those who have enlisted to desert? The Tories! Who harbor those who do desert? The Tories! In short, who wish to see us conquered, to see us slaves, to see us hewers of wood and drawers of water? The Tories!"

It is little to be wondered at that the Whigs, who believed in this terrible indictment, were ready to deprive these desperate characters of all the natural rights of law-abiding citizens. They must, of course, deprive them of all those political rights which might help them to ruin the state. They must place such restrictions upon them as would protect their neighbors from their malevolence. Every privilege must be denied them that might lend aid to their "wicked designs." The popular definition of a Tory intimated very plainly the only fate of which they were thought worthy. "A Tory is a thing whose head is in England, and its body in America, and its neck ought to be stretched."

On the ground that only citizens should be allowed the right to vote, and that those who had not taken an oath of allegiance were not citizens, the Tory was early deprived of his vote in every state.[1] To prevent his voting, the inspectors of election were made liable to a heavy fine if they did not make certain by some reliable voucher that every voter was of Patriot sympathies. The Loyal-

---

[1] See analysis of laws in the appendix. I shall omit references in this chapter, as facts may be verified in the appendix.

ist who ventured to vote in spite of this prohibition could be prosecuted and heavily fined or imprisoned.

The right to hold any office of trust or profit in the state was also prohibited. No man who could speak of the members of Congress indiscriminately as "ambitious incendiaries" or as "indigent men, bankrupt both in fortune and character" could be given any chance to influence their fortunes, however remotely. These "parricides," who had "plunged their once happy country into a flood of miseries," therefore enacted a law[1] which debarred all men, who had not given proof of their fidelity to the United States, from holding any office, civil or military under Congress.[2]

In the courts of law, not even the rights of a foreigner were left to the loyalist. If his neighbors owed him money, he had no legal redress until he took an oath that he favored American independence. All legal action was denied him. He might be assaulted, insulted, blackmailed or slandered, though the law did not state it so baldly, yet he had no recourse in law. No relative or friend could leave an orphan child to his guardianship. He could be the executor or administrator of no man's estate. He could neither buy land nor transfer it to another.

---

[1] In February of 1778.

[2] In the law of Pennsylvania, which excluded Loyalists from all other offices, was a curious clause which stated that this did not exempt them from serving as supervisor of the highways, collector of public taxes and overseer of the poor. It is very strong evidence that these offices were not considered desirable.

The legal right to dispose of his own fortune at his death was refused him. Even his deed of gift was invalid. Except for the divine sanction implied, it was worse than excommunication. His property was left completely at the mercy of his fellow men. There is good evidence that confiscation, though delayed until the general issue was more certain, was early in the minds of prominent patriots, and this accounts for the effort to prevent the Loyalist from selling his property.

It was only when the war fever ran the highest, in the eastern and southern states and in Pennsylvania, that the laws reached the degree of severity indicated in the preceding paragraph. Massachusetts and the several central states did not carry the attack on the Loyalist to this extreme. Rhode Island, however, went so far as to enact that all executions, already issued to persons who had not taken the oath, be returned to the officers unsatisfied, and even persons already committed on such executions were to be discharged from prison.

Most of the states forbade anyone to serve as a juryman who had no certificate of his fidelity to the state. Any violation of this law was punished with fine and imprisonment. No man, however, who was known to have Tory tendencies, was likely to be chosen on a jury. That these prohibitions are to be found in the laws is important chiefly, because it proves that such measures had the approbation of men high in authority. It is not strange that, in the rage of civil war, the rabble should make all practical justice impossible for its opponents, but that theoretical justice should be refused by the legislators shows the bitterness of the civil strife.

Legislative efforts to prevent Tory influence in the courts not only restricted the use of legal machinery, but placed disqualifications upon legal practitioners. The state of New York made a well-defined attack upon Tory members of the bar.[1] Every man of the legal profession, who had been licensed to plead or practice in the courts, must produce a certificate of his attachment to the "liberties and independence of America." Those who failed to do so, and others already guilty of overt acts had their licenses suspended. To regain their privileges they might apply to the superior court, and it would order a sheriff to summon eight to sixteen freeholders, for an inquisition. This body decided the status of the individual and restored him to his privileges, if he proved himself a faithful Whig.

Two years before, New Jersey had closed her courts to councillors and attorneys-at-law who were known as Loyalists. Pennsylvania added clerks, notaries and sergeants-at-law to the proscribed list. The ministerial as well as the advisory legal system was thus purged. The Loyalist had said bitterly that the new Patriot officials had rather "rule in Hell, than serve in Heaven," with the suggestion that the service of Great Britain was the celestial em-

[1] In October of 1779.

ployment referred to. The Patriot retort was the prohibition of legal practice to the Loyalist.

The forbidding men to pursue their professions, outside of the law, was a refinement of persecution to which most of the thirteen legislatures refused to give their sanction. Maryland and Pennsylvania were the most noteworthy exceptions. The legislation of the former preceded by several months the action of the latter on the subject, but the act of Pennsylvania was more comprehensive.

While the British were in Philadelphia, and the legislature's wrath was at its height, an " act for the further security of the government " struck a blow at every Loyalist of influence. Some of the trustees of the College of Philadelphia had already had their powers suspended; but they were now incapacitated in law from holding the office. All rectors, professors, masters and tutors of any college, if they had Tory sympathies, might be prosecuted for performing their duties. The prosecutor was encouraged by the promise of one half the penalty of £500 that might be inflicted. The same penalty was incurred by any schoolmaster who pursued his vocation without a certificate of his love of America and her independence.

A New Jersey law, passed several months previously, made the same prohibition, but the lawmakers felt constrained to explain their action. They stated that it was " of the last moment to a free and independent state that the rising generation

UNDER THE BAN OF THE LAW. 197

should be early instructed in the principles of public virtue and duly impressed with the amiable ideas of liberty and patriotism, and at the same time inspired with the keenest abhorrence of despotic and arbitrary power." They emphasized the fact that " public teachers and instructors may be greatly instrumental in tincturing the youthful mind with such impressions either in favor of a just and equal administration or of a slavish submission to lawless rule, as in their riper years are not easily obliterated." The sentimental defense as well as the law were quite unnecessary, for no Patriot, at that stage of the war, would knowingly send children to a Tory schoolmaster. The Pennsylvania law had added druggists and apothecaries to the list of professions denied the Tory, but rumor and slander, aided by personal spite, had already taken care of the Tory apothecaries. It was common gossip that they wittingly made mistakes, and that all their drugs were more or less poisoned. How could any one trust a Tory, who was a "son of that infernal monster" which "bestrides our harbor, shading the ocean with his lowering brow, and yawns with horrid jaws for the innocent blood of this continent"?

The same may be said of loyal physicians or surgeons. Many a story of a lucrative practice ruined was told to the British commissioners when they heard the Loyalist claims after the war. A Maryland surgeon, who evidently was not a rabid

Loyalist, testified that his business gradually declined until he had none. People were afraid to employ him, he said.

Merchants and traders did not escape this searching legislative persecution, but it was needless. A Tory was a social leper, and it was only by great sacrifice that he kept up any commercial activity. For the execution of this prohibitive legislation the law always provided a most zealous agent. Half of the heavy fines, for continuing any profession without taking an oath, went to the prosecutor. Every prosperous man was sure to have jealous rivals who would seize upon any opportunity to accomplish his downfall and diminish his fortune. "Every eye was intuitively suspicious," wrote a Loyalist who suffered much at this time.

Another kind of attack upon the Tory was the legislative prohibition of free speech and the free press. As a war measure, it had every excuse. As the preambles of many laws of the time stated, there were men ever ready to discourage others from enlisting in the American army, or to urge them not to continue in the service. The ignorant were frightened with stories that the King had hired 50,000 Russians to subdue America. These terrible Cossacks would spare neither man, woman nor child. Their leaders were "masterpieces of inhumanity." There was no salvation from the King's wrath but to join the British army. These "artful devices of the enemies of America" were met by the interdiction of all speech or writing against the states or Congress. The Continental Congress[1] urged the states to "frustrate these mischievous machinations" and prevent "honest and well-meaning but misinformed people" being "deceived and drawn into erroneous opinion."

Connecticut had already acted. In a law dated "Anno regni regis Georgii tertii, decimo sexto," the last law headed with the regnal year and published under the royal arms, the attack was made. Any person who wrote, or spoke, or by any overt act libeled or defamed Congress, or the acts of the Connecticut General Assembly, should be brought to trial. If convicted, he might be fined, imprisoned or disfranchised, and must pay the cost of prosecution. There are abundant proofs in the Connecticut records that the law was vigorously executed.

A pamphlet entitled: "A Discourse upon Extortion" became the subject of a special resolution of the legislature. It was denounced as containing many insulting reflections on civil government, tending to sedition, bloodshed and domestic insurrections. As it was expected soon to be published and dispersed among the people, to the great danger of public peace, the sheriff was ordered to seize and hand it over to the State attorney. The resolution was a kind of literary bill of attainder. "Papinian" well expressed the Tory sentiment toward such laws, when he sneered, "There is more

[1] January of 1776.

liberty in Turkey than in the dominions of Congress."

Five of the remaining states acted in the following year, and the rest, as the exigencies of the war forced the issue upon them.[1] They contracted the freedom of speech and press still further. Not only should men refrain from evil speaking and writing upon the delicate subject of Congress and the Colonial Assemblies, but they must not affirm that the King or Parliament of Great Britain had any authority over the United States. This was not to be done even under the pretense of prayer; for some did under "that guise wish for the success of the King's arms and that he might vanquish and overcome all his enemies."

To speak in a derogatory way of the Continental currency was sternly forbidden. In preaching or praying, in public or in private discourse, no one was to be allowed to discourage people from supporting the Declaration of Independence. The raising of the Continental army must not be discountenanced.

The cupidity of the Loyalists' neighbors was wrought upon to make such laws effective. As mentioned before, half of the enormous fines[2] that were imposed as penalties went to the prosecutor. In other instances, the town treasury or the poor

[1] In 1777 and 1778.
[2] The limit of the fines was in some cases as high as $20,000. In March, of 1781, New York went so far as to threaten with the death of a felon any one acknowledging the King of Great Britain as his sovereign.

in the almshouse got the benefit. In Massachusetts, the obligation to prosecute was laid upon the selectmen, the committee of correspondence, sheriff, constable, grand juryman or tithingman. If one of them complained of an individual to the justice of peace, the latter issued a warrant to the sheriff to bring the accused for examination. If found inimical, he must furnish heavily-bonded sureties for his good behavior.

In the execution of these laws, the patriots often went to the most fantastic extremes. All wit and humor which had for its object the Patriot cause must be hushed. Congress and the flag were shielded from the Tory wag who asserted that Mrs. Washington had a mottled tomcat with thirteen yellow rings around his tail, and that his flaunting it suggested to the Congress the adoption of the same number of stripes for the rebel flag. There is an authentic case of the trial, before the South Carolina provincial Congress, of a Loyalist who had given his word not to injure the American cause. He was accused of intimating that Americans had no right to make any demands of the Prince and Parliament. His open offence, however, was that by way of burlesque he had called his stray dog "Tory," thus intimating, presumably, that the Tory led a dog's life. On the plea that he was intoxicated when he said these things, he was only reprimanded from the chair.

The Continental paper money, more than anything else, needed protection from Tory wit and aspersion. The subject was mentioned in nearly every general law directed against freedom of speech. Most of the states, upon the recommendation of Congress, passed special acts. "Disaffected and evil-minded persons" had sought to destroy the credit and circulation of the Continental bills and the bills of the state. Thereafter, no one was to demand a higher price in bills than in coin. The truth was that Loyalists were no greater sinners in that regard than Patriots, but, at that time, Loyalists were scapegoats for every ill in the state. The Patriot, however, confined *his* disapproval to refusing the bills or allowing[1] about two cents on a dollar. He did not advertise it as a particularly cheap form of papering for the walls of a house, nor urge its use for kindling fires and lighting pipes, as did the satirical Tory. John Adams, on shipboard off Newfoundland, overheard a woman of Tory principles speaking of the currency as "nasty, poison paper money." She gave orders not to "put that nasty money with our other money."

The Patriot leaders were ever unearthing "gigantic plots" to depreciate the Continental money. "Our grand enemy," wrote Henry Laurens," have . . . a device . . . for depreciating the value of money issued by the authority of Congress... . . The pernicious stratagem . . . appears more glaring from a late publication in Philadelphia, sub-

[1] In 1780.

scribed to by a very great number of those misguided persons who chose to remain in the city and welcome the enemy to rivet their fetters." [1] As if a "device" or "pernicious stratagem" were necessary to depreciate currency for which there was so slight hope for redemption!

Those whose patriot principles were not in doubt might refuse to accept the paper money at par, but the suspected Tory had the "worthless rags" forced upon him at every turn. His rents were paid in it. For his produce, he was obliged to accept paper money at par, and then purchase his necessities with hard money or the currency at a terrible sacrifice. He was made the sink for all this financial refuse. He dared not protest against this persecution for fear of the more violent attack that would sweep away all his wealth at once. The only result of this temporizing was that ruin crept more slowly into his fortunes. The long-wished-for victory of the British never came, and, at last, the wretched Tory fled, penniless, to the British lines. Such was the story told with many variations by the claimants before the British Commissioners for granting them compensation.

Concurrent with these legislative restrictions upon the expression of loyal or anti-revolutionary sentiments were limitations upon the personal action of Loyalists. They were forbidden to travel or to go near the enemy's lines. Men were subjected to

[1] In December of 1777.

the penalties of Toryism if they refused to join the militia and appear regularly at muster. Of course, these were simply war-measures, and were as necessary to control the Patriot as the Loyalist, but the latter bore the opprobrium of having made the law necessary. Occasionally the fact was recognized that " lukewarm friends of the American cause " did carry on trade with the British army, but usually it was " evil-minded and disaffected persons." The Whig legislators, " those zealous votaries of the bubble, popularity," as Governor Martin termed them, were careful not to offend their constituents by intimating that there was any sordid element in patriotism. They could not openly direct their laws against the Patriots who grew rich by trading with the British. They preferred to aim at the Loyalist and, if, perchance, the Patriot were hit, that was no business of the lawmaker.

The presence of many spies, in the states where the war centered, made the identification of strangers most necessary. The Council of Safety of Connecticut resolved:[1] "Whereas many persons inimical to the United States of America do wander from place to place with intent to spy out the state of the colonies and give intelligence to their enemies, whereby confederacies may be formed and strengthened," that no unknown or suspected person, whether he appeared in the character of gentleman, express carrier, traveller or common beggar,

[1] In July of 1776.

should travel in the state unless he produced a certificate from some Congress, Committee of Safety, or of Inspection, or other specified civil or military officers, stating whence he came and whither he was going. There must also be a guarantee that the traveller was friendly. The recommendation was made to the larger towns to keep proper watches to seize the persons who might travel by night. The same precautions were taken in several other states. A formal statute in New Jersey contained all the above regulations, and added that the innkeepers, ferrymen, and stage drivers must make sure that their patrons had the necessary certificate. They should forfeit £20 for the neglect of this duty.

Prohibitions of trade with the British army were most necessary in those states where the enemy were long encamped. Washington fairly pled with Rhode Island and New York to stop that "abominable traffic." The most desperate struggle against the evil was made by New Jersey. Law after law was passed, with ever more rigorous penalties. From threats of very heavy fines, the severity increased until the offender, besides being fined, was to be pilloried, cropped or imprisoned during the war. In one county, where the enemy was encamped, the driving of cattle was forbidden altogether. Live stock driven within five miles of the enemy's camp could be seized by the American authorities. But the business seems to have gone on to the end of the war. Men could not be deterred from so profitable a trade by impotent legislative threats. As suggested above, the British paid gold for provisions, while the Americans paid paper; and it was a hardy patriot who could resist the temptation to acquire British gold. When the British wintered in Philadelphia, they had no difficulty in getting fresh provisions from all the country round. At the same time the American army at Valley Forge was starving, and Washington had to use high-handed measures to get what provisions he had.

Compulsory military service was another subject that cried for legislative action. That service might interfere with the personal liberty of the American sympathizer as well as the Loyalist, but it was only the latter who was compelled to aid the cause he hated. The refusal to join the militia was early regarded as evidence of Tory sympathies. Religious scruples were regarded as the only acceptable excuse; and any one who refused on that ground should have a record for piety, in the past, that was unimpeachable. As the struggle grew more fierce, the exemption even on a religious ground was denounced. Heavy fines were imposed for non-attendance in arms at the regular muster. The payment of the fines was in many cases refused and measures for enforcing the payment were loudly demanded.

In a moment of generosity or piety, the Rhode Island Assembly passed a law for the relief of persons of tender consciences. They were to be excused from military service upon making the affirmation : " I, (A. B.) do sincerely affirm and declare that the art of war and fighting, and the use and exercise of arms therein, either offensively or defensively, is utterly inconsistent with my belief as a Christian ; and that I do not decline and refuse the use thereof out of obstinacy or singularity, but for conscience sake. And this affirmation I make and give without evasion or mental reservation." The records show that the act was followed by an epidemic of tender consciences. Two months later the assembly was obliged to amend the act by requiring those who thus escaped military duty to hire a substitute.

However rigorous the laws might be made for compelling military service, there were many who would not yield to legislative threats. The unruly were taken in charge by the militia officers themselves. Sometimes the comforting assurance was given them that the Tories were to be put in the forefront of the battle. A Pennsylvania Quaker related an incident which well illustrates the fate of the recalcitrant. Fourteen Quakers, who were drafted under the militia law, had been forcibly taken from their homes to the militia encampment. They refused to partake of the provisions allotted to themselves and others, or to handle any of the muskets. They were forced to move in military order for some distance. Then half of them, who were exhausted, were allowed to return home. The others continued the march — several with muskets tied to their bodies. In camp, they were obliged to stand sentinel for many hours together — evidently kept there by the actual sentinel. Again, four Quakers were taken from their homes by the militia and, with drum and music, paraded through the streets.

The treatment of the members of religious sects who refused military service was always milder than that accorded the known Loyalists. For the latter there was ever ready the "tar and feathers and thousand other ills that loyalty is heir to." James Allen asserts, in his diary, that the "dragging out the disaffected to serve in the militia is attended with every species of violence and depredation." Another asserted that the Loyalists were often drafted "through pique."

Not only was conscience outraged and loyalty persecuted by compulsory military service, but soldiers were quartered in the homes of peace-loving Friends and unwilling Loyalists. There may have been an element of maliciousness in the selection of such homes, at times; but the evident wish of those in command was that the physical comfort of the soldiers should be the sole motive for the choice. It is, however, axiomatic that war does not recognize the amenities of peace.

The proclamation by the Continental Congress of a day of fasting and humiliation and prayer was the signal for the persecution of those who refused to obey. The Committees of Safety, the country over, watched narrowly how doubtful persons observed the day. Even before the arrival of the fast, solicitous committeemen waited upon ministers of the Gospel to learn whether they would preside at the ceremonies. Of the hundreds of Loyalist clergymen the majority dated the commencement of their troubles from the first fast day.[1]

One clergyman was visited by the committee to request and entreat him to perform divine service in his church on a Continental fast day and deliver a sermon. But their entreaties were in vain. He gave as a reason that he was one of the missionaries of the honorable Society for Propagating the Gospel in Foreign Parts. He would render himself obnoxious to the Ministry and, of course, lose his mission. The day after the fast, the committee, taking into consideration the unaccountable behavior and conduct of the reverend gentleman in deserting his congregation when almost all ranks and denominations of Christians among them were assembled at church by the order of the Continental Congress to humiliate themselves before God by fasting and prayer, resolved that the vestry of the parish be earnestly requested to suspend the offender from his ministerial function and stop the payment of his salary. And he was suspended, as was also his salary.

If a day of celebration was not entered upon with becoming zeal, the person guilty of the neglect was

[1] On July 20th of 1775.

suspected at once of having the political cloven hoof. The stamp of "Tory" was at once put upon him, and he or his property suffered. The Quakers were especially ill-used in this matter. The records of the Philadelphia Friends[1] contain the complaint of abuse by " the rude rabble, for not joining with the present rulers in their pretended acts of devotion ; and conforming to their ordinances in making a show of that sort in shutting up our shops and houses, professedly to observe a day of humiliation and to crave a blessing on their public proceedings, but evidently tending to spread the spirit of strife and contention." They also suffered "because Friends could not illuminate their houses and conform to such vain practices and outward marks of rejoicing to commemorate the time of these people's withdrawing themselves from all subjection to the English government, and from our excellent constitution under which we long enjoyed peace and prosperity." There seems to be in the spirit of these entries something nearer akin to Loyalty than mere Quaker aversion to strife.

If we regard the sum of these restraints, the wings of Loyalist freedom seem to have been very closely clipped. The Tory could not vote or hold office. He had no legal redress for his wrongs, and, if he had, no Loyalist member of the bar could defend him ; he was denied his vocation, and his liberty to speak or write his opinions; he could not travel or

[1] In July of 1777.

trade where he chose, and he must pray and fight for the cause he hated. But, it must be remembered, that all of these restrictions were not to be found in any one place, nor at any one time. Nor were they rigorously enforced except where the cloud of war hung most threateningly. Viewed from the distance of a hundred years, the necessity of such severity is not apparent. The Patriots themselves can best defend their use of the "iron hand." Washington, in approval of such laws passed in Connecticut, wrote,[1] "the situation of our affairs seems to call for regulations like these; and I should think the other colonies ought to adopt similar ones. . . . Vigorous measures, and such as, at other times, would appear extraordinary, are now become absolutely necessary for preserving our country against the strides of tyranny making against us."

The preambles of the laws always contain some defense couched in the florid rhetoric common to most productions of their kind. A Maryland act which attacked the Loyalists' liberties was defended by the statement that the clemency of the state toward those inimical to its freedom had not had the desired effect of reclaiming them from their evil practices; "but, still pursuing their dark and criminal designs of enslaving America, they continue to encourage and promote the operation of our enemies." Since "every hope of uniting to the interests of

[1] January 6, 1776.

their country the affections of these its unnatural and implacable enemies is extinguished, and great disadvantages have arisen, and still more dangerous consequences may be apprehended from a delay of effectual measures to suppress them " — because of this, their liberties are curtailed.

It was perfectly true that Maryland and other states had shown clemency at first, and, even after the harsher measures began, there were legislative retreats to a more lenient position. The spirit of uncompromising persecution was not manifested until near the close of the war.

The early vacillating policy of the states, in regard to the Tory, forces the belief upon us that conversion was the consummation devoutly to be wished. The incorrigibility of the Loyalist was not established, and it was hoped that the cumulation of ills might at last force the Tory into the Whig ranks.

CHAPTER X.

RECONCENTRATION CAMPS AND BANISHMENT.

THE efforts of the Whigs to restrict the civil rights of the Tory, thus limiting his power to harm the revolutionary cause, proved a failure. They soon discovered that the " Plague of Toryism " infected the whole state. There was no remedy but political quarantine or the establishment of reconcentration camps. The fear of Tory insurrections confronted Congress and the States at every turn. Tories became a menace to the success of military movements. In some parts of the country they seemed to have a majority in political contests. Even as a minority they were troublesome, because they always were, or seemed to be, plotting. Their very neutrality was a bad example. Plainly, some way had to be contrived to rid the state of this "pest."

Exclusion from public favor was the first step in the political purification. This social ostracism was at first informal. After the first violent agitation and discussion there was a breaking of old bonds. Loyalists were sent to coventry by their townsmen. Old friends did not speak as they met; neighbors ignored neighbors; Whig and Tory drifted further apart, because neither modified the views of the other by friendly argument. But every community contained many men who listened to either side with a ready ear. To gain this floating element became the object of both parties.

Soon after the battle of Lexington, the Whigs had begun to exercise the governmental power in their hands, and the formal ostracism of Tories was announced. In North Carolina, the respective district and parochial committees were empowered to take cognizance of, and to question those persons who should presume to violate or refuse obedience to the authority of Congress. They were to declare such persons "objects of the resentment of the public." This was effectually to expose them to be treated as "enemies to the liberties of America."

The committees took up the commission eagerly. The records abound with examples of a ready use of the power. A week after the proclamation, James Hepburn was declared a "False, scandalous and seditious incendiary, who, destitute of property and influence as he is of principle, basely and traitorously endeavors to make himself conspicuous in favor of tyranny and oppression . . . to raise a fortune to his family upon the subversion of liberty. Let the friends of liberty avoid all intercourse with him." Another was denounced, in like manner, for resenting a Whig's assertion that the throne of King George was "built of the bones of his fellow creatures," and that he had carried war into the

East Indies "that he might snuff the spices of the East and repose his sluggard limbs on the sofa of a nabob."

Where this ostracism was approved by a large majority of the inhabitants of a town, the victim was practically expelled from the community. None dared give him lodging or food or comfort. He was a pariah, and to countenance him was to incur public wrath. After the war, many proved their loyalty to the British government by producing advertisements in which they were held up to the world as "incorrigibles."

There are several instances in the Revolution where a whole county or section was cut off because it had offended. Congress, at one time, resolved,[1] since a majority of the inhabitants of Queen's County, New York, "were incapable of resolving to live and die freemen," and had deserted the American cause by refusing to send deputies to the New York convention, that all who had refused to vote for the deputies be put out of the protection of the United Colonies. All trade and intercourse with them was to cease. None of them were permitted to travel or abide in any part of the United States. No attorney could defend them in any action at law. They had avowed "an unmanly design of remaining inactive spectators of the . . . contest" and it was reasonable "that those who refused to defend their country should be excluded

[1] In January of 1776.

from its protection." Those in the county who had not offended could regain all lost privileges by means of a certificate of their allegiance. The inhabitants of Richmond County, New York, gave a like offence and the same interdiction fell upon them. They repented, however, and elected deputies. In February, Congress recommended that the New York Convention receive the new deputies, if they and the majority of the people of the county would sign the association.

The next stage in political quarantine was to confine the Loyalist to his own house and yard, as if he had some contagious disease. In the rural district, the range of freedom was greater than in the cities. It was a common provision that the unfriendly person " be confined to his farm and the limits of one mile thereof." To get this mark of favor, however, the Loyalist was obliged to give his parole not to transgress the bounds assigned, or to hold any correspondence with the enemies of the United States. If he broke the parole, the sheriff forthwith seized him and placed him in jail. Nor was the privilege of remaining at home likely to continue long. Suspicion was sure to fasten upon the unlucky Tory, and then exile or imprisonment followed.

The approach of the enemy, any unwonted activity among the Tories, or the mere suspicion that there was any concerted action among them, usually resulted in an effort to secure all of the

Loyalists in that section. When Lord Howe was expected in Philadelphia, and when Washington's army was so continuously retreating that a Tory satirist suggested putting, a brass collar on the leader, with the inscription " They win the fight that win the race," the Pennsylvania Council became so alarmed that they ordered the seizure of all suspected persons. James Allen wrote that " Houses were broken open, people imprisoned, without any color of authority, by private persons, and, as was said, a list of 200 disaffected persons made out who were to be seized, imprisoned and sent off to North Carolina." He said that his house, which was some distance from Philadelphia, was surrounded by a guard of soldiers with fixed bayonets. The officer produced a warrant from a council of safety, and Mr. Allen went with them to Philadelphia. Later, he commented bitterly upon these measures. " The most discreet, passive and respectable characters are dragged forth and, though no charge can be made, yet a new idea is started . . . of securing such men as hostages." Patriots did not, however, put this interpretation upon the seizure of the Loyalists. They regarded the measure as a means of preventing coöperation with the British.

After the battle of Moore's Creek in North Carolina, it became necessary to dispose of the captured Loyalists, so that they could not spread disaffection to the Patriot cause. The Provincial Congress resolved to publish a declaration stating that, out of a regard for public safety, the prisoners must be removed. There was much to be apprehended from their personal and family influence. They might delude the ignorant, wicked and unwary into dangerous measures. The unhappy families of the prisoners were assured that every indulgence, which humanity and compassion could give, should be extended to those in the power of the Congress. The treatment of the prisoners, however, would depend largely upon the future good behavior of those who still remained in the province.

The declaration, when drawn up, contained these words in regard to the exiles: "We have their security in contemplation, not to make them miserable. In our power, their errors claim our pity, their situation disarms our resentment. We shall hail their reformation with increasing pleasure, and receive them to us with open arms." As to the wives, the magnanimity continued: "We war not with the helpless females which they left behind them; we sympathize in their sorrow. They are the rightful pensioners upon the charity and bounty of those who have aught to spare from their own necessities to the relief of their indigent fellow creatures; to such we recommend them." In the six counties from which the prisoners came, commissioners were appointed, who were to prevent the waste and embezzlement of the estates of the exiles, and at the same time see that the women and children did not want the common necessaries of life.

The committee of secrecy, war and intelligence wrote to John Hancock, President of Congress, saying that they "thought it expedient to send the prisoners taken during the late commotions, some to Maryland, some to Virginia and some to Philadelphia. . . . These last are such as appear to us from their rank and influence over an ignorant and restless part of our inhabitants to be capable of doing us the most mischief. . . . We are sorry to be compelled to an act of such severity as this of sending these men at such a distance from their unfortunate families, but . . . their pernicious influence . . . might and probably would prove fatal." There was an apologetic manner in the execution of this early act of political exile, which was not found at a later period of the war.

These North Carolina Loyalists were exiled and imprisoned, because they had actually made war upon the Patriots, but this was by no means the usual reason for such measures. In the majority of the states, the prophetic eye of the legislature saw the danger while it was yet in the seed. A writer in the *Providence Gazette* had urged that words did not "convert lions into lambs, serpents into doves or Tories into Sons of Liberty." From this truism he inferred that the oath of allegiance was not enough; the Tories must be placed where they could do no harm.

Massachusetts, when anticipating an invasion of the State,[1] gave the Council power to issue, under the great seal and signed by the President, a warrant to apprehend and commit suspicious persons. The sheriff might require aid from any subject of the state. The persons so seized were to remain in prison without bail, until discharged by an order of the Council.

A few months later, Virginia passed an act indemnifying the Governor and Council for removing and confining suspected persons when the British fleet appeared in Chesapeake Bay. A law was passed,[2] later, giving such powers to the Governor and Council, that, if the State should be invaded or if there should be an insurrection, the disaffected persons might be confined or removed.

In New York, there were dangerous persons living near the military posts and passes. There was reason to believe that they communicated intelligence to the enemy. The Governor was given power[3] to remove them to such places in the state as he chose. In their place of exile, farms were to be rented to them by the commissioners of sequestered estates in that district. Property had been sequestered in almost every part of the state, so that it was not difficult to find farms for the exiles. They were to be assigned land of approximately

[1] In 1777.
[2] In May of 1780.
[3] In April of 1778.

the same value as the land they were compelled to abandon.

South Carolina also granted extraordinary powers to the Governor, on the ground that, in time of invasion, the hands of the executive must be strengthened.[1] No person confined by the Executive was to be bailed or tried until ten days after the next meeting of the legislature.

The opinion of contemporaries seems to be that the extraordinary power thus placed in the hands of the executive was not abused. It was a dangerous experiment, but there is no evidence that the decrees of the executives were ever unnecessarily tyrannical. They were expected to take all due precaution for the safety of the new state, and they did it with as little violence as possible. The agents who carried out the will of the executive were often rough, over-zealous men, and they, doubtless, at times used their little brief authority in no gentle manner.

The other states, which took the precaution of removing Tories from the places where they might become dangerous, gave the power to committees and local officers. Connecticut chose the latter method, but, in one special case, sent out a committee. It had been represented to the Assembly that there were a number of persons in the western towns of the state who were inimical, that they in-

[1] This ordinance was issued in October of 1778 and renewed in August of 1779.

stigated dangerous insurrections and tried in various ways to aid the enemy and bring on anarchy. Five persons were chosen to visit these western towns, convene all dangerous persons, and send them under guard to safe places. General Wooster was directed to assist the committee with his troops.

The provincial governors and councils of safety frequently received memorials from towns, the inhabitants of which were nervous because of the number of Tories dwelling among them. They set forth the fears and apprehensions they were under, and prayed the board to take the matter up and to decree that such suspected persons be removed. The Tories were not only dangerous in themselves, said the Whigs, but they spread abroad terrifying reports. Ignorant men were informed that the king intended to open the next campaign with 90,000 Hessians, Negroes, Japanese, Moors, Esquimaux, Persian archers, Laplanders, Feejee Islanders, together with a most tremendous and irresistible fleet. Men who circulated such horrifying tales ought to be exiled.

New Jersey made the most abnormal delegation of this power to exile. Judges of the Inferior Court were to order the removal of all suspected persons residing near the enemy's lines; though this was not to be done, except on the oath of six well-affected freeholders that the person to be removed was dangerous. Only the Council of Safety could remove them without this preliminary oath. New York, in desperation, passed an act to remove the families of persons who had joined the enemy. The exiles returned secretly to their homes, it was said, and were harbored by their families.[1]

Not only the militia but the regular army was called upon to aid in seizing and conveying the Loyalists to places where they would be harmless. It was generally conceded that the civil authority should give the orders, and the military officers would execute them. In May, 1776, Washington issued orders to General Putnam to aid the Provincial Congress of New York in a scheme for seizing the principal Tories in Long Island and New York City. Upon hearing of the partial success of the committee on Long Island, he wrote congratulating them, and promising all the aid in his power "to root out or secure such abominable pests of society." A few days later, he wrote with approbation of the seizure of the Tories in the counties of Princess Anne and Norfolk, in Virginia. Later, he expressed disappointment that nothing had been done in Philadelphia, and feared they might therefore have internal as well as external enemies to contend with.

Washington wrote [2] Brigadier General Livingston that "the known disaffection of the people of Amboy and the treachery of those of Staten

[1] July 1, 1780. See "Laws of New York."
[2] In July of 1776.

Island who after the fairest professions have shown themselves our most inveterate enemies" had induced him to order all doubtful persons removed from places where they might correspond with the enemy, and this had been done. He told Livingston that he might return those for whom he was willing personally to vouch. "But," Washington concluded with a warning, "my tenderness has often been abused. . . . I would show them all possible humanity and kindness, consistent with our own safety, but matters are now too far advanced to sacrifice anything to punctilios."

It was to the military power that Congress looked, either mediately or immediately, to remove troublesome Loyalists. When the Tories of Somerset and Worcester counties, Maryland, were turbulent and aggressive, the legislature was requested[1] to send militia to secure all leaders of the Tory faction. This not having the proper effect, and Sussex, Delaware, being also in Tory hands, the Congress "those Thirty Tyrants of Athens" resolved[2] to ask the two states to remove all "persons of influence or of desperate characters" to some remote, secure place within the states. No person was to have access to them unless by license from the proper officer. Again, when an invasion of Delaware was expected,[3] Congress ordered Brigadier Smallwood to secure

[1] In February of 1777.
[2] In April of 1777.
[3] In March of 1778.

the disaffected and send them under guard to a safe place. The government of the state was at that time in such a condition that Congress regarded it as unable to exercise such powers as were absolutely necessary for its preservation, and, for this reason, the usual *recommendation* was dispensed with.

That Congress was sometimes too slow to suit the more eager military men is evident in letters of the several commanders. Charles Lee, in the early days before jealousy had made him an execrable traitor, wrote Washington:[1] "New York must be secured, but it will never, I am afraid, be secured by the direct order of Congress, for obvious reasons." He suggested that Washington should send him into Connecticut to get some volunteers, and with these Lee hoped to effect the "expulsion or suppression of that dangerous banditti of Tories, who have appeared in Long Island with the professed intention of acting against the authority of Congress. Not to crush these serpents, before their rattles are grown, would be ruinous." Lee's plan was approved and he was sent to New York, as he requested, though with only indifferent success.

When a state exiled its Tories to the territory of a sister state, the guard which accompanied the exiles carried a letter from the Committee of Safety of the one state to that of the other. The note

[1] "Correspondence of the Revolution," Sparks ed., Vol. I., p. 107

contained a statement of the number of Tories consigned and a few words about the dangerous character of the prisoners. The Committee usually "lamented" the necessity of troubling a sister state with persons of this stamp, but the "peculiar and dangerous situation of the state" must apologize for a measure dictated by the most cruel necessity.

In the earlier stages of the war, New York and New Jersey sent many of their most dangerous Loyalists to Connecticut. The latter seemed to have plenty of prisons, and, except in the western part of the state, few Tories of its own. Pennsylvania received some of New York's exiles, and in turn sent into Virginia her own loyalists and Quakers of doubtful sympathies. There was an active interchange of prisoners between North and South Carolina, though the former sent many of her political offenders northward. Some of the states merely transported the disaffected to places remote from the scene of war — "into the back country" as the phrase ran.

There was undoubtedly a discrepancy between the actual treatment of Tories, during their enforced journey, and the theoretical treatment prescribed by the committees. Whether this was any greater than the difficulties of travel, the uncertain temper and character of the agents, and the stress of weather would unavoidably cause, cannot be determined. We have the greatest divergence of opinion on the subject. The Loyalist was ready to take his oath that he was treated with utmost cruelty, and that he and others were driven like herds of cattle into distant provinces; but the Patriot guard asserted that every kindness and amenity possible was practiced. We can only conclude that the truth lies somewhere between the best that the Patriot can claim and the worst that the Loyalist could charge.[1]

When the suspected Philadelphia Quakers were to be exiled to Augusta, Va., the instructions,[2] given to the persons in charge of the escort, certainly indicated good intent. The exiles were to be placed in light, covered wagons, and not crowded. Care was to be taken to secure every suitable accommodation for them on the way. A proper degree of firmness and watchfulness, as well as politeness, would be necessary. At Reading the prisoners were to be delivered over to another officer, who, under like directions, was to conduct them further. Five hundred dollars was provided to defray all expenses.

A diary was kept by the Friends, while on the journey, and, though there is a querulous and fault-seeking tone throughout, there does not appear any good reason for complaint. In the towns where they passed the night, Friends were allowed to

---

[1] One writer claimed that in exiling the lower classes of Tories "it was customary to chain 10, 15 or 20 together and drive them some hundreds of miles." See *Rivington's Gazette*, May 29, 1779.

[2] "Pennsylvania Archives," Vol. V., 607.

entertain them. Only once do they even state that friends were denied admission to them, and then there appears no good reason for the privilege being granted. The guards allowed delays that the baggage might come up, because, as the diary ingenuously stated, none of the company had "a second shirt." In Reading, an angry mob threw stones at them, but no one was reported injured, and the stoning, evidently not of a dangerous character, was not the fault of the guards. The impression given by the reading of the journal is, that, granting the justice of exiling them, there was nothing in the execution of the order which might be deplored.

The respectable position of these Philadelphia Quakers and the uncertainty whether their religion or political sympathies had brought upon them the disfavor of Congress and the Executive Council, did doubtless mitigate their treatment. There is, however, an account of the transportation of a number of Tories which is perhaps nearer the typical case.

John Connolly,[1] a zealous Loyalist, who had attempted to arouse the Indians in the western part of Pennsylvania, and to organize loyal opposition to the Patriots, was captured at the instigation of a Whig committee, and, with other Tories, taken to the eastern part of the state. The night before the journey began was passed in the house of the Colonel of the Minute-men. Connolly did not complain of

[1] See a "Narrative of the . . . Imprisonment . . . of John Connolly," etc., London, 1783.

the lodging or diet, but "the clamorous gabble of the raw militia was eternal and noisy beyond conception." The next morning, the party set out for Philadelphia, a journey of 160 miles. The escort was a party of military dragoons. "The spurs were taken off," wrote Mr. Connolly, "our horses placed parallel like coach horses, with their heads tied together in a very confined manner, and a horseman with a long rope attached to the intermediate cord, rode before, rudely conducting us in whatever direction he thought proper. My servant was allowed to follow with my portmanteau, but not having taken off his spurs the populace ran violently up to him, and cut through his boot and stocking to tear them away."

The journey that day was painful to remember. The road was rough, there was but a narrow track broken through the snow and ice, and the horses constantly pushed each other to keep in the broken path. The knees of the riders were thus bruised, and their legs in danger of being broken. "Sorry I am to say," Connolly commented, "it rather afforded cause of merriment to our conductors, than any scope for the exercise of benevolence. For the honor of humanity, however, it should be observed that our guard consisted of the lowest and most irrational of the inhabitants . . . and their captain a common surgeon barber."

At Yorktown, a committee assembled to decide how to lodge the Tories. They determined on a room in the county jail. There was "a dirty straw bed, a little covering and . . . no fire." The "new made soldiers were so fond of fife and drum" that they entertained the prisoners all night. The next morning they were led to the tavern by an officer's guard and a drum beating the Rogue's March. It was the first of January, and they were ironically and vociferously complimented with many wishes of a happy new year. The guard exhibited them "in terrorem to all Loyalists." When they set out again, a multitude rode with them some distance "for the novelty of the sight." Several days later, they reached Philadelphia, and were placed in prison.

It seems from this account, that the inclemency of the weather, the wretched roads and the exuberance of American humor, were the discomforts of which Connolly most complained. The treatment of the Loyalist in exile depended so much upon the time and place, the exigencies of war, the character of the exiled individual, and of the persons having him in charge, that no general judgment can be made as to its rigor or lenity. From the Tory pen we have a picture of an inexorable reign of terror; from the Patriot, a story of gentle indulgence that would make exile a pleasure. There are, however, perfectly authentic facts, which, with proper coördination, may reveal the approximate truth for the vast majority of cases. The records of various committees and councils of safety, who had immediate oversight of the Tories in exile, contain entries stating the privileges to be allowed or the limitations to be placed upon the prisoners. There could have been no reason for guile, no object for deception in making these entries; it was a simple record of a business transaction.

Omitting, for the present, the Loyalists who were imprisoned for some overt act in support of the British, and who were, in consequence, treated as criminals, the political exiles may be divided into two classes. There were very influential and active Loyalists, who were, as a rule, confined in jails, and closely guarded, but having due attention paid to the preservation of their health. They were allowed exercise in the jail yards, during the daytime, and often a greater range, accompanied by a guard. Under parole and a heavy bond, greater liberty of action was allowed. Often the freedom of the town was obtained in that way; the only requirement being that the prisoner was to report to a guard every day between certain hours. Friends were allowed to send food and clean clothing to the prisoners. They might have any delicacy that was purchased with their own means. Servants were allowed to attend them, and keep the room and bed clean, as the master pleased to direct. The directions, however, for the care of Tories of extremely dangerous character contained prohibitions of the use of pen, ink and paper. They were allowed to converse with no one except in the presence of a magistrate, and then only in the English language.

The second class were those who had little influence, but who talked too freely about the mistakes of Congress, or the virtues of the British government; in fact, often their only offense was a refusal of the oath. The aim of the Patriots was to coerce these men, or, at least, remove them from localities too thickly populated with persons of like views. After transportation, they were little heeded. They were allowed to work by day, but must pass the night in the jail. There was at least one example of a Tory allowed to continue his business—which was to sell rum—until he was complained of by the townspeople, because he was apt to babble over his cups. The exiles were obliged to support themselves, even to paying for lodging in the jail. The mildest of offenders were allowed, under the care of a resident, to find a lodging in the town of their exile. Frequent complaints were made to the committee-men that no one would give a Tory lodging. Feeling ran so high that to rent a room to a Tory was sure to call forth abuse of the landlord by his fellow townsmen.

For this milder type of Tory, the parole would secure almost any privilege. On promising to return, he was often allowed to go home to his farm, either because his health demanded it or to gain a sustenance for his family. Sometimes a Loyalist was permitted to go home and bring back part of his family to live with him in exile. A promise to return, in a given number of weeks, secured the temporary freedom of many. One was permitted to go home and get a gentleman of equal rank to return in his place. Where there were many Loyalists from the same locality, two or three were allowed to go home and get clothes and other necessities for their fellows. The prisoners always paid the expenses of the journey. The committees sometimes reported " large numbers of Tories" present at their meeting, and the minutes of the meeting show that all were there to request favors, and that they usually obtained them.

The diary of Thomas Vernon,[1] a Rhode Island Loyalist, gives us the most intimate acquaintance with the life of an exile. Vernon was one of the mildest of political offenders, but he refused to approve of the revolutionary measures, and the reformers could not tolerate even mild opposition. He and three other Loyalists were, by order of the assembly, removed to a distant town and lodged with a farmer. A dinner of salt pork, dried beans, and corn rather lowered their spirits, but, resolving to make the best of the situation, they were soon in perfect harmony with the family. Their efforts to prevent the new life becoming a dreary monotony were recorded in the diary with the greatest detail. Mr. Vernon made a weather vane, watered the garden and caught some fish. Then they all drank punch, chatted and read, and finally tried the effect of cider on monotony. The next day was whiled

[1] See "Rhode Island Hist. Tracts, No. 13, Providence, 1881."

away by making a flower-garden, helping the landlord rake hay, killing a snake and a bird, whittling a cane, and finally lamenting the lack of books. The neighbors came and stared at the Tories, and expressed a fear of having them in the neighborhood. The next day they were removed to a house in a town near by, where the townspeople were, for the most part, New Light Baptists. Soon the landlord told them that the town was very uneasy at their stay, and he wanted them to move to another house. Mrs. Vernon sent her husband some tea and some delicacies, and, as the landlord's family helped consume them, the departure was not urged for a time. Mr. Vernon, however, had an argument with an old man "whose mind was much poisoned with the disorder of the country," and, soon after, the landlord reported that the townspeople would destroy his house, if he continued to entertain the Tories. Meanwhile, the exiles were writing and using every influence with the Legislature to get relief from their exile. The Governor sent them word that something would soon be done. The agitation against them in the town continued. They tried to get a weaver to make some handkerchiefs, but the weaver's wife was afraid to do work for a Tory. At last, the landlord came with great trepidation, and said that forty men were coming with a leader to get "those Tories." They must go, the landlord urged, or he would be ruined. "I must observe," Vernon comments, "that the whole famliy have almost lived upon our provisions for eight or nine days past. It seems they can digest Tory victuals very well." Soon the sheriff came, with a warrant to remove them to some other house. He was, however, unable to find any other house that would entertain the outcasts. They were thus left to their own resources, and started to walk to Newport. Friends met them on the way, but the whole party were overtaken, and compelled to go to Providence, where they were cast into jail. One night of the "dismal, overcrowded jail," with "no bedding," determined them to get back into the country on their parole. Fortunately their troubles were then nearly over. After getting shelter with friends, an act of the assembly allowed them and other exiles to return home.

Such an experience was half amusing as compared with the fate of those Tories who, because of the bitter feelings engendered by war, were regarded as criminals. Tories who had been active in the service of the British, and, thereafter, fell into the hands of the Whigs, were more apt to be thrown into the common prisons which, in that day, were places of horror. One of the most terrible prisons in which they were confined was the famous Simsbury mine in Connecticut. A Loyalist, who was imprisoned in that hole, has left a graphic description of its horrors. On approaching the dungeon, he and his fellow victims were first conducted through the apartments of the guards, then through a trap door down stairs to a room in the corner of which opened another large trap door, covered with bars and bolts of iron. Two guards hoisted this by means of a tackle. The hinges grated, as they turned on their hooks, and opened the jaws and mouth of what they called Hell. They then descended about six feet by means of a ladder which led to a large iron grate or hatchway locked down over a shaft of about three feet in diameter, sunk through the solid rock, which led, the guards informed them, to the bottomless pit. Here they bade "adieu to the world," and descended the ladder about thirty-eight feet more, when they came to what was called the landing. Then they marched step by step, until, descending about thirty feet more, they came to a platform of boards laid underfoot, with a few more put overhead to carry off the water, which kept continually dropping. Here they found the inhabitants of the "woeful mansion" exceedingly anxious to know what was going on above. The inmates were obliged to make use of pots of charcoal to dispel the foul air which was only partially drawn off by means of a ventilator or auger hole bored through from the surface, and said to be seventy feet perpendicular.[1] It can readily be imagined that this prison might have been made quite as horrible as the British prison ships — especially if the jailer chose to enrich him-

---

[1] Moore's "Diary," Vol. II., 435.

self like the monster Cunningham by "feeding the dead and starving the living."

This prison was, however, undoubtedly the worst in America, and, although others were so overcrowded as to endanger the health of the prisoners, and the inmates sometimes lacked things necessary for the comfort of persons of their station, yet there seems no good proof of deliberate cruelty to Tory prisoners. The records of the committees of safety show that they intended to provide decent jails for the detention of their political enemies.

The Loyalist, who was exiled to another state or to a remote part of his own state, was looked upon as one having a contagious political disease from which he might recover and then become a very useful member of society. Loyalists, however, who joined the British army and refused all offers of pardon, if they would return, became, in the eyes of the Patriots, political lepers, who ought to be sent out of their country and forbidden to return. During the war, eight of the thirteen states formally banished certain prominent Tories either conditionally or unconditionally. The remaining states, Connecticut, New Jersey, Delaware, Maryland and Virginia, accomplished the same result in different ways.

North Carolina and Massachusetts began the formal banishment of Tories in April and May of 1777. Actual hostilities had begun earlier in both states. There had been reasons for a more rapid growth of Tory antipathy in these states than the others. That they should be first to act is precisely what the logic of events would seem to dictate.

In Massachusetts, a very perfect piece of machinery was at once invented for weeding out Tories. The selectmen of each town were to "warn a meeting" of the inhabitants. Some person firmly attached to the American cause was to be chosen by ballot. The person thus elected was charged with the duty of laying before the courts evidence to prove the inimical character of any inhabitants whom the freeholders charged with favoring the British cause. The selectmen were to make out a list of men who had shown Tory sympathies since the Battle of Lexington. Any one present at the meeting might suggest a name to the moderator or chairman. This name was to be added to the list, if the majority of those present so voted. The completed list was given to two or more justices of the peace who issued warrants for the arrest of the proscribed persons. The trial followed at a special session of the court. On conviction of being dangerous to the public peace, the Loyalist was to be sent to the Board of War, and by them sent on board a guard-ship. As soon as possible the prisoner was to be transported to Europe or the West Indies at his own expense. He might carry off his personal estate, if he were accompanied by his family. In less legal but more sentimental phrase the cry of the mob was:

> "That Tories with their brats and wives,
> Should fly to save their wretched lives,
> From Sodom into Goshen." [1]

If the exile went alone, he was allowed only money enough for his immediate support. To prevent the accused person converting his wealth into a more portable form, his real estate could not be transferred in any way to another.

This act was to remain in force until the first of January, 1778. About that date, Massachusetts enacted her "test" law, and the penalty of refusal to sign the oath of allegiance was banishment. Forty days after refusal, the offender was sent by order of the Council to some port in the British dominions. Vessels were hired for that purpose, and paid for out of the personal estate of the banished man. He was allowed to sell his personal estate, and take with him what money remained after paying all his debts. An attorney might do this for him, which was a kindly provision, inasmuch as the forty days between refusal of the oath and banishment was passed in jail. Both the above laws threatened death without the benefit of clergy to any one who returned after banishment.

Later in the year, not content with the above stringent measures, a proscription of about 260

[1] *Rivington's Gazette*, June 26, 1779.

Loyalists was made. Fifty-three merchants, sixty "esquires," twenty-four mariners and traders, sixty-three yeomen and gentlemen, a number of former state and crown officers, and a few people in the humbler walks of life who had left the state were named in the act. These and all others who had joined the enemy were to be seized, committed to jail by the Justice of Peace, and sent out of the state by the Board of War. Death without benefit of clergy was the penalty for returning. The master of any ship who knowingly brought them back was fined five hundred pounds. The ministers at the French Court were to receive five hundred handbills containing this act, the object being to convince France that America was in earnest.

New Hampshire and Georgia passed proscriptive acts in the same year, and Rhode Island in 1780. In October of 1779, New York banished about sixty officers, merchants and yeomen and confiscated their estates at the same time. Her test act[1] had already ordered the banishment, to the enemy's lines, of all who refused the oath. In like manner, the same end had been attained by other states without passing an actual proscriptive act. Pennsylvania, in her act for the punishment of treason, made the provision that persons sentenced to death might have the sentence commuted by the President and Council to banishment. North and South Carolina made the refusal of the oath a sufficient cause for

[1] June, 1778.

banishment. Under certain conditions, the non-jurors might sell their estates, but a failure to do this within a certain time subjected the estates to forfeiture.

Those states which did not, by enactment, banish the Loyalists left the matter to the natural social forces and the effect of persecutions. How potent these forces were, to that end, may be judged from the large number of refugees to British territory and the British army. "A good and wholesome law of tar and feathers," as some grim humorist expressed it, was a powerful agent for this purpose. The Tory was constantly threatened with violence, even if it were not meted out to him. A facetious writer of the day, advertised an "Anodyne Elixir for quieting fears and apprehensions," and recommended it as " very necessary for Tories in all parts of America."

A large number of Loyalists told the British claim commissioners [1] that, after being imprisoned, they were given their freedom upon the promise to leave the country. Some were compelled to give bonds never to return. One had his bonds placed as high as four thousand pounds. Many, to escape military service, paid fines until they were ruined, and then fled to the British lines. Those whose professions were denied them, were often forced by

[1] Who were sent after the war by the British Government to determine what compensation the Loyalists were entitled to for their losses.

want to join the British army. The story of a flight from an angry mob, followed by weeks of skulking in the woods and swamps, and the final escape to the British camp, constantly recurs in the records of the Loyalists. The life to which they fled is the theme of another chapter.

CHAPTER XI.

LIVING IN EXILE.

THE banished Loyalists had the wide world before them. They departed from their houses, said one of the pious victims, "as Abraham from the land of the Chaldees" not knowing whither they went.[1] He wished that he too might have the kind protecting hand that guided that good old patriarch. Many of the exiles went to England to watch the course of the war, and others fled to the West Indies and the Bahamas, or some part of Canada; but the far greater number awaited the outcome in one of the American cities then in control of the British.[2] Of these places, New York was the chief city of refuge and longest retained that character.[3]

The first arrival within the British lines was a happy moment for the refugees. They looked back upon official and unofficial persecution in the colonies with a sense of horror. They had been threatened, boycotted and plundered; committees had summoned them to examinations from which

[1] Curwen, "Journal," p. 65.
[2] New York, Newport, Charleston, Savannah, and, for a few months, Philadelphia.
[3] From September 15, 1776, to November 25, 1783.

they had escaped perhaps with a recantation and a reprimand, or, more likely, they had been ostracized or paroled and compelled to find a surety willing to forfeit some extravagant amount if they committed any breach of Whig law. Then, apprehensive neighbors denounced them, or drew up petitions to have them removed, and gave the authorities no rest until they were disarmed. They had been obliged to accept at par the depreciated money, and had stood in terror of the law of the maximum. Finally, a test act had demanded of them an oath which they could not take, and refusal had brought upon them fines, disabilities, special taxation, and even whipping and imprisonment. Where the partizan struggle was hottest, the persecutors had already resorted to proscription, outlawry and confiscation. Never, since the days of Nimrod, thought one Tory, was there such a land of oppression and tyranny as America. After being whirled in this torrent of persecution the outraged Tory was glad to rest in the quiet pool of protected loyalty.

The exile, from whatever direction he might come, readily found, in New York, friends and acquaintances. The refugees from the several provinces had formed societies which looked after the interests of fellow colonists; for the Loyalists, like the Patriots, had the narrow and particularistic interest in their respective colonies, rather than in America as a whole.

These societies called their provincial meetings in some favorite tavern, at Hicks', in Broadway, or at Lenox', the sign of Joseph Brandt; and the notice in the *Gazette* hinted darkly at secret and important business which all should attend.[1] Gathered around loyal tables and smoking "monstrous good smoaking tobacco," bought of the Tory printer, they discussed the war, and took comfort in the reflection that most rebellions, in the past, had failed, and, even when the rebels had won, they had been worse off than before. They drank toasts "to the speedy revival of civil authority and a happy reinstatement of the loyal refugees." A rhymster in the crowd would assure them that,

"Old England's lion now once more shall roar;
   Be heard from Pole to Pole and shake each trembling shore."[2]

and a whimsical statistician would demonstrate that the guns of England's navy, placed at the extent of each gun's range, would, with one shot from each, circumscribe the earth, or, pointed upward, might do considerable damage to the moon.[3] Thus did fancy and reason sustain the Tory in his hour of trial.

The business, if there was any to be transacted, usually concerned some loyal address to the king or his military representatives in America. These

[1] Pennsylvania refugees met at Birket's Tavern, near Maiden Lane; the Jersey refugees at Leonard's Tavern; Massachusetts, at Hicks' Tavern, and those of Virginia at the Queen's Head Tavern, etc. See advertisements in *Rivington's Gazette*, during 1779.
[2] *Rivington's Gazette*, May 11, 1782.
[3] *Ibid.*, April 6, 1782.

addresses were curious medleys of warm assertions of devotion to the king's sacred person, complaints of the discomforts of military rule, and bad estimates of the Patriot resources. In the later years of the prolonged stay in New York, they often requested returning commanders to carry indignant protests to the king, because of the representations made to Parliament concerning the Loyalists. He could not, ran one of the protests, be ignorant of the causes which formerly depressed the spirit of loyalty, and prevented it from becoming so usefully extended as it otherwise might have been.[1]

This protest alluded to the fact that the Loyalists had not been properly encouraged to form militia companies. Petitions of Tories who wished to rise in aid of the British had been neglected.[2] Their aid had been scorned as of no value. The British officers and soldiers preserved a cold tolerance of the Loyalists, and never gave them a warm and sincere reception. The loyal as well as rebellious Americans were "our colonists," not equals. Galloway, who rendered the British greater service than any other genuinely American Loyalist, always smarted under Howe's neglect. The two men, the greatest of the Loyalists and the commander of the British forces, lived side by side for seven months in Philadelphia, and Howe called on Galloway but once in all that time.[3] This low

[1] *Rivington's Gazette*, August 25, 1779.
[2] *Ibid.*, September 17, 1779. See Address.
[3] *Ibid.*, November 10, 1779.

estimate of the Americans, both Tory and Whig, cost the British dearly. Much of Cornwallis' early success was owing, thought a Tory writer, to the fact that he treated a Loyalist like a friend, embarked in the same cause. If the meanest of them had business with him, he attended them himself, and asked them to eat and drink with him.[1]

Mere neglect was not the only injury which the Loyalists suffered from the British armies. Though, for political reasons, the British officers sought to spare the Tories from plunder, yet the soldiers held all Americans in contempt, and were hard to restrain. Many Loyalists were plundered while they held their certificates of protection in their hands. When Newport was in British power, the soldiers robbed the fields and gardens of Loyalists, and the loot was sold by the soldiers' wives. The shameful practice reached such proportions that a proclamation was issued, ordering that all roots, vegetables and fruits exposed for sale be seized, if the venders could not tell where they were procured.[2] Galloway said that Loyalists had come to him with tears in their eyes, complaining that they had been plundered of everything in the world, even to the pot to boil their victuals.[3] A British officer explained this unpleasant fact by the assertion that, upon the approach of the British, the Whigs secreted everything that could be of use;

---
[1] *Rivington's Gazette*, February 28, 1781.
[2] *Newport Gazette*, September 9, 1779. The offenders were to be expelled from the garrison.
[3] *Rivington's Gazette*, October 3, 1779.

while the Tories, confident of protection, took no precaution, and thus were exposed to be plundered: as a result they were frequently the only sufferers.[1] A Committee of the Continental Congress, to investigate the wanton destruction of property by the British in the march through New Jersey, affirmed that both Whig and Tory suffered indiscriminately.[2]

Outrages of this kind were, however, incidental to the times of hurried marches and to the confusion of active military campaigns. Within the British lines at New York, the Tories found themselves better protected by the officers from abuse by the soldiers. There were thousands of loyal tradesmen and farmers whose homes were within the British lines, and many of the refugees had been permitted to cultivate for their own benefit the lands of Whigs who had fled at the coming of the British.[3] Some erected temporary habitations, and others appropriated the dwellings of the exiled Whigs. To protect those who tried to raise garden produce for sale, the commander issued emphatic orders that their fences were not to be destroyed, nor their crops and cattle taken. There was not much complaint on that score, but a source of continual friction was caused by the issuing of orders billeting the British officers upon the citizens.

[1] Stevens' "Facsimiles," No. 2102.
[2] *Pennsylvania Evening Post*, April 24, 1777.
[3] *Rivington's Gazette*, March 10, 1779. The favored persons were compelled to give certificates of loyal character before taking possession and to receive a permit. See Onderdonck's "Revolutionary Incidents of Long Island," Vol. II., No. 648.

The haughty boarders expected the same subservience in their hosts that they would have found in England, but "our colonists" had ideas of their own as to their obligations, and the two standards of hospitality clashed. The officer would clap his host into the mainguard, and then the prisoner and his friends would enter an indignant protest with the commander-in-chief.[1] Although the officers were reprimanded, yet the citizen had no legal redress, and, as a result, began to long for civil rather than military government.

With almost pitiful reiteration the Loyalists in New York petitioned for the establishment of civil government.[2] Men high in the loyal ranks assured the British ministry that the Americans in New York, whether Loyalists or helpless rebels, would grow impatient under a Government perfectly military.[3] It could not impede military operations, they urged, to restore the blessing of civil government, and the sooner that desirable event should take place, the better would the British government be prepared to receive under its protection those who were weary of the sanguinary conflict in the colonies.[3]

At one time in 1780, the government was on the eve of establishing the long-desired system, and even issued a proclamation to that effect suggesting appointments for a council, and promising soon to

[1] *Rivington's Gazette*, November 11, 1780; November 23, 1779.
[2] For one of the most elaborate petitions see Stevens' "Facsimiles," No. 1226, November 25, 1778.
[3] *Ibid.*, I, 116.

open the courts and convene a loyal assembly.[1] There was powerful opposition to this move by Tryon who feared that civil government might come too early,[2] and by General Robertson who thought that affairs ran smoothly enough with loyal magistrates and arbitrators, who prevented or settled all differences between loyal citizens.[3] The changing phases of the war, also, made the policy of such an action too doubtful. As a result, the civil system never came, and the Loyalists lived under military rule to the end.

If at any time the Loyal citizens became desperate under this régime; if the farmers became enraged over a military order to preserve all their grain and forage " for the King's use," and sold it to any one else at their peril; if they were obliged to cut their wood and even sacrifice their orchards to warm the King's troops; if every citizen was threatened with imprisonment or banishment for failing to enroll in the loyal militia;[4] or if he was commanded never to appear in the streets before reveille or after eight o'clock in the evening, without a "lanthorn;"[5] and if, worse than worst, every tradesman was obliged to submit to the law of the

[1] *Rivington's Gazette*, April 19, 1780. It is significant of the nationality of many of the refugees that most of the proclamations were printed both in English and German.

[2] "Documents Relating to the Colonial History of New York," Vol. VIII., 767, 799.

[3] "The Remembrancer," Vol. III., 225.

[4] *Rivington's Gazette*, January 22, 1780.

[5] *Pennsylvania Evening Post*, January 8, 1778.

LIVING IN EXILE. 251

maximum, and even the bakers had to stamp their loaves with their initials and sell at so many coppers for a given weight [1] — if this military despotism grew unbearable, the Tory could always find comfort in the stimulating and optimistic pages of the loyal gazettes.

There was a fool's paradise for the hopeful Tory in every issue of these journals. Dr. Franklin was reported desperately wounded by a secret enemy, and there was no prospect of his recovery.[2] Again, this "chief prop of rebellion" was dead, and his end had been hastened by the late ill success of the rebels.[3] Another day brought the golden tidings that Robert Morris[4] had left Congress in disgust, having first made a motion "for rescinding independency." Wild reports got abroad that Washington had been made Lord Protector, or, again, this "Cæsar," this "Cromwell," was dead or, at least, captured.[5] Sometimes "court cookery" prepared for the gazette the news of a treaty with Russia by which 36,000 Cossacks — a most plausible number — had been taken into British service. The King of Prussia, too, had yielded to British diplomacy.[6] "Poor Rivington," sneered a Boston editor, was

[1] *Rivington's Gazette*, March 6, 1782. According to police regulations a two-and-one-half-pound loaf sold for fourteen coppers, and if deficient was seized and sent to the almshouse.
[2] *Ibid.*, March 7, 1778.
[3] *Ibid.*, January 31, 1778.
[4] *Ibid.*, January 3, 1778.
[5] Curwen, "Journal," p. 125.
[6] *Rivington's Gazette*, November 1, 1777.

hard put to it to keep up the spirits of the Loyalists in their confined district in New York.[1] Another editor observed that the printer of the *London Gazette* had been thought the greatest liar on earth, but Rivington far exceeded in this curious art his more respectable brethren in England.[2]

Not only did the loyal papers publish these cheering items of news, but they gave to a hungry world morsels of political argument filled with bold antithesis, turbulent eloquence and the "cant of passions which the writers never felt." The peaceful citizens of New York, in nightly terror of the sailors from the British ships, who rioted in the streets and disturbed the loyal slumber,[3] were told of the terrible scenes of anarchy in the Whig centers. The refugee, groaning under the war prices, which were fast consuming the few funds that he had brought with him, was made content by the tale of grinding taxes in the provinces. There was, asserted one writer, hardly one article of live or dead stock, or of the produce of the earth or waters, or the result of industry or labor that was "exempt from the fangs of those devouring locusts," the Whig legislatures. America was mortgaged for ages to come. They had incurred this intolerable burden because, forsooth, England had laid that "most exorbitant and grievous tax of three pence on a pound of tea."[4]

[1] *Rivington's Gazette*, December 1, 1779.
[2] *North Carolina Gazette*, December 12, 1777.
[3] *Rivington's Gazette*, April 14, 1779.
[4] *Ibid.*, March 20, 1782.

The Tories lived in constant terror of an attack by Washington's forces on their city of refuge, but Rivington comforted them with stories of the illimitable resources of the British army. One hundred thousand men had been raised for the internal defense of England; not that an invasion was apprehended, but just to let the world see what a plenty they have of men and money. In spite of the war, trades were flourishing and taxes light. "Was there ever such a nation as this?" queried a Whig journal. "Its fleets are most victorious when they flee, . . . its inhabitants can fight and manufacture at the same time! The higher the taxes, the richer it grows; and the more you exhaust its resources, the more they increase! What can the United World do against such a nation? . . . France, Spain and America together are not half a breakfast for it. It is the very giant of Pantagruel, and can swallow as many windmills as any other giant can poached eggs. There was a panic," the writer declared, "in the very sound of Rivington's paragraphs."

The Tory writers had now given up, for the most part, any attempt to convince the Whigs of their error. The die had been cast, and there was left nothing but recrimination, invective, direful prophecy and terrible threats. It was pointed out in the Tory press that Whigism never had been anything more than the privation of every fixed principle in politics. The Whigs of Charles I.'s time were "regicides and republicans," and in Cromwell's they were "levellers," and in the time of Charles II., Puritans. Now, if the Whigs establish their republic, they "will reduce all men into a state of nature," and perhaps the next step would be to cut off the legs of the tallest, that no man might look over the head of his neighbors.[1] Nothing but destruction could come to such a rash, foolish people, augured the Tory, and, when one day an eclipse occurred, the loyal fancy assumed that it "was the devil spreading his wings over . . . the rebellious colonies," and hopefully concluded that, "if they do not repent, the next time he will certainly fly off with them all."[2]

In spite of all the efforts of the loyal press, however, it was impossible to make the thousands of refugees forget the physical want, to which many of them were reduced. As early as the summer of 1778, Sir Henry Clinton wrote that nothing distressed him so much as the applications he hourly received from great numbers of refugees who crowded to New York from every quarter of America. Many, he said, had been reduced from affluent circumstances to the utmost penury by their attachment to the king. He urged that humanity and good policy required that at-least a temporary relief be afforded them. The necessity of immediate assistance had so strongly appealed to him, that

[1] *Rivington's Gazette*, December 1, 1779; January 12, 1782.
[2] Curwen, "Journal," p. 298.

he had used the funds in hand, and then asked for approval and aid from his government.¹ In consequence of this request, Clinton was authorized to use his discretion in aiding the distressed, giving, as the circumstances dictated, either money or allotments of rebel lands.²

By the autumn of 1783, the provision for the temporary support of Loyalists cost the British government 40,280 pounds annually. This sum merely included the pensions given to some 310 persons, ranging from ten pounds, given a tide-waiter, to 800 pounds given to Eden, the exiled governor of Maryland.³ But, in addition to these pensions, thousands of Loyalists had been employed in the pay of the British, either in civil or military capacity.⁴

Not only those refugees who were under British protection in America, but the many who had fled

---

¹ Stevens' "Facsimiles," No. 1121, dated July 25, 1778.
² "New York Documents," Vol. VIII., 765, 768, 774, 801.
³   124 pensioners received 100 pounds.
        34   "   "   200   "
        58   "   "   50   "   or under.
        39   "   "   50   "   to 100 pounds.
        30   "   "   100   "   " 200   "
        18   "   " over 200   "

       303

The last were governors and men in high station. See MSS. Transcript of Loyalist papers, "Old Claims for Temporary Support."

⁴ For example, Joseph Galloway was Magistrate of the police while the British were in Philadelphia, with a salary of £300 per annum. He was also Superintendent of the Port at £770 per annum. See "Bulletin of New York Public Library," Vol. IV., No. 1, p. 8.

to England, became pensioners by the stress of ill-fortune. If possible, the latter were in worse straits than the former, for their letters to America were intercepted, as one expressed it, by the order of the "amphyctionic states of America," and thus their friends knew no more of their circumstances than as if "they were in the region of the moon." They found London a "sad lickpenny," where, as Curwen asserted, they "could not breathe the vital air without great expense."[1] Begging, this good loyalist soliloquized, is a meanness, and starvation is stupid; and his only comfort was that he was fast declining into the vale of life, wherefore his miseries could not be of long duration.[2]

Nothing can better reveal how truly American the moderate Tories were, than the journal of the patriotic Curwen, who, though he was heartily opposed to the revolution, confessed that he and his friends supped at a tavern in Bristol and passed their time "talking treason and justifying American Independence."[3] When the news of Bur-

---

[1] Curwen, "Journal," pp. 61, 102. As early as July, 1775, he wrote that there was "an army of New Englanders in London," pp. 32–39.

[2] *Ibid.*, p. 63.

[3] *Ibid.*, p. 79. They had many favorite places of meeting, especially certain famous taverns in London. Jerusalem Tavern and St. Clemen's Coffee-house rang with their denunciations of the rebels, or discussions of the latest pamphlet of the nature of "An inquiry whether Great Britain or America is most in fault." See "Journal," p. 53. The "Adelphi," on the Strand, was also a resort of the Tory "New England Club." See "Journal," page 47.

goyne's defeat reached him, he had become so exasperated with British underestimation of America's[1] strength, that he wrote in exultation, "What do you think, now, . . . of laying the colonies at the minister's feet? Of Lord S.'s boast of passing through the continent, from one end to the other, with 5,000 British troops? Of the raw, undisciplined, beggarly rabble of the northern colonies?"[2] His warm patriotism appeared even in the expression of his Tory principles, "For my native country I feel a filial fondness, her follies I lament, her misfortunes I pity, and to be restored to her embraces is the warmest of my desires."[3]

The story of the wanderings of these exiles and their efforts to obtain support from the British government is best told in their own letters and journals. They came to England, complained one of them, "only to suffer hunger and nakedness in the comfortless mansions of the wretched."[4] Curwen wrote bitterly in the midst of his trials, "Seneca and the moral writers, luxuriating in the midst of

[1] He was not made very welcome, either, and was suspected of being a spy. See "Journal," page 242.
[2] Curwen, "Journal," p. 178. Still, he saw what it meant for him and wrote, page 176: "God knows what is for the best, but I fear that our perpetual banishment from America is written in the book of fate; nothing but the hopes of once more revisiting my native soil, enjoying my own friends, within my own little domain, has hitherto supported my drooping courage." Now that prop seemed taken away, and his distress was great.
[3] *Ibid.*, p. 283.
[4] *Ibid.*, p. 101.

plenty, have written elaborate . . . and edifying treatises on contentment and the duty of submission. Let Seneca . . . be brought to the mouth of the cave of poverty; let hunger, thirst and nakedness, in all their grisly, terrifying shapes stare him in the face;" then let him a write a treatise on these ideal doctrines.[1]

Not all of the exiles, however, viewed the situation so gloomily. Harrison Gray, a prominent Loyalist, wrote from London[2] that he was sorry his brother's spirits were so low, but he was confident that the glorious period was hastening when " you will be emancipated from the tyrannical, arbitrary, congressional government under which you have for some time groaned. A government for cruelty and ferocity not to be equalled by any but that in the lower regions, where the prince of darkness is President, and has in his safe custody a number of ancient rebels who are reserved in chains of darkness to the judgment of the great day."

Jonathan Sewall, filled with buoyant confidence as to the outcome of the war, wrote to a friend in America in a rather sardonic vein. " Dear Johnny, don't be frightened at seeing a letter from an old Tory friend lest it should come under the inspection of your high and mighty committees, as I suppose will be the case in your *free* and independent state." He then facetiously made an affidavit that

[1] Curwen, "Journal," p. 101.
[2] March, 1777.

he had never had any treasonable word from his friend since leaving America. "Thus much to prevent any mistakes which might expose you to the perils of tarring and feathering, Simsbury mines, a gaol or a gallows." After hoping that it would not offend "committees or congresses or parsons or generals," if he said that he was alive, he added, "I suppose by this time you have entered so thoroughly into their mad scheme, that it will afford you no pleasure to hear your quondam friends on this side the Atlantic are well. However, I will mortify you by assuring you that they are all in good health and spirits, and government has liberally supplied the wants of all the Tory refugees who needed its assistance; and none here entertain the penumbra of a doubt how the game will end." A little banter about a friend intervened, and a wish for "one peep" at his house, which he supposed he should not know again. "Sic Transit gloria mundi. I shan't break my heart about it. Every dog, they say, has his day, and I doubt not I shall have mine. Ah, my old friend, could you form a just idea of the immense wealth and power of the British nation, you would tremble at the foolish audacity of your pigmy states."[1]

It must be remembered, in comparing Curwen's pessimism with the cheerful confidence of Gray and Sewall, that the latter were high in political in-

[1] "Life of E. Gerry to the Close of the American Revolution," pp. 268-272.

fluence, and were never for a moment threatened with poverty. Position assured them of favor during the war and ample compensation for their losses if the struggle ended unfavorably. The less fortunate exiles complained that, too often, the relief granted by the government was improperly and injudiciously distributed. Interest, influence, and a sounding title, or mere presumption and boldness, secured aid, while character, merit and real losses went uncompensated.[1] An examination of the lists of pensioned persons [2] indicates plainly that there was much justice in the charge, for the larger percentage of the pensioners were men who had held government offices or high social positions in the colonies. However, it is not to be forgotten that there were other means of relief provided for the Tory democracy, which, as a rule, remained in New York or some other American city protected by the British.

Under the direction of the royal commanders, the Tory leaders had early organized schemes for the relief of the destitute refugees. Orders were given that these loyal charity boards were to receive the proceeds of the fines paid by the farmers who had asked a price higher than the legal maximum for their wheat, rye, Indian corn, and buckwheat.[3] The rent paid by those who lived in Whig houses,

[1] MSS. "Transcript . . . of . . . papers . . . of American Loyalists," Vol. I., Information, p. 87.
[2] See " Old Claims for Temporary Support " in MSS. Transcript, etc.
[3] *Rivington's Gazette*, January 23, 1779.

the licenses of tavern keepers, and of the retailers of liquors, as well as the ferry rents, were set aside for charitable purposes.[1]

Finally, loyal collectors waited upon the "gentlemen of the Army and Navy, who subscribed in the most liberal manner for the relief of the refugees," [2]

[1] General account of receipts and disbursements from November 1, 1777, to April 30, 1782, of all moneys raised for the support of the Almshouse and other charitable purposes and the exigencies of New York.

Cash paid overseers of poor for Almshouse Out-pensioners.	£35,732	Received for rents of houses, the property of persons out of the lines	£35,281
Salaries of city officers appointed by proclamation	9,788	Licenses to tavern keepers and retailers of liquors	12,961
Repairs of buildings, ferries, pumps, fire-engines,	4,261	Brooklyn ferry rents	3,386
		Lotteries	10,314
Cleaning and repairing streets	5,717	Fines and forfeiture	1,474
			£63,419
Contingent expenses, carting, etc	1,090	(N. B. Shillings and pence are omitted.)	
Different charities, itinerant distressed objects, passage money to ship off some	435		
Wages for work on Governor's Island	691		
Repairing arms of militia	733		
Rent of houses to accommodate garrison	2,033		
Fines and forfeitures repaid by order	578		
Balance in hand of Treasurer	2,355		
	£63,419		

May 30, 1782, *Rivington's Gazette* published above account.

[2] *Rivington's Gazette,* December 16, 1778, and April 10, 1778. For an advertisement of the lottery see the *Gazette,* February 14, 1778.

and several extensive lotteries were created to tease the needed funds from the purses of men who could best be approached in that way. Over 10,000 pounds was raised by that seductive method alone. Thus, as Rivington gracefully phrased it, proof was given that "the hand of charity" in the loyal metropolis was ready to aid those "suffering for their attachment to our most gracious sovereign." How noble this was, he moralized, compared with " our unrelenting enemies," who, contrary to the dictates of humanity, have driven from their habitations a large number of helpless women and children without the means of subsistence.[1]

The work of distributing the money obtained was left to a loyal vestry, and their action was, in the later years, influenced by a "Board of Directors of the Associated Loyalists." This board had been formed by a federation of the particularistic societies which, during the first few years of war, had shown how strong was the local prejudice, and how provincial an American colonist remained even in exile. The Board was given authority to look after all the interests of the Loyalists. Their work in directing the military activities of the Loyalists has already been noted.

After united action on the part of the Tories from the different provinces had been secured, there sprang up a new source of faction. At a meeting to appoint a committee to correspond with friends

[1] *Rivington's Gazette*, February 14, 1778.

in England, it was moved that no person be elected " who has ever been known to act on the part of the Rebels, either as a member of Congress, convention or committee," or who in any way " took a public acting part with the rebellious Americans."[1] The motion gave voice to an idea that had long been in the minds of those who from the first had been ultra-Tories. The consistent Loyalists were jealous that they, who had borne the burden and heat of the day, should get no better reward than those who came within the British lines only to avoid the evils outside. Loyalty, they argued, is out of the question for these *converted* men. They are time-servers who come in only to save their estates (" the few who had estates ") or to get hard money. Such " cowards, despisable wretches," after blowing up the fire, do not stay and fight, but come here to enjoy themselves at ease, while the deluded suffer.[2] This difference between consistent loyalty and that which was only developed by the oppression and tyranny of the Whigs was never forgotten by the British government nor by the few, whom Curwen likened to Abdiel, who retained his " primitive loyalty amidst hostile bands of fallen spirits."[3]

The Whigs outside of New York quickly learned of this schism among the " sons of despotism," as

[1] *Rivington's Gazette*, August 19, 1780.
[2] *Ibid.*, August 19, 1780.
[3] Curwen, " Journal," p. 62.

they delighted to call them, and their editors loosed many shafts of wit and ridicule at Tory expense. But, remarked Rivington, "these squibs and crackers, which they are continually throwing, are perhaps scarcely noticed by those who are up to ears and eyes in Concerts, Plays, Balls and Charades,"[1] and his picture of gaiety was quite true, for, as has so often been the case in besieged cities, the inhabitants tried to forget their anxiety in a mad whirl of pleasure.

Every existing place of amusement was utilized. The theaters produced the most startling dramas, and one might choose on any night between "The Mock Doctor, or the Dumb Lady Cured" and the more serious production "Devil to Pay, or Wives Metamorphosed." After the drama, the seeker after pleasure could retire to the King's Head Tavern, which was connected with "an elegant garden, with arbors, bowers, alcoves, grottos, naiads, dryads, hamadryads,"[2] and where genteel liquors and good dinners were renowned. A band of music would attend, and "God Save the King will be played every hour."

On the occasion of a celebration of His, or Her Majesty's birthday, the host made especial efforts to be entertaining. A pyramid of lamps rose from the base to the top of the flagstaff of Loosely's tavern,

---

[1] *Rivington's Gazette*, January 5, 1782.
[2] Onderdonck, "Revolutionary Incidents of Long Island," Vol. I., 161.

and there were fireworks, one piece of which was
" George Rex with a crown imperial, illumined and
finished with a globe of fire." [1] But the chief glory
was within, where 200 wax lights illumined the
scene, and in the center of all was a transparent
painting of their majesties " with a crown supported
by angels elegantly illuminated by different colored
lights." Above was a canopy of state splendidly
decorated, " which shone like their Majesties' virtues conspicuous to the world." To the left of the
queen were the figures of Hibernia and Bellona; also
a British sailor trampling on the 13 stripes, signifying that, by the bravery of the navy, American Independence should be no more.[2] On the other
side, the " generous indignation " of the Loyalist was
aroused by a view of Congress, " whose ambition
has almost ruined this unhappy country." It was
" very apropos of the painter to place the devil at the
president's elbow, who tells him to persevere, with
so significant a grin as seems to indicate his having
no manner of doubt of their making his house their
home in the infernal regions." The statue of William Pitt, without its head, was placed near the Congress "as being one of their kidney and gave a hint
of what ought long ago to have been done." [3]

Amid these symbols of loyalty,

> "the festive Board was met, the loyal band,
> To Church and King devote each heart, each hand,"

[1] *Rivington's Gazette*, June 10, 1780.
[2] *Ibid.*, June 4, 1778.
[3] *Ibid.*, January 24, 1778.

as the poet of the occasion expressed it. And, when the dinner was begun, a standard appeared, on one occasion, with a representation of the British flag above that of France, with the lilies reversed.[1] Then the company joined in song,

> "Inspired by this auspicious morn,
> When George the Great, the Good, was born."

There was a note of challenge in the lines declaring that,
> "Aspiring France, and haughty Spain,
> With envy swol'n shall join in vain
> To give rebellion aid;
> Britannia's rage they soon shall feel
> Her seamen's thunder, soldiers' steel,
> A George's wrath displayed."[2]

These lines were sung with special vigor at the carnival which celebrated Rodney's famous victory over the French fleet in the Caribbean Sea.[3] Loosely, "the Boniface of Brooklyn," announced to his patrons that, since tyranny and its republic were no more, and monarchy was again firmly established, he would "produce a dinner fit for a conquering sovereign." When his "approved good masters" repaired to the dinner, they were entertained with such amusements and decorations as

[1] *Rivington's Gazette*, May 8, 1782.
[2] *Ibid.*, June 4, 1778.
[3] The famous Meschianza given in Philadelphia to Howe before his departure for England was rather a British army than a Loyalist affair, though the latter took part. See Moore's "Diary," Vol. II., 52.

illustrated the glories "won by his majesty's arms."[1] Nothing had surpassed the occasion except the splendid entertainments at the time of the visit of Prince William Henry. On that august occasion, a sentimental Loyalist wondered that Rebellion should not "sink at the approach of so fair a representative of the Royal Virtues."[2] No evidence of joy was omitted. There was a ball and a *feu de joie* in the evening, and the taverns rang with loyal toasts and songs, until the early morning.

Into the midst of all this gaiety, deadening all the mirth and silencing the song, came the news that a treaty of peace was being negotiated, accompanied by a fearful rumor that the Loyalists were to be abandoned to their fate. In vain the loyal gazettes seized upon every worthless opinion or anonymous tale, however insignificant or ridiculous, which seemed to indicate that England would not grant independence. Schemes were suggested by which the Loyalists alone should conquer America.[3] But, in spite of every effort, the Loyalists awaited, in utmost anxiety, the arrival of the vessel with dispatches, announcing the result of the Paris negotiations for peace.

[1] *Rivington's Gazette*, May 29, 1782.
[2] *Rivington's Gazette*, September 29, 1781. On that occasion a poem appeared which hailed the Prince with the lines,

"Rising o'er the Atlantic main,
William, the star of Morn, appears."

Upon the appearance of the poem, a critic remarked that "so far is this curious piece from being of standard weight, that it is fit only to be converted into Continental money."

[3] *Rivington's Gazette*, January 4, 1783.

CHAPTER XII.

CHARGED WITH TREASON.

THE thought of peace, except that which would come with the complete overthrow of the Revolution, was filled with terror for the Loyalists. In most of the states they had been proscribed as traitors; in all, their property had been confiscated. Throughout America, the people had given unmistakable evidence that no Loyalist would be tolerated among them. Even those refugees — and there were many of them — who, upon hearing of the surrender of Cornwallis, had fled from the British lines and joined the American army, had been none too graciously received. As a result, a peace on terms of American independence could mean for the adherents of the British crown nothing but perpetual banishment and the loss of all their worldly possessions.

The legislators of the several states had not left the Loyalists in doubt as to their status. The laws plainly defined a traitor as one who adhered to the king of Great Britain. He, who by preaching, teaching, speaking or writing, maintained that the king had authority over the state of New Jersey, or who acknowledged allegiance to Great Britain, should suffer death without benefit of clergy.[1] Such severity came only when loyalty had become particularly odious, near the end of the war; but, even in the year of independence, the giving aid to Great Britain had been made by law an act of treason.[2] In Pennsylvania, any resident of the state became a traitor if he accepted a commission from the king or enlisted in his army or persuaded others to do so, and, if convicted of such an offense, he should suffer death and the forfeiture of all his property.[3] Later, " divers traitors" were attainted if they did not surrender to the state authorities before a given date. The laws of the colonies to the south of Pennsylvania were of about the same degree of severity, and, in the actual treatment of the Loyalists, differed in no remarkable particular. In general, the states which were the seats of war, and these in times of great stress, persecuted the Loyalists most vigorously.

That the laws against treason, and the bills of attainder, were not without effect is shown by the famous "Black List" of Pennsylvania, which contained 490 names of persons attainted of high treason.[4] The larger number of these never re-

[1] Laws of New Jersey, March 30, 1781. The courts might change the sentence to serving on the ships of war of the United States. Vol. I., 370, laws compiled by R. Wilson, 1784.

[2] October 4, 1776. Laws of New Jersey, p. 4.

[3] Laws of Pennsylvania, Vol. X., 103, February 11, 1777. The president and Council of the State might commute to banishment.

[4] "The Black List," Philadelphia, 1802. Of these 71 "surrendered and were discharged," 13 were "tried and acquitted."

turned to the state, while some established their innocence, and others were pardoned. Only a few actually suffered the penalty. Among these were two citizens of Philadelphia, Mr. Roberts and Mr. Carlisle, who had shown great zeal for the British while the king's army was in Philadelphia. When the British army evacuated they remained, although warned of their danger, and were at once seized and brought to trial by the returning Whigs. They were condemned to be hanged.[1] Mr. Roberts' wife and children went before Congress and, on their knees, supplicated for mercy, but in vain.

In carrying out the sentence, the two men, with halters round their necks, were walked to the gallows behind a cart, "attended with all the apparatus which makes such scenes truly horrible." A guard of militia accompanied them, but very few spectators.[2] At the gallows, Mr. Roberts' behavior, wrote a loyal friend, "did honor to human nature," and both showed fortitude and composure. Roberts told his audience that his conscience acquitted him of guilt; that he suffered for doing his duty to his sovereign, and that his blood would one day be required at their hands. Turning to his children he charged

[1] For a report of the trial see "Pennsylvania Packet," Nov. 7, 1778. See also Pennsylvania Archives, Vol. VII., 22, also Dallas, Vol. I., 39, 42, Wharton ed., Hazard ed.

[2] The punishment for treason, which at the outbreak of the Revolution was the same as in England, was changed in America, because, Livingston is quoted as saying, that of England "none but a savage or a British subject can think of without horror." See also Laws of New York, March 30, 1778, Vol. I., 43.

and exhorted them to remember his principles, for which he died, and to adhere to them while they had breath. He suffered with the resolution of a Roman, wrote a witness. After the execution, the bodies of the two men were carried away by friends, and their burial was attended by over 4,000 people in procession.[1]

In this particular case the offenders were tried by a civil tribunal, but, more often, their fate was decided by court-martial,[2] or by committees "for detecting and defeating conspiracies," to the sittings of which the victims were brought by armed bands of rangers who scoured the country in every direction in search of these "traitors." In New York, over 1,000 were tried and sentenced, and some 600 were released on bail. A number were released on taking the oath of allegiance to the state, and others were confined in prison for refusing such an oath.

Some of the more heartless leaders of the revolution defended this severity of treatment, and thought that "hanging the traitors" would have a good effect and "give stability to the new government." One suggested that the Tories seemed designed for this purpose by Providence.[3] The more thoughtful leaders, however, denounced the trial of Loyalists for treason, and Washington feared

[1] Galloway's "Examination," p. 77.
[2] In New York such a condemnation had to be approved by the state legislature. For particulars of a trial by court-martial see "Public Papers of Geo. Clinton," Vol. I., 741.
[3] "Records of North Carolina," Vol. XI., 561.

that it might prove a dangerous expedient. It was true, he granted, that they had joined the British after such an offense had been declared to be treason, but, as they had not taken the oaths nor entered into the American service, it would be said that they had a right to choose their side. "Again," he added, "by the same rule that we try them may not the enemy try any natural-born subject of Great Britain taken in arms in our service? We have a great number of them, and I, therefore, think that we had better submit to the necessity of treating a few individuals who may really deserve a severer fate, as prisoners of war, than run the risk of giving an opening for retaliation upon the Europeans in our service."[1]

Other prominent patriots took a more sympathetic view, and disapproved of such trials because of the impossibility of rendering justice. "We shall have many unhappy devils to take their trials for their life next Oyer court," wrote a patriot to Gov. Caswell. "I must confess I feel myself deeply interested in this matter." He thought that the governor must view the present situation of the country in as deplorable a light as he did. "An exasperated jury and a lay judge. My God!" he exclaimed, "What may we not expect? Law should be strictly attended to, severity exercised, but the doors of mercy should never be shut."[2]

[1] "Washington's Writings," Ford Ed., Vol. VI., 241.
[2] "Records of North Carolina," Vol. XI., 552.

It is true, however, that the actual number of executions was very small as compared with the number either found guilty of treason by actual trial or attainted with that crime. Many joined the British and never returned, others escaped after trial, and many were pardoned by tender-hearted legislators. In fact, for every severe enactment to be found in the session laws of the several states, there are ten acts of pardon or abatement of the severer clauses of the original law. Many, indeed, were only pardoned on condition of joining the patriot army, and, as this same alternative was sometimes granted to a forger or a horse-thief, the quality of the mercy may seem strained.[1]

Not only were the refugee loyalists debarred from the hope of returning to their homes because they had been attainted with treason, but they had no property with which to resume the old life, even if permitted to return unmolested to their former dwelling places. Every vestige of their possessions had been taken from them, at first by a nibbling system of fines and special taxation, and later by an all-devouring rage for confiscation.

Very early in the Revolution, the Whigs tried to drive the Tories into the patriot militia or into the Continental army by fines and by obliging them to hire substitutes. The families of men who had fled from the country to escape implication in the impending war were obliged to hire substitutes, and

[1] "Colonial Records of Pennsylvania," Vol. XII., 222.

then were fined for the misdeeds of the mercenary whom they had engaged. Fines were even imposed upon neutral and unoffending persons for not preventing members of their family from entering the British service. If the fines were refused, the property was recklessly sold to the amount of the fine and costs of action. In addition to this drain on Tory property there quickly followed the fines and amercements for refusing the test oath or for acts aiding the British. Loyalists, convicted of entering the enemy's lines, could be fined as high as 2,000 pounds, and even the unsuccessful attempt to enter might be punished by a fine of 1,000 pounds.[1] Persons abusing the use of passports suffered a like amercement. If the property of the offender failed to answer for his offences, he became subject to corporal punishment; whipping, branding, cropping the ears, and exposure in the pillory being resorted to in some of the states. Every possible mode of manifesting loyalty was subjected to a fine. Speaking or writing favorably of Great Britain had its price. Dissuading any one from entering the Continental army or speaking ill of the Continental currency was punished by a fine.

In New York and South Carolina, the Loyalists were obliged to make good all robberies committed within their county, and were specially taxed for that purpose. The supposition was that the enemies of independence encouraged the robbers in order

[1] "Acts of New Jersey," October 8, 1778, p. 60.

to hurt the American cause. In Maryland and Virginia, a treble tax was placed on the estates of all non-jurors and absentees. Permission was generally given to appropriate loyalist property for Continental purposes, such as using the timber on Tory lands to build Continental vessels.

As the war progressed the greed for Loyalists' property was less restrained. The financial straits of the states tempted them to look upon Tory property as a source of revenue, and, under the conviction that they wished only to make neutrality expensive, or to punish internal enemies, or compel absentees to pay their proportion of the war expenses, the states began to amerce loyal estates, and then to declare them forfeited altogether to the offended commonwealth.

That the Whigs had early had a covetous eye upon the Tory property seems hardly dubitable; for the legislative bodies had hastened to pass such laws as would prevent those suspected of Toryism from transferring their property either by real or pretended sale. They also made efforts to stop the plundering of the estates of absentees — which was rather an interested benevolence than a shining example of revolutionary altruism. These efforts were made to prevent individual plunderers enriching themselves by preying upon the Tories, but the disposition of the property was such that, if the Revolution succeeded, the proceeds would fall into the coffers of the state.

The state interference was, no doubt, needed, for the depredations were carried so far that the powerless Tories were robbed of their common house and kitchen utensils, and even of their wearing apparel. Friends, who tried to guard the property of refugees, nailed up the doors that led to rooms containing valuable furniture, but were obliged, by bullying committeemen, to remove their barricades and give up their treasures. The members of one wealthy refugee's family were reduced, in their housekeeping, to broken chairs and tea cups, and to "dipping the water out of an iron skellet into the pot as cheerfully as if they were using a silver urn."[1] The furniture had been removed, though the family pictures still hung "in the blue room," and the harpsichord stood in the passage way to be abused by the children and people who passed through.

In towns containing a minority of Tories, desirable articles of their personal property were often raffled off by the authorities. The militia, too, plundered without ceremony all who in any way were suspected of Toryism. Horses, cows, poultry, and every movable possession of a Tory became regarded as contraband of war. Loyal farmers complained that soldiers from neighboring camps cut their timber and burned their fences, until the once beautiful lands looked like "an unfrequented desert." The vandals appropriated everything they fancied — furniture, dishes, liquors,

[1] "James Murray, Loyalist," p. 245.

and even the family chaise. Washington forbade the soldiery molesting any one on the pretense that he was a Tory, but his command came, said a Loyalist, like Venetian succor — rather late. It was noted, too, when men were actually tried for theft, that the act was condoned if the victim had been *mistaken* for a Tory, and altogether excused if actually shown to be of that political persuasion.[1]

When, however, the idea had gained ground that the confiscation of Loyalists' estates would provide the sinews of war, and it was realized that a vulnerable point of attack upon the refugees was the real estate they had left behind, the state governments began in a most thorough manner to confiscate all manner of Tory wealth, and to protect it from further vandalism. The vigorous and resourceful author of "Common Sense," the pamphlet which, it was said, "turned Tories Whigs, and washed blackamores white," had urged, even before the Declaration of Independence, that the Patriots should seize all the property of their opponents to carry on the war. That gave the idea wide circulation, and some of the states began the work before the famous resolution of Congress, late in 1777,[2] recommended that the states confiscate and sell the real and personal property of persons who had for

---

[1] For an example see "George Clinton Papers," Vol. I., 530.
[2] Nov. 27. See "Journals of Congress," Philadelphia, 1880, Vol. III.

feited "the right to protection," and to invest the money arising from these sales in Continental loan certificates. The approval of Congress gave the plan widespread popularity, and, though in some of the states the measure met bitter opposition,[1] all, in time, seized the loyalist property for the uses of the commonwealth.

The mode of confiscation varied in different provinces. Some states gave the Loyalists a preliminary warning of the stroke that would come in case they did not take the oath and conduct themselves as patriots. Others granted an alternative, while the remainder made a sudden legislative onslaught upon the coveted property, giving the owners no opportunity to recant and save their possessions. An invidious class hatred of the Loyalists as the largest landowners, and even personal spite, in some cases, lent a peculiar zeal to these attacks on the Tory property.

The execution of the work of confiscation shows some differences in the manner of seizure. Some states gave the owners the right of trial by jury to determine the legality of the seizure, while others confiscated in a peremptory manner by attainder. Sometimes, the work was left to the regular executive officers in the state, such as the sheriffs and constables; while, in other places, special commis-

---

[1] See *Rivington's Gazette*, January 26, 1780, for trouble in Maryland, also see "North Carolina Records," XIII., 578, 612, 863, 870, 872, 898, 930, 963, 977, 989, 991.

sioners[1] were appointed for the work, or trustees were selected by the judges of probate. The method of selling the confiscated estates was usually prescribed in the law, which authorized sales by auction or the slower method of holding until a purchaser presented himself. Provision was made for selling on credit, though in that case bonds were exacted. In some cases the payment could be made in certificates, which were issued by the treasurer to the persons loaning their money to the state treasury. At the sales these certificates could be used as specie. It was the same plan that was later resorted to by the French revolutionary government, when it pledged the confiscated property of the clergy for the redemption of its paper issues.

To prevent "dangerous monopolies of land," the estates were to be divided and sold in small tracts. Finally, none but persons who had taken the test oath were permitted to buy. This not only rewarded patriotism, the laws declared, but prevented collusive purchases of land by the friends of the forfeiting Loyalists. In nearly every case, a charitable clause in the confiscation laws provided for the care of the wife and children of the offender out of the proceeds of the estate. In practice, however, even this charity degenerated, and we hear of two aristocratic ladies using their coach house as their dining room, and the "fowl house" as

[1] See for a good account of their work Flick's "Loyalism in New York," Chapter VII.

their bed-chamber. The picture continues in character, "the old lady looks as majestic even there, and dresses with as much elegance as if she were in a palace." [1]

In spite of the great opportunities for corruption, and the plain evidence that these opportunities were improved,[2] great sums came into the state treasuries as the proceeds of these sales of forfeited lands. In New York, alone,[3] over $3,600,000 worth of property was acquired by the state, although lands in New York City, Long Island and Staten Island practically escaped confiscation, because that territory was in British power until 1783, and then the zeal for confiscation had abated. The important and lasting result of confiscation, however, in New York and elsewhere, was that large manors and estates were cut up into small lots and sold to the common people, thus leveling, equalizing and making more democratic the whole social structure.[4]

The justice of the confiscation laws was defended in their preambles. The Virginia House of Delegates made a defense of confiscation the object of a special resolution, which asserted, "That confiscation laws, being founded upon legal principles, were strongly dictated by that principle of common justice

[1] "James Murray, Loyalist," p. 253.
[2] Curwen asserted that not two pence in the pound came into the Massachusetts treasury from the lands confiscated there. See Curwen, "Journal," p. 147.
[3] See Flick, "Loyalism in New York," p. 159.
[4] See Flick, *Ibid.*, p. 160.

which demands that, if virtuous citizens, in defence of their natural rights, risk their life, liberty and property on their success, vicious citizens, who side with tyranny and oppression, or cloak themselves under the mask of neutrality, should at least hazard their property and not enjoy the labors and dangers of those whose destruction they wished."[1] Such was the general trend of the arguments for defense, though they usually added a long account of the "murders, rapine, and devastation" of which the Loyalists had been guilty,[2] and to avenge which the confiscations were justifiable. Washington approved heartily of the confiscation acts, and thought the state of affairs demanded such severity.

The effect upon the Loyalists was overwhelming. They pled in vain the injustice of it. Grant, they argued, that the opponents of independence were necessarily removed from among the people where their influence might do harm, but why add to their banishment any punishment affecting their property? By removing the man the measure of public justice is full; by adding to that punishment, it runs over. The one derives its justice from a regard to self-preservation, which, when well-founded, is right; the other is an act of vindictive justice, which is due only to overt acts, and transgressions of known laws. Confiscation perpetuates the of-

[1] Almon's "Remembrancer," Vol. 10, 92, 2d part; date Dec. 17, 1782.

[2] See, for example, "Laws of Georgia," Philadelphia, 1800, C. T. Cole, p. 242. Law dated May 4, 1782.

fender's punishment down to innocent posterity, and can there be a more melancholy spectacle than a whole family overwhelmed with misery from the crime of their chief?[1]

Realizing, however, the futility of argument, the Loyalists tried intimidation. Stories got abroad of men who bought confiscated houses having their throats mysteriously cut in the night while sleeping in their new possessions. Notices appeared in the loyal gazettes, whence they were derisively published in the patriot papers, threatening the severest persecution upon the return of peace if any one bought the writer's confiscated estate.[2] Another refugee threatened "that august body, the Executive Council of Pennsylvania." He had noticed their late advertisement for selling estates and his was "luckily" among them. "Luckily," he explained, "because he was sure from the great quantity of old rags which they had the modesty to call money, that his estate would sell for at least twenty times its real worth, though a good title could not be obtained without his consent. If he liked the bargain, he would insist upon it, but the purchaser must remember that he must be paid in good, hard, Spanish milled dollars. *Soft* money would not satisfy such a *hardened* Tory. He hoped that the purchaser would be a good warm Whig

---

[1] "Life of Peter Van Schaack," p. 114. See, however, "James Murray, Loyalist," p. 171.

[2] *Rivington's Gazette*, August 3, 1782.

with a good hoard of hard dollars, for reprisal was his maxim."[1]

Such laughable and impotent threats were naturally of no avail, and, when the full meaning of the confiscation acts came upon the Loyalists, they realized their desperate straits and turned to the consideration of a means of saving their worldly possessions, with honor.

As a tentative measure, a number of the victims sent a memorial to the commissioners from the king, setting forth that, since the reconciliation of the "friends of government" with their country had become an object of the attention of his Majesty's Commissioners, and, as it was doubtful whether the Commissioners would be able to negotiate with the American Congress or even with the individual states, would it not be well for the Loyalists themselves to try to make terms with the American states, agreeable, of course, to the British government? Would this not help the general reconciliation? Could not the Loyalists, even if the war continued, better help to eventual conciliation? Their estates, in their own hands, would contribute less to aid the American cause than in the patriot hands. This was, of course, merely a suggestion, and they would do as the Commissioners directed. They closed with an appeal requesting that it be remembered that they had left their families and fortunes, friends and connections in the country;

[1] *Rivington's Gazette*, April 28, 1779.

that the war had occasioned separation from these for more than three years, and that their happiness and prosperity must depend upon their being enabled at some future time to return to their country. It must surely be acknowledged that the time, manner and terms thereof are objects of the last importance and such as call for the indulgence of that government to which they had adhered at the risk of their lives and fortunes.[1] They enclosed with this proposal to the commissioners a copy of the sort of memorial that they wished to send to the state government. In this document, after an eloquent appeal for a conciliatory reception[2] they suggested, without raising again the subjects of dissension, that they draw over them a veil of mutual forgiveness and perpetual oblivion. They had, it was true, differed in opinion, but both, doubtless, desired the happiness of their country. They did not believe that the state government would want concessions inconsistent with their manliness, and offered the following terms: (1) The state should make the refugees the subject of an act of amnesty and naturalization, which should include all who would comply with the conditions. (2) The state should restore the Loyalists to their property and recommend the people of the state to receive the returning refugees and protect them. On the part of the memorialists, they would become

[1] Stevens' "Facsimiles," No. 1128, dated August 20, 1778.
[2] Stevens' *Ibid.*, No. 1129.

peaceable subjects of the state's law and government, and would pay their proportion of the debt on account of the war. Should these terms be rejected they called upon God to witness that they did not occasion further war.

Whether this protocol would ever have received the serious consideration of the state legislatures is a matter of conjecture, but they were never given the opportunity, for the commissioners objected to any reconciliation except upon the terms offered by themselves to the American Congress. When this hope was thus extinguished, the Loyalists gave themselves up to watching the progress of the war and yearning for a favorable outcome. In such a state, then, with absolutely no salvation but in the complete victory of the British arms, it is not strange that the news of a treaty, which did not guarantee the restoration of their property, threw them into the depths of despair.

CHAPTER XIII.

EXPATRIATION.

On March 26, 1783, Rivington's "Royal Lying Gazette," as the Whigs called it, published in New York the first authentic news of the treaty of peace. The interest of the refugees centered in the fifth and sixth articles of the treaty. The fifth, besides providing for the restitution of the confiscated property of the British subjects, stipulated that "persons of any other description" — meaning Loyalists — might go into any part of the United States, for twelve months, unmolested, in the effort to obtain the restitution of their confiscated estates. Congress agreed earnestly to recommend the states to revise their confiscation laws, to make them consistent with the spirit of conciliation, which should prevail upon the return of peace. The states should be asked to restore the confiscated property to the Loyalists who would refund the price paid by the persons now holding such property. The sixth article was designed to guard the Loyalists against any future confiscations or persecutions on account of the part they had taken in the war. Neither should they suffer any future loss, nor should those then in confinement be held after the ratification of the treaty.¹

The commissioners who had negotiated the treaty, had long and bitterly discussed the question of amnesty and compensation for the Loyalists. The French minister, even, had urged it, moved, it was thought, by the idea that the presence of the Tories in America would keep up two rival parties whose antagonism the French might use to their advantage.² John Adams favored compensating "the wretches how little soever they deserve it, nay, how much soever they deserve the contrary,"³ but the commissioners hesitated "to saddle" America with the Tories, because they feared the opposition at home, especially by the individual states. The British demands had finally been met with the mere promise that Congress would *recommend* to the states a conciliatory policy with reference to the Loyalists.

This solution neither satisfied the Loyalists nor the more chivalrous Englishmen. One declared that the whole peace was a shame which only proclaimed the British as beaten cowards incapable of protecting the adherents to their wretched fortunes.⁴ Another thought the provision concerning the Loyalists was "precipitate, impolitic" and "cruelly

---

[1] Journals of Congress, September 3, 1783.
[2] John Adams' "Works," Vol. II., 307.
[3] *Ibid.*, Vol. IX., 516.
[4] Stevens' "Facsimiles," 1055.

neglectful of our American friends."[1] A Loyalist wrote bitterly, in the *Gazette*, that "even robbers, murderers and rebels are faithful to their fellows and never betray each other," and he asked if Britain was to be more perfidious than they. A rhymster cried,

> "'Tis an honor to serve the bravest of nations,
> And be left to be hanged in their capitulations."[2]

But all the cavilling was unreasonable and hasty, for England had gotten for the Loyalists the utmost attainable in the treaty and, later, proved honorable and generous in the highest degree by compensating the Loyalists out of her own treasury.

Whatever the Loyalists might think of the care taken of them by the British peace commissioners, the fact of a treaty of peace made their immediate departure from New York imperative. They had been assured by the king, through Sir Henry Clinton, that no place in which there were Loyalists and British troops would be surrendered upon terms which discriminated between them, and that refugees might rely upon the utmost attention being shown to their safety and welfare;[3] but it was plain to all that, when the troops went, the refugees must go also or be left to the mercy of the uncertain temper of the returning Whigs.

The British posts at Charleston and Savannah had already been evacuated. Some 3,000 of the

---
[1] Stevens' "Facsimiles," 1054.
[2] G. W. Greene, "Hist. View," etc., p. 431.
[3] *Rivington's Gazette*, March 9, 1782.

loyal inhabitants had left the former place for Jamaica, St. Augustine, Halifax or New York, which was the last loyal refuge in the United States. Fifty of the two hundred sail which left Charleston came to New York.[1] Some 7,000 persons, besides the British soldiers, left Savannah, and about 5,000 of these were negroes, property of the wealthy, loyal planters. Most of these sailed for St. Augustine, and the remainder reached Charleston just in time to swell the number of Loyalists about to leave that post.[2] By this gradual reduction of the number of British posts, the entire company of refugees in America was concentrated in New York.

Early in 1782, bands of Loyalists had begun to leave New York. Sailing boats bound out advertised for emigrants, and boasted particularly of their armament. The newspapers began to be filled with offers of property for sale. "Genteel furniture" was at a great discount, as were all goods difficult to move, such as china and glassware. Houses and stores were also offered for sale because the owners had little faith in the promises of Congress or the will of the states to obey them. Merchants urged their debtors to pay their accounts at once; and Loosely, the tavern keeper, issued an address which urged those gentlemen who were about to

[1] *Rivington's Gazette*, January 8, 1783, November 30, 1782.
[2] *Ibid.*, August 28, 1782. Arrived in Charleston, July 30, 1782.

leave the country not to forget with what generosity he had always treated them. Rivington, the printer, showed his appreciation of the coming evacuation by an apology to the public. He was, he said, "Sensible that his zeal for the success of his Majesty's Arms, his sanguine wishes for the good of his country, and his friendship for individuals, had at times led him to credit and circulate paragraphs without investigating the facts so closely as his duty to the public demanded. Hereafter he would err no more."

This conversion from "yellow journalism" was greeted with derision by the Whig papers outside of New York. A wag advertised Rivington's excess stock of the letters R E B E L for sale. Many hundred weight worn out in his Majesty's service would be sold for the value of the metal. Another proposed making Rivington's whole carcass into portable soup for the use of the lady and gentlemen Tories bound for England.[1] In spite of these wag-

[1] James Rivington's "Reflections" appeared in the *Freeman's Journal*, December 4, 1782.

"The more I reflect, the more plain it appears,
If I stay, I must stay at the risque of my ears,
I have so-be-peppered the foes of our throne,
Be-rebeled, be-deviled, and told them their own,
That if we give up to these rebels at last
Tis a chance if my ears will atone for the past.
  [If there is an evacuation.]
Yet still I surmise for aught I can see
No Congress or Senates would meddle with me.
For what have I done, when we come to consider,

gish attacks, and others more vicious, Rivington tried to conciliate the Whigs, and continued the publication of his *Gazette*, after the Whigs returned to New York, but was obliged to give way before the popular antipathy.

Long before the actual evacuation by the British troops, the departure of the Loyalists began. The

> But sold my commodities to the best bidder?
> If I offered to lie for the sake of a post
> Was I to be blamed if the king offered most?
> > [Ridicules Honor and Fame when compared with emolument]
> > [True the Tories might defend New York, but he doubts it]
> > . . . As a very last shift
> We'll go to New Scotland and take the king's gift.
> Good folks do your will — but I vow and I swear
> I'll be boiled into soup before I'll live there :
>
> . . . .
>
> Of all the vile countries that ever were known
> In the frigid or torrid or temperate zone,
> (From accounts I have had) there is not such another ;
> It neither belongs to this world or the other.
> A favor they think it to send us there gratis
> To sing like the Jews at the river Euphrates.
> And after surmounting the rage of the billows
> Hang ourselves up at last with our harps on the willows.
> Ere I sail for that shore may I take my last nap ;
> Why it gives me the palsy to look on its map.
> And he that goes there (tho' I mean to be civil)
> May fairly be said to have gone to the devil.
> Shall I push for old England and whine at the throne?
> Alas they have Jemmies enough of their own !
> Besides such a name I have got from my trade,
> They would think I was lying whatever I said.
>
> . . . .
>
> In short, if they let me remain in this realm,
> What is it to Jemmy who stands at the helm?"

King offered to transport all loyal subjects who had lived within the British lines for twelve months. If the refugee could prove a residence for that length of time, show that the house assigned to him was in good repair and the rent paid to date, he might, after paying his debts and listing the property that he wished to move, be entered on the books of the adjutant general for transportation in some one of his Majesty's ships.

Previous to their embarkation, they were supplied from the King's stores with provisions, sufficient for their support for a full year. An allowance of twenty-one days' rations was made for their passage. The government also furnished comfortable clothing for the men, women and children, together with an assortment of medicines, various kinds of husbandry tools, various arms and ammunition for hunting and defence.[1] Thus equipped, the transports would set sail under a strong convoy.

In the anxiety to escape the predicted merciless persecution by the Whigs, the nature of the land to which they were going had not been very carefully studied. Some of the King's Rangers, who had preceded the mass of the emigrants, had published a highly colored account of the attractions of the Island of St. John. The soil was good, well wooded, and free from rocks, they claimed. The climate was good, the harbors spacious, safe and numerous. The waters abounded with shell and

[1] *Rivington's Gazette*, October 19, 1782.

fish. The taxes were few, the government mild, and the lands finely situated and reasonable in price. Cattle were plentiful, and the story about starvation was nonsense.[1] From Nova Scotia, the agents for the Loyalists sent most favorable accounts. There were, they said, great business opportunities, as well as the mere necessities for subsistence. Sawmills could be erected and a great lumber business carried on with the West Indies. The fisheries would develop into a great industry. Cattle and poultry were far cheaper than on Long Island.[2] In fact, they were assured, they might there, under the protection of a good government, quietly enjoy the fruits of their labor, freed from the "detestable tyranny of seditious demagogues."

Lured by such representations and sped by the fear of the Whigs, who were about to come into the possession of New York, over 29,000 refugees left that city within a year. Some entered the new life with zest and endured the privations with good humor; but, soon, there were signs of discontent, and complaints, by some, that they had been deceived. One wrote, a year later, "all our golden promises are vanished in smoke. We were taught to believe this place was not barren and foggy as had been represented, but we find it ten times worse. We have nothing but his Majesty's rotten pork and

[1] *Rivington's Gazette*, January 22, 1783.
[2] Onderdonk's "Long Island," pp. 255, 256. *Rivington's Gazette*, March 29, 1783.

unbaked flour to subsist on. 'But can't you bake it, seeing it is so wooden a country?' Only come here yourself and you will soon learn the reason. It is the most inhospitable clime that ever mortal set foot on."[1] The winter, it was said, was of almost insupportable length and coldness. There were but a few spots to cultivate, and the land was covered with a cold, spongy moss instead of grass. The country was wrapt in the gloom of perpetual fog.

The Whigs heard with delight the tales of discontent from Nova Scotia. They nicknamed the land "Nova Scarcity." It was a land, they said, that belonged neither to this world nor the other. It was enough to give one the palsy, just to look at the map. However, it was no more than the Tories deserved, for, in addition to their crimes during the war, one must consider their conduct on leaving New York. They had left the churches filthy and dirty from the uses to which they had been put; they had raided the Whigs who returned before the British evacuated, and had harried the country about New York, burning barns and haystacks, and extorting money from the Whigs by beating them.[2] Every violence which was the result of the unsettled political and social condition was confidently laid at the door of the Tory.

[1] Onderdonk's "Long Island," p. 256.
[2] For a good account of the evacuation of New York and the departure of the refugees, see McMaster, "With the Fathers," p. 274.

In spite of the recommendation of Congress, which had been made in accordance with the terms of the treaty, little moderation could be seen in the legislation concerning the Tories. Confiscation still went on actively; governors of the states were urged to exchange lists of the proscribed persons, that no Tory might find a resting place in the United States; and in nearly every state they were disfranchised,[1] while in many localities they were tarred and feathered, driven from town and warned never to return.[2] In the South where the partizan warfare had been most bitter, the Tories fled for their lives, and a few of the bolder ones who attempted to return to their homes, were warned and then attacked; eight being murdered and the rest fleeing from the country. In New York, the legislature passed a Trespass Act, in which all persons, who had been driven from their homes at the coming of the British, were given the legal right to recover damages against those who had used their property during the British occupation. The act declared that a military order — the usual justification of such use — would be of no value for defence in the courts.

Many Whigs hastened at once to secure indemnity from the Tories who had used their prop-

---

[1] As late as 1801 Tories were disfranchised in Pennsylvania; see "Black List," New York, 1865, p. 7. See also Flick's "Loyalism in New York," p. 164.

[2] For a full account of this persecution see McMaster's "History of the United States," Vol. I., 106-128.

erty, and who still remained in New York, hoping thus to save the little property that the war had spared them. After many cases had been decided in favor of the Whig prosecutors, a case came up for trial in which the plaintiff was a widow, and the defendant a rich Tory merchant. 'To the disgust of the Whigs, Alexander Hamilton appeared as counsel for the Tory. Indignation ran high, and, when the verdict was rendered in favor of the Tory, Hamilton had lost tremendously in popularity and gained little credit because of his brilliant display of forensic ability.

Hamilton had undertaken the defence, because he, with other eminent Whigs, thought the Tories ill-treated. Only a short time before, he had received a letter from John Jay, then in Paris, declaring that "violence and associations against the Tories pay an ill compliment to government, and impeach our good faith in the opinion of some, and our magnanimity in the opinion of many."[1] "The Tories are almost as much pitied in these countries as they are execrated in ours; an undue degree of severity toward them would, therefore, be impolitic as it would be unjustifiable. They, who incline to involve that whole class of men in indiscriminate punishment and ruin, certainly carry the matter too far. It would be an instance of unnecessary rigour and unmanly revenge, without a parallel, except in the annals of religious bigotry

[1] Hamilton's "History of the United States," Vol. III., 10.

and blindness. What does it signify where nine tenths of these people are buried? Victory and peace should in my mind be followed by clemency, moderation and benevolence, and we should be careful not to sully the glory of the revolution by licentiousness and cruelty."

Patrick Henry, when making a plea that the Tories might return unmolested, had been told that they were dangerous, and at this he exclaimed: " Afraid of them ! — what, sirs, shall *we* who have laid the proud British lion at our feet, now be afraid of his whelps?"[1] Many reasons were advanced, by those who reasoned about the matter, for a generous treatment of the Tories. John Adams feared that any trouble the United States might have with Canada or Nova Scotia, concerning the fisheries, would arise from American severity toward the Tories. The same observation might apply to the fur trade and the posts upon the frontier.[2]

Such ideas, however, appealed very little to the great mass of the victorious Whigs. The memory of Tarleton's raids, of the Wyoming Valley massacre, of the prison ships and churches of New York, and of cities burned by the marauding Tories were still fresh in mind, and were not to be reasoned out. Indeed, it was many years before the hatred of the Tories was mitigated, and the War of 1812 had

[1] " Library of American Literature," Vol. III., 218.
[2] John Adams' " Works," Vol. VIII., 237.

been fought before laws against the Tories had disappeared from the statute books.

Thousands of inconspicuous Tories did nevertheless succeed in remaining in the United States, especially in large cities, where their identity was lost, and they were not the objects of jealous social and political exclusion as in the small towns.[1] The mass of those who had taken any part in the war were, however, at some time during the revolution, or immediately after, driven into exile, for the most part in the British territory lying to the north of the United States.[2]

Throughout the war, various routes through New York were followed by the escaping Loyalists, all leading to and over the northern and western border. As a rule, voluntary exiles, the loyal provincial troops, and those driven out by persecution, went during the war to some place in Canada; the Niagara frontier, Montreal and Quebec being the favorite centers. In 1778, provision having been made by the British government, some three thousand moved into upper and lower Canada. During the next four years hundreds were banished from the colonies, and joined the earlier groups. These were for the most part the Tory democracy;

[1] In and about New York City, thousands pled that their Toryism had been forced, under the stress of British occupancy. As their assertions could not be disproved, and as they were in a majority, the hostile minority was not able to wreak its vengeance.

[2] For a full and detailed account of this migration see Flick's "Loyalism in New York," Chapter VIII.

for the aristocratic Tories generally fled to England to await the outcome. With the treaty of peace there came a rush for British American territory. The numbers were increased in Canada to some 25,000 during the next few years and those in Nova Scotia and other British territory swelled the number to 60,000.[1]

Most of these exiles became in one way or another a temporary expense to the British government, and the burden was borne honorably and ungrudgingly. The care began during the war. The Loyalists who aided Burgoyne were provided with homes in Canada, and, before the close of 1779, nearly a thousand refugees were cared for in houses and barracks, and given fuel, household furniture, and even pensioned with money. After the peace, thousands of exiles at once turned to the British government for temporary support. The vast majority had lost little, and asked only for land and supplies to start life. The minority who had lost lands, offices and incomes demanded indemnity. As for the members of the humbler class the government ordered that there should be given 500 acres of land to heads of families, 300 acres to single men, and each township in the new settlements was to have 2,000 acres for church purposes

---

[1] See Flick's "Loyalism in New York" where the details and references are so fully given that there is no need of repetition here. I have investigated these questions for myself, and, as I agree substantially with Mr. Flick, have no reason for duplicating his work.

and 1,000 for schools. Every colonist was to be exempted from fees and quit rents for ten years. Building material and tools — an axe, a spade, a hoe and a plow — were furnished each head of a family. Even clothing and food were issued to the needy, and, as late as 1785, there were 26,000 entitled to rations. Communities were equipped with grindstones and the machinery for grist and sawmills. In this way nearly $5,000,000 were spent to get Nova Scotia well started; and, in Upper Canada, besides the three million acres given to Loyalists, some $4,000,000 were expended for their benefit before 1787.

But there was a far greater burden assumed by the British government, in granting the compensation asked for by those who had sacrificed everything to their loyalty.[1] Those who had lost offices or professional practice were, in many cases, cared for by the gift of lucrative offices under the government, and Loyalist military officers were put on half pay, but there were many not to be thus cared for. To those who could not be employed grants of pensions had been made even during the war, but the number increased so greatly in 1782 that Parliament suspended all donations until a Committee could investigate both old and new claims. This committee struck nearly a hundred from the

---

[1] The fullest and most reliable account of this subject is found in Wilmot's "Historical View of the Commissioners for Enquiring into the Losses . . . of . . . Loyalists from each Colony."

list, but added four times as many, and the burden was heavier than before.

After the peace, over five thousand Loyalists submitted claims for losses, usually through the agents appointed by the refugees from each American colony.[1] In July of 1783, a commission of five members was appointed by Parliament to classify the losses and services of the Loyalists. This commission divided the Loyalists into six classes : (1) Those who had rendered services to Great Britain ; (2) those who had borne arms against the Revolution ; (3) uniform Loyalists ; (4) Loyalists resident in Great Britain ; (5) those who took oaths of allegiance to American states, but afterwards joined the British ; (6) those who took arms with the Americans and later joined the English army and navy. They then examined the claims with an impartial and judicial severity which the Loyalists denounced as an inquisition. The claimant entered a room alone with the commissioners, and, after telling his services and losses, was rigidly questioned concerning fellow claimants as well as himself. The claimant then submitted a written and sworn statement of his losses.[2] After the results of both examinations were critically scrutinized, the judges made the awards. They refused to consider

[1] See Wilmot, p. 82. They were the arch-loyalists from each colony.

[2] The memorandum books which the commissioners used in making notes while conducting the examinations in Nova Scotia and Canada are now in the MSS. Department of the Library of Congress.

losses for lands bought or improved during the war; for uncultivated lands; property mortgaged to its full value or with defective titles; for ships captured by Americans or damage done by British troops, or for forage used by or furnished to them. Losses due to a fall in the value of provincial paper money, robbery, runaway negroes, crops left on the ground or evaded rents, were discarded. Nothing was allowed for expenses or suffering in prison, fines paid for refusing to drill with the patriot militia, or the cost of living in New York city during the war. Anticipated professional profits, and losses in trade and labor were thrown out. Claims were allowed only for losses of property through loyalty, for offices held before the war, and for the loss of actual professional income.[1]

The commission sat at first in England, but soon realized that, to give fair opportunities to all classes of claimants, it would be necessary to go to them. Thereupon, Dundee and Pemberton went to Nova Scotia, and John Anstey to New York. Between the years 1785 and 1789, these commissioners sat in Halifax, St. John's, Quebec and Montreal. In the whole course of their work, they examined claims to the amount of forty millions of dollars, and ordered nineteen millions to be paid.[2] At first

[1] See Wilmot's "Historical View," pp. 69-78.
[2] In the most complete list to be obtained of the claims admitted by the commissioners, there are some noteworthy statistical facts concerning the distribution and character of the Loyalists. 941 out of 2,560 had been residents of New York when the war broke out.

the per cent. that was granted was not fixed, but, later, Pitt's plan was adopted which fixed by schedule the per cent. of approved losses to be paid, giving greater consideration to the small losers than the great. If, to the cost of establishing the Loyalists in Nova Scotia and Canada, we add the compensations granted in money, the total amount expended by the British government for their American adherents, was at least thirty millions of dollars. There is every evidence that the greatest care, that human ingenuity could devise, was exercised to make all these awards in a fair and equitable manner. The members of the commission were of unimpeachable honesty. Nevertheless, there was much complaint by the Loyalists, not only because of the awards of the commission, but because of the partial failure of the general scheme

Over one third, then, in a miscellaneous list of Loyalists, were from New York ; and the next state in order was South Carolina, with only 321, or one third the number in New York.

LOYALISTS BY PROVINCE.

Complete list of those claiming of British government.

Vermont,	61	New York,	941	Virginia,	140
New Hampshire,	31	New Jersey,	208	N. Carolina,	135
Massachusetts,	226	Pennsylvania,	148	S. Carolina,	321
Rhode Island,	41	Delaware,	9	Georgia,	129
Connecticut,	92	Maryland,	78		2,560

Again, a rough estimate shows that nearly two thirds were not natives of America. In other words, the active Tory of the American Revolution was such, in a majority of cases, because he had not become a thorough American, had not yet fully imbibed American ideas.

for giving the loyal exiles a new start in life. The task was no easy one, to transfer a disheartened people to a strange land and a trying climate, and let them begin life anew.

What the experiences of these exiles were, their hopes, defeats and triumphs, may be more clearly seen by following the fortunes of one community, though, perhaps, ultimately an unfortunate one. The town of Shelburne at Port Roseway in Nova Scotia is best suited for the purpose.[1] As the ship bearing the Loyalists entered the harbor, the eyes of the exiles could see no spot along the shore where even a tent could be set, except where a pioneer and a few neighbors were encamped. When the surveyors had selected a site, and the plan of the town was agreed upon, they set about laying out five long parallel streets, crossed by others at right angles. The shore was to be cut up by small lanes and divided into small lots, that each settler might have a town and a water lot. Away from the town each was to have a fifty-acre farm lot. Parties now went about cutting the trees and clearing the lands, and soon tents were pitched and huts erected. Within two months the division of the lands was begun, and ownership determined by lot, so that, at last, each head of a family might point out a certain collection of rocks, stumps and

---

[1] See the article by Rev. T. Watson Smith in the "Collections of the Nova Scotia Historical Society" for the year 1887–88, Vol. VI., Halifax, 1888.

swamps as his own. They had hardly completed these formalities when they were perplexed by the arrival of five thousand exiles more, some of whom were most unwelcome neighbors. However, new streets were run on the land reserved for commons, and each newcomer settled down in his tent or hut on his own land. The winter was, fortunately, mild at Shelburne, but, inland, a Loyalist settlement suffered terribly. "Women, delicately reared, cared for their infants beneath canvas tents, rendered habitable only by the banks of snow which lay six feet deep." "Strong and proud men wept like children, and lay down in their snow-bound tents to die." Some of the Nova Scotia exiles died of starvation because the supply ships failed to arrive before the closing of navigation. At Shelburne, however, British agents issued rations all winter to nearly ten thousand people.

In the spring, the work of settlement went on slowly. There were bickerings and dissensions among themselves, and general dissatisfaction with the provincial government. Heavy duties were imposed on imported goods, though the new colonists were hardly able to exist with the aid of the British government. Political strife broke out, embittered by personal ambitions and social intolerance. The "mixed crowd" recently exposed to all the unhallowed and unsettling influences of a long civil war, was very hard to control. "Whoever had human form," especially sailors and fishermen, had been encouraged to stay because the colony needed them.

So great was the need of workingmen to develop the colony that the poor roads were considered a blessing, and, when one was opened that led to a fertile neighboring valley, the rapid depopulation of the town put an end to roadmaking. It was said that the people staid only because poverty brought them there, and poverty kept them there. Except the King's supplies of flour and pork, the food was limited to fish and the few vegetables brought by irregular coasting vessels. Fresh meat was rarely tasted. Nor did this condition improve, for the heart and enterprise seemed to have been taken out of the exiles. They neglected the opportunities, which their fine harbor and timbered shores offered, of a lumber and shipbuilding trade, and simply existed on fishing, while the town gradually dwindled. As the deserted dwellings increased in number, the town became repulsive in itself. It became a city of untenanted houses. A visitor said, "it had all the stillness and quiet of a moonlight scene. It was difficult to imagine it was deserted. . . . All was new and recent. Seclusion, and not death and removal, appeared to be the cause of the absence of inhabitants." Many years later the houses had disappeared. "Some had been taken to pieces and removed to Halifax or St. John; others had been converted into fuel, and the rest had fallen a prey to neglect and decomposition. The chimneys stood up erect, and . . . bespoke the size of the tenement and the means of its owner. In some places they had sunk with the edifice, leaving a heap of ruins; while not a few were inclining to their fall. . . . Hundreds of cellars, with their stone walls and granite partitions, were everywhere to be seen like uncovered monuments of the dead. Time and decay had done their work."

Failure of this kind led many to brave the terrors of persecution and return to the United States, but many thousands remained, and, when, years later, they had made of the land of their exile a mighty member of the great British empire, they began to glory in the days of trial through which they had passed. To-day, their descendants, organized as the United Empire Loyalists, count it an honor that their ancestors suffered persecution and exile rather than yield the principle and the ideal of union with Great Britain.

The cause of the Loyalists failed, but their stand was just and natural. They were the prosperous and contented men, the men without a grievance. Conservatism was the only polity that one could expect of them. Men do not rebel to rid themselves of prosperity. Prosperous men seek to conserve prosperity. The Loyalist obeyed his nature as truly as the Patriot, but, as events proved, chose the ill-fated cause, and, when the struggle ended, his prosperity had fled, and he was an outcast and an exile.

APPENDIX A.

A DECLARATION OF INDEPENDENCE BY THE LOYALISTS.

When in the course of human events it becomes necessary for men, in order to preserve their lives, liberties and properties, and to secure to themselves, and to their posterity, that peace, liberty and safety, to which by the laws of nature and of nature's God they are entitled, to throw off and renounce all allegiance to a government, which under the insidious pretences of securing those inestimable blessings to them, has wholly deprived them of any security of either life, liberty, property, peace, or safety; a decent respect to the opinions of mankind, requires that they should declare, the injuries and oppressions, the arbitrary and dangerous proceedings, which impel them to transfer their allegiance from such their oppressors, to those who have offered to become their protectors.

We hold these truths to be self evident, that all men are created equal; that they are endowed by their Creator with certain rights, that among those, are life, liberty, and the pursuit of happiness; that to secure those rights, governments are instituted; that whenever any form of government becomes destructive to these ends, it is the right of the people to alter or to abolish it, or to renounce all allegiance to it, and to put themselves under such other government, as to them shall appear best calculated and most likely to effect their safety and happiness; it is not indeed prudent to change for light and transient causes, and experience hath ever shewn, that men are disposed to suffer much before they can bring themselves to make a change of government; but when a long train of the most licentious and despotic abuses, pursuing invariably the same objects, evinces a design to reduce them under anarchy, and the distractions of democracy, and finally to force them to submit to absolute despotism, it is their right, it becomes their duty, to disclaim and renounce all allegiance to such government, and to provide new guards for their future security.

Such have been our patient sufferings, and such is now the necessity which constrains us to renounce all allegiance to Congress, or to the governments lately established by their direction.

The history of Congress, is a history of continued weakness, inconsistency, violation of the most sacred obligations of all public faith and honour, and of usurpations, all having in direct object the producing of anarchy, civil feuds, and violent injustice, which have rendered us miserable, and must soon establish tyranny over us, and our country.

To prove this let facts be submitted to the candid world.

They have recommended and caused laws to be passed, the most destructive of the public good, and ruinous to individuals.

Availing themselves of our zeal and unanimity to oppose the claims of the British Parliament, and of our unsuspecting confidence in their solemn professions and declarations, they have forbidden us to listen to, or to accept any terms of peace, until their assent should be obtained.

They have refused to accept of, or even to receive proposals and terms of accommodation and peace, though they know the terms offered exceeded what the Colonies in America had unanimously declared would be satisfactory, unless the Crown would relinquish a right inestimable to it and to the whole empire, and formidable to Congress only.

They have excited and directed the people to alter or annull their ancient constitutions, under which, they and their ancestors, had been happy for many ages, for the sole purpose of promoting their measures.

They have by mobs and riots awed Representative Houses, repeatedly into a compliance with their resolutions, though destructive of the peace, liberty, and safety of the people.

They have by their misconduct, reduced us to all the dangers and distress of actual invasion from without, and to all the horrors of a cruel war within.

They have not only prevented the increase of the population of these states, but by fines, imprisoning, and banishments, with the losses by war, they have caused a rapid depopulation.

They have corrupted all the sources of justice and equity by their Tender Law, by which they destroyed the legal force of all civil contracts, wronged the honest creditor, and deserving salary man of his just dues, stripped the helpless orphan of his patrimony, and the disconsolate widow of her dower.

They have erected a multitude of new offices, and have filled them with men from their own body, or with their creatures and dependants, to eat out the substance of the people; they have made their officers dependant on their will for the tenure of their offices, and the payment of their salaries.

They have raised a standing army and sent it into the field, without any act of the legislature, and have actually rendered it independent of the civil power, by making it solely dependant on them.

They have combined with France, the natural and hereditary enemy of our civil constitution, and religious faith, to render us dependant on and subservient to the views, of that foreign, ambitious, and despotic monarchy.

They have suffered their troops to live repeatedly on free quarters on the inhabitants, and to strip them by force of the necessaries of life, and have protected them from either trial or punishment under the plea of necessity, which necessity if real, was caused by their treacherous views, or unpardonable negligence.

They have ruined our trade, and destroyed our credit with all parts of the world.

They have forced us to receive their paper, for goods, merchandise, and for money due to us, equal to silver and gold, and then by a breach of public faith in not redeeming the same, and by the most infamous bankruptcy, have left it on our hands, to the total ruin of multitudes, and to the injury of all.

They have driven many of our people beyond sea, into exile, and have confiscated their estates, and the estates of others who were beyond sea before the war, or the existence of Congress, on pretence of offences, and under the sanction of a mock trial, to which the person condemned was neither cited or present..

They have abolished the true system of the English constitution and laws, in thirteen of the American Provinces, and established therein a weak and factious democracy, and have attempted to use them as introducing the same misrule and disorder into all the Colonies on the continent.

They have recommended the annihilating of our charters, abolishing many of our most valuable laws, and the altering fundamentally the form of our government.

They have destroyed all good order and government, by plunging us into the factions of democracy, and the ravages of civil war.

They have left our seas unprotected, suffered our coasts to be ravaged, our towns to be burnt, some of them by their own troops, and the lives of our people to be destroyed.

They have without the consent or knowledge of the legislatures, invited over an army of foreign mercenaries to support them and their faction, and to prevent the dreadful scenes of death and desolation from being closed by an honourable peace and accommodation with our ancient friend and parent.

They have fined, imprisoned, banished, and put to death some of our fellow citizens, for no other cause but their attachment to the English laws and constitution.

They have countenanced domestic tumults and disorders in our capital cities, and have suffered the murder of a number of our fellow citizens perpetrated under their eyes in Philadelphia, to pass unnoticed.

They first attempted to gain the savage and merciless Indians to their side, but failing in making them the presents promised and expected, have occasioned an undistinguished destruction to ages, sexes, and conditions on our frontiers.

They have involved us in an immense debt, foreign as well as internal, and did put the best port and island on our continent, into the hands of the foreigners, who are their creditors.

They have wantonly violated our public faith and honor, and destroyed all grounds for private confidence, or the security of private property, have not blushed to act in direct contradiction to their most solemn declaration, and to render the people under their government, a reproach and a bye word among the nations.

In every stage of these proceedings, they have not been wanting to throw out before us, specious excuses for their conduct, as being the result of necessity and tending to the public good.—In every stage since their public conduct, began to contradict their public declarations, our minds have been overwhelmed with apprehensions; and as our sufferings have increased, our tears have flowed in secret. It has been dangerous and even criminal to lament our situation in public. The unsuspecting confidence which we with our fellow citizens reposed in the Congress of 1774, the unanimous applause, with which their patriotism and firmness were crowned, for having stood forth, as the champions of our rights, founded on the English constitution; at the same time that it gave to Congress the unanimous support of the whole continent, inspired their successors with very different ideas, and emboldened them by degrees to pursue measures, directly the reverse of those before adopted, and were recommended, as the only just, constitutional and safe.—Congress in 1774, reprobated every idea of a separation from Great-Britain, and de-

APPENDIX A.

clared that they looked on such an event as the greatest of evils.—They declared that a repeal of certain acts, complained of, would restore our ancient peace, and harmony.—That they *asked but for peace, liberty and safety.—That they wished not for a diminution of the royal prerogative, nor did they solicit the grant of any new right.* And they pledged themselves in the presence of Almighty God, that they *will ever carefully and zealously endeavour to support and maintain the royal authority of Great-Britain over us, and our connection with Great-Britain—and our councils had been influenced only by the dread of impending destruction.*

The acts complained of have been repealed, yet how have Congress given the lie, to these their most solemn professions! In 1774, they declared themselves concerned for the honour of Almighty God, whose pure and holy religion, our enemies were undermining—They pointed out those enemies, and the danger in which our holy religion was by their complaints of the establishment of the Roman Catholic religion in Canada; they say, "It is a religion which has deluged the Island of Great Britain with blood, and dispersed impiety, persecution, murder, and rebellion through every part of the world." We find the present Congress not only claiming a new right, and hazarding every thing valuable in life, to the present and future generations in support of it, but we also find them, leagued with the eldest son of this bloody, impious, bigoted, and persecuting church, to ruin the nation from whose loins we sprung, and which has ever been the principal bulwark in Europe, against the encroachments and tyranny of that church, and of the kingdoms devoted to her: we think it not too severe to say, that we find them as intoxicated with ambition of Independent sovereignty, as that execrable Roman Daughter, who drove the wheels of her chariot over the mangled body of her murdered father, in her way to the capitol.

We find that all their fears and apprehensions from the Roman Catholic religion in Canada, have vanished, or sunk to nothing, when put in competition with their political views, and that they have attempted to seduce the Canadians to their side, by promises of still greater religious establishments; and to shew that they were in earnest, have countenanced this impious religion by attending its ceremonies and worship in a body. — We find them at one time boasting of their patriotic and religious ancestors, who braved every danger of unknown seas, and coasts, to preserve civil and religious freedom, and who chose rather to become exiles, and suffer every misery that must await them, on a savage and unexplored coast, than submit to civil, but above all religious innovations — at another time we find them destroying the British Constitution, the pride of their ancestors, and encouraging a religion which they held in abhorrence, as idolatrous and tyrannical. — We find them contending for liberty of speech, and at the same time controlling the press, by means of a mob, and persecuting every one who ventures to hint his disapprobation of their proceedings.

We find them declaring in September 1779, that to pay off their paper money, at less than its nominal value, would be an unpardonable sin, an execrable deed. "That a faithless bankrupt Republic would be a novelty in the political world, and appear like a common prostitute among chaste and reputable matrons," would be " a reproach and a bye-word among the nations, &c."

APPENDIX A. 317

We find the same Congress in March following, liquidating their paper debt at 2½ per cent. or 6d. in the pound.

We should fill volumes, were we to recite at large their inconsistency, usurpations, weaknesses and violations of the most sacred obligations — We content ourselves with the above brief recital of facts known to the world and attested by their own records

We have sufficiently shewn that a government thus marked and distinguished from every other, either despotic or democratic, by the enormity of its excesses, injustice and infamy, is unfit to rule a free people.

We therefore, Natives and Citizens of America, appealing to the impartial world to judge of the justice of our cause, but above all to the supreme Judge of the World for the rectitude of our intentions, do renounce and disclaim all allegiance, duty, or submission to the Congress, or to any government under them, and declare that the United Colonies or States, so called, neither are, nor of right ought to be independent of the crown of Great-Britain, or unconnected with that empire; but that we do firmly believe and maintain "*That the Royal Authority of the Crown of Great-Britain over us, and our connection with that kingdom ought to be preserved and maintained*, and that we will *zealously endeavour to support and maintain the same;*" and in the support of this declaration, with a firm reliance on the protection of Divine Providence, we mutually pledge to each other, and to the crown and empire of Great-Britain, our lives, our fortunes, and our sacred honor.[1]   Dated, &c.

[1] The "Declaration" appeared in *Rivington's Royal Gazette*, November 17, 1781.

APPENDIX B.

ANALYSIS OF THE TEST LAWS PASSED BY THE LEGISLATURES OF THE THIRTEEN COLONIES DURING THE REVOLUTIONARY WAR.

NEW HAMPSHIRE.
(Laws of New Hampshire in C. Tower Coll., pp. 63, 90.)

Date of Test Laws.	Affected Persons.	Penalty of Refusal.	Persons Executing the Laws.
Nov. 8, 1777.	Civil and Military officers, barristers and attorneys at law.	Suspended from office.	Commissioners.
March 14, 1778 (an addition to above act). (Time limit extended.) (Affirmation instead of oath allowed.)			Justices.

MASSACHUSETTS.
("Laws of Massachusetts, 1775-80," pp. 31, 159, 161, 168, 184.)

1776.	Every male person above 16.	Disarmed, unable to hold office, ministers and school masters lose salaries—also governors of Harvard College.	Committee of Corres., Safety, Justice of Peace, Sheriff.
Jan. (?), 1778.	Persons suspected of being inimical (except Mandamus Councillors who accepted office, and all who since April 19, 1775, have joined the enemy or enlisted men for, etc.).	Committed to gaol (costs to be paid out of the estate of person). Within 40 days sent to British territory. Death penalty if return.	Justice of Peace (upon representation made by member of Council, H. of R.). Civil or military officer, selectman, or member of any Committee of Corres. or any two substantial free-holders.

318

APPENDIX B.

MASSACHUSETTS (continued).

Date of Test Laws.	Affected Persons.	Penalty of Refusal.	Persons Executing the Laws.
Jan. (?), 1778.	Members of General Assembly, civil and military officers, attorneys at law.	Not allowed to practice.	Two or three of the Council.
June (?), 1778.	Every military officer under the commanding officer of regiment.		Commanding officer of regiment of militia.
April (?), 1778, addition to act of Jan., 1778.	Every military officer under the commanding officer of regiment.	(Forty days' limit; "as soon as conveniently may be.")	

RHODE ISLAND.
("Col. Recs.," Vol. VII., pp. 566, 585, 611.)

June, 1776.	All male inhabitants above 16 years, who are suspected of being inimical.	May be summoned to give reason. Arms and ammunition seized (state to pay for arms).	Members of upper and lower house of assembly.
July 18, 1776.	Male person aged 21.	Cannot petition to set aside judgment or stay execution. Suit, action, bill, or plaint dismissed. Not vote in town meeting.	
Sept., 1776.		Cannot hold office, civil or military.	Inferior Court (may fine).
Nov. 21, 1776.		No execution to be issued on any judgment of any court. Executions already issued to be returned to officers (see Vol. VIII., pp. 39, 187, 247, 291).	

CONNECTICUT.
("Public Recs. of Conn.," Vol. I., p. 4.)

Oct. 10, 1776.	Members of the general assembly, civil and military officers, freemen.	Deprived of office. Disfranchised.	Magistrate or justice of peace. Inrolled by town clerk.

CONNECTICUT (continued).

Date of Test Laws.	Affected Persons.	Penalty of Refusal.	Persons Executing the Laws.
May 8 (?), 1777.	All persons over 21 years. Freemen.	Shall hold no office. Disfranchised.	Assistant or justice of peace (oath taken in open freeman's meeting).
Oct. 11, 1777.	All persons who wish to hold offices or vote, be an executor or guardian.		
May 12, 1777.	Those charged with treason or misprision of treason.	Subject to prosecution for previous acts of disloyalty to the state.	Justice of the peace.
May 18, 1779.	(See "Public Records of Conn.," Vol. II., p. 279.)		

NEW YORK.
("Laws of New York," Vol. I., p. 252.)

Date of Test Laws.	Affected Persons.	Penalty of Refusal.	Persons Executing the Laws.
Dec. 27, 1776 (res. of a convention).	Inhabitants of Westchester county.	Treated as open enemies.	Militia and committeemen.
March 13, 1780 (an act to relieve certain persons of Westchester).			
June 30, 1778.	All persons of neutral and equivocal characters who have influence sufficient to do mischief.	Removed to any place within the enemy's lines. Names recorded. Those failing to appear on summons guilty of misprision of treason. Lands double taxed.	Commissioners for enquiring into, detecting and defeating all conspiracies against the liberties of United States.
March 26, 1781.	All public officers and electors.	Disfranchisement or incapacity to hold office.	Presiding officer at elections.
April 11, 1782.	Suitors in the courts of the State.	Incapacity to sue.	Justices of the peace, etc.

APPENDIX B.

NEW JERSEY.

("Acts of New Jersey Territory," 1784, pp. 1, 18; 1776–'83, p. 27.)

Date of Test Laws.	Affected Persons.	Penalty of Refusal.	Persons Executing the Laws.
Sept. 19, 1776.	All civil and military officers.		
June 5, 1777 (an oath giving chance for reconciliation).	Persons "who have been seduced from their allegiance," but "since become sensible of their error."	Forfeit personal estate. Not allowed to transfer real estate.	Justice of Supreme Court (who gives a certificate—for 2 shillings).
Oct. 6, 1777.	Counsellors, proctors, solicitors, attorneys, jurymen, public teachers and instructors.	£5–£20 fine.	Any persons (may sue), judges and justices.
Oct. 1, 1778 (a provision for those who have scruples against the oath).			

PENNSYLVANIA.

("Laws of Pennsylvania," 1777-81, Vol. X.)

Date	Affected Persons	Penalty of Refusal	Persons Executing the Laws
June 13, 1777.	Male, white inhabitants above 18 years. Travelers (except Delegates for Congress, prisoners of war, officers, soldiers, merchants and mariners).	Unable to hold office, serve on jury, sue for debts, elect or be elected, buy, sell or transfer lands or tenements. Disarmed.	Justices (paid 1 s. for each certificate issued). Lieutenants of city or county.
October 12, 1777 (supplements above).	Every inhabitant above 16 years who travels out of Philadelphia or the country in which he resides. Persons suspected of being unfriendly.	Committed to gaol, without bail. Jailed (costs levied on his goods).	Justices.

PENNSYLVANIA (continued).

Date of Test Laws.	Persons Affected.	Penalty of Refusal.	Persons Executing the Laws.
April 1, 1778.	All persons over 18 (provision made for prisoners of war, unable to take the oath). Delegates in Congress (had been exempt) now included.	Same as in Act of June 13, 1777; disabled to sue, etc., or be guardian or administrator of any estate, cannot receive legacy or deed of gift or make will, and shall pay double tax. (All trustees, provosts, rectors, professors, masters, tutors, etc., merchants, traders, sergeants-at-law, councillors-at-law, barristers, advocates, attorneys, solicitors, proctors, clerks or notary, apothecary or druggist, physician or surgeon) shall be incapacitated and upon prosecution may be fined £500 (half to go to the estate and half to the prosecutor), (persons summoned and refusing) committed to jail for 3 months or pay £10. Disarmed; if by force, pay double the value of the arms.	Justices. Inspectors of election (fined if they allow non-jurors to vote).
Dec. 5, 1778 (supplement above) (a new oath).	All present and future officers of Pennsylvania. Persons who have neglected previous oath.	Not elect or be elected or serve on juries (other penalties removed) except non-jurors paying double tax.	Commissioners, (feed 7s. 6d.).

(See also modifications of the law on April 2, 1779, and October 1, 1779. The latter returns to the more rigorous law.)

APPENDIX B. 323

DELAWARE.
(Session Laws of Del., in N. Y. Bar Assoc. Library.)

Date of Test Laws.	Persons Affected.	Penalty of Refusal.	Persons Executing the Laws.
May 18, 1778.	Every male white person 21 years old. (Officers and soldiers in pay of U. S. excepted.)	Unable to hold office, civil or military. Disfranchised. Unable to serve on jury.	The "Justice in the hundred." (1s. 6d. paid for a Certif.)
June 26, 1778.	Inhabitants of the state that have levied war against it (except some 46 proscribed persons).	Estates confiscated. (Those who took oath were denied franchise and right to hold office.) (Incapacity removed Jan. 27, 1790.)	Justice of Supreme Court or Justice of Peace.

MARYLAND.
(Laws of Md., 1775-80.)

Date of Test Laws.	Persons Affected.	Penalty of Refusal.	Persons Executing the Laws.
Before Dec. 3, 1777. (Additional clauses not concerning the oath.)	Every free male above 18 years of age (except Quakers, Mennonites or Dunkers, who only declare). (Soldiers and officers excepted.) Refugees to the state. (Imprisoned.)	Pay treble tax in all public and county assessments during life. (Tax to follow the property.) Cannot sue. Fined, if acting as a merchant (without oath). Not to practice law, physics or surgery or apothecary, nor preach or teach or hold office or vote.	County or city magistrate. Constable (to make out a list of free males in his Hundred).
Between Mar. 17 and Apr. 22, 1778. (Supplements above.)			County Clerk (to make list annually).
Between July 22 and Aug. 15, 1779.		(Treble tax suspended until Nov. 10.)	
Nov. 0, 1779.		(Treble tax suspended to Dec. 30.)	
June 12, 1780.		Treble tax to be collected on absentees.	
1781		Persons returning from abroad, take oath, not pay tax.	

MARYLAND (*continued*).

Date of Test Laws.	Persons Affected.	Penalty of Refusal.	Persons Executing the Laws.
Between Nov. 5, 1781, and Jan. 22, 1782.		(Treble tax suspended and disability to sue for debts, practice physic, or carry on merchandise removed).	

VIRGINIA.

(Laws of Virginia, "Hennings," IX., 281; X., 22.)

Date of Test Laws.	Persons Affected.	Penalty of Refusal.	Persons Executing the Laws.
May, 1777.	All free-born males above age of 16 (except imported servants). Persons coming from any of the other States.	Disarmed (but must attend muster). Incapable of holding office, serving on jury, suing for debts, buying lands. Travelers committed to jail.	Justice of the peace, county clerks (to receive register of signers), county courts (to appoint members to receive oath), county lieutenant (to disarm).
May, 1783 (repeals the part subjecting Quakers and Mennonites to penalties).			
May, 1779.	Every person by law required to give assurance of fidelity. Governor and Privy Council.		Court of record.
May, 1779 (providing for those who have scruples against oaths).			
Oct., 1780.	Persons in the counties of Henry, Bedford, Pittsylvania, Botetourt, Montgomery and Washington who have taken oath to Great Britain since 1776 and who have not added any overt act criminal by law.	Prosecuted if taken (pardoned if they take the oath).	Justice.

APPENDIX B.

North Carolina.

("Laws of North Carolina," 1750–90, p. 281; "Records of North Carolina," Vol. XI., p. 363.)

Date of Test Laws.	Persons Affected.	Penalty of Refusal.	Persons Executing the Laws.
Nov. 22, 1776 (an opportunity to recant).	All who by taking arms against United States, or adhering to, comforting or abetting the enemy. Persons using disrespectful words about United States or of this State. Does not extend to persons now in open enmity.	Incapable of bringing any suit in any court. Cannot be sued, plead or make defence, prosecute indictment, purchase or transfer lands, tenements, etc. Same to be forfeited to State.	Court, judge or justice.
Jan., 1777.	Members of Council of State.		

South Carolina.

("Statutes at Large of South Carolina," 1838, Vol. IV., pp. 338, 450, 468.)

Date of Test Laws.	Persons Affected.	Penalty of Refusal.	Persons Executing the Laws.
April 6, 1776 (oath of office).	All persons not having commissions, who, by the laws of Great Britain, have hitherto taken oaths of office. State officers, President, Privy Councillors.	Loss of office.	
March 28, 1778 (repeals old law).	Commander-in-chief and members of Privy Council.		
Oct. 17, 1778.	Members of Senate and House of Representatives.		
March 28, 1778.	Every free male above certain age.		Justice of peace.
Oct. 9, 1778 (enlarges the time for taking oath of March 28, 1778).		Must sell or dispose of estate and depart. Death if they refuse to leave or return.	Justice of peace. Captain of company and colonel of each regiment of militia (a heavy fine is imposed for neglect of this duty). Courts of law.
Feb. 17, 1779 (extension of time).			

GEORGIA.
("Digest of Laws of Georgia," 1800, p. 237.)

Date of Test Laws.	Persons Affected.	Penalty of Refusal.	Persons Executing the Laws.
Aug. 20, 1781.	Those who took oath to the British, but have since shown loyalty to U. S.	Regarded as guilty of "certain high crimes and misdemeanors." (Banished, if they later take sides with the British.)	Army officers.

APPENDIX C.

A CLASSIFICATION OF THE PRINCIPAL LAWS DIRECTED AGAINST THE LOYALISTS DURING THE AMERICAN REVOLUTION, EXCEPTING THE TEST LAWS WHICH ARE IN APPENDIX B.

Laws Against Freedom of Speech and Action.

New Hampshire.

January 17, 1777.

An act for preventing and punishing such offences against the State as do not amount to treason or misprision of treason.

Massachusetts.

August (?), 1777.

An act for preventing or punishing crimes that may be committed against the public safety below the degree of treason and misprision of treason.

Rhode Island.

August (third Monday in), 1775.

An act to punish persons, who shall pilot any armed vessels in or out of any of the harbors . . . in this colony, excepting vessels belonging to some one of the British colonies in America. . . .

October–November, 1775.

An act for the punishment of persons who shall be found guilty of holding a traitorous correspondence with the ministry of Great Britain or any of their officers or agents, or of supplying the ministerial army or navy that now is, or may be, employed in America against the United Colonies, with provisions, cannon, arms, ammunition, warlike or naval stores, or of acting as pilots on board any of their ships and vessels.

July, 1776.
  An act to punish persons who shall acknowledge the King of Great Britain to be their sovereign.

July, 1776.
  An act to prevent the depreciation of the Continental Currency, etc.

March, 1781.
  An act more effectually to prevent illicit trade, commerce, and correspondence with the enemies of this and the other United States of America.

Connecticut.

December 14, 1775.
  An act for restraining and punishing persons who are inimical to the liberties of this and the rest of the United Colonies. . . .

July 18, 1776.
  Resolve for stopping suspected persons, etc.

February 12 (?), 1778.
  An act more effectively to prevent illicit trade.

New York.

April 13, 1782.
  An act more effectually to prevent illicit trade with the enemy.

July 22, 1782.
  (Same as above.)

March 21, 1783.
  (An act to limit above acts.)

New Jersey.

February 11, 1777.
  An act for more effectually preventing disaffected and evil minded persons destroying the credit and circulation of the Continental bills of credit. . . .

February 13, 1777.
  An act to prevent the counterfeiting or forging the tickets of the United States lottery.

October 8, 1778.
  An act to prevent the subjects of this State from going into, or coming out of, the enemy's lines without permissions or passports. . . .

December 11, 1778.
  (Amendment of above.)
December 25, 1779.
  (Another amendment.)
June 10, 1779.
  An act to prevent persons from passing through this State without proper passports.
June 13, 1780.
  An act more effectually to prevent the passing of counterfeit bills of credit.
June 17, 1780.
  An act more effectually to prevent desertion and for the punishment of persons harboring prisoners of war or purchasing the clothing and accoutrements of the soldiers of the army and for the repeal of a certain act therein mentioned.
December 22, 1780.
  An act more effectually to prevent the inhabitants of this state from trading with the enemy, or going within their lines, and for other purposes therein mentioned.
June 24, 1782.
  An act for preventing illicit trade and intercourse between the subjects of this State and the enemy.
December 24, 1782.
  (Amends above.)

Delaware.

May 20, 1778.
  To prevent the inhabitants of this State from dealing and furnishing the enemy thereof with supplies. . . .

Virginia.

May, 1780.
  An act affixing penalties to certain crimes injurious to the independence of America, but less than treason, and repealing the act for the punishment of certain offences.

South Carolina.

April 11, 1776.
  An act to prevent sedition and punish insurgents and disturbers of the public peace. (Estates of offenders confiscated.)

Laws Disfranchising the Loyalists or Removing Them From Office.[1]

New York.
March 27, 1778.
    An act to regulate elections within this State.

October 9, 1779.
    An act making it necessary for the attorneys, solicitors and counsellors-at-law, who have been licensed to plead or practice in any of the courts of law or equity within the late colony of New York to produce certificates of their attachment to the liberties and independence of America.

May 12, 1784.
    An act to preserve the freedom and independence of this State and for other purposes.

Rhode Island.
October–November, 1775.
    An act declaring the office of governor of this colony vacant.

Maryland.
July 3, 1776.
    (Resolutions of provincial convention. See Laws of Maryland, 1765–84, Chapter XXVIII.)

South Carolina.
February 6, 1782.
    An act for settling the qualifications of the electors and elected in the next general assembly.

North Carolina.
November, 1784.
    An act to describe and ascertain such persons who owed allegiance to this State and to impose certain disqualifications. . . .

[1] I have included here only such laws as were *directly* intended to disfranchise or remove. See in Appendix B where the penalties for not meeting the requirements of the laws are of this nature. Disfranchisement and removal were common penalties in the Revolutionary laws.

APPENDIX C.

Laws Suppressing, Quarantining, Banishing and Exiling the Loyalists.

New Hampshire.

June 19, 1777.
   An act for taking up, imprisoning, or otherwise restraining persons dangerous to this State.

November 19, 1778.
   An act to prevent the return to the State of certain persons therein named, and of others who have left or shall leave this State or either of the United States of America and have joined or shall join the enemies thereof.

Massachusetts.

May 10 (?), 1777.
   An act for securing this, and the other United States, against the dangers, to which they are exposed by the internal enemies thereof

May 27–September 16, 1778.
   Act to prevent the return of certain persons therein named and others who have left this State or either of the United States and joined the enemies thereof.
   (See also Laws of Massachusetts 1775–80, pp. 103, 186, 187, 210, 220, 231.)

Rhode Island.

July, 1780.
   An act to prevent certain persons therein named . . . from being admitted within this State.

Connecticut.

October 10 (?), 1776.
   An act for apprehending and securing such inimical persons as shall be deemed and adjudged dangerous to the State.
   (Amended May 8, 1777.

New York.

February 5, 1778.
   An act appointing commissioners for detecting and defeating conspiracies and declaring their powers.
   (Amended April 3, 1778, October 29, 1778, June 14, 1780.)

April 1, 1778.
 An act to enable the persons administering the government of this State . . . to remove certain disaffected and dangerous persons and families.

March 22, 1781.
 An act to accommodate the inhabitants of the frontiers with habitations. . . .

March 20, 1783.
 An act to protect the persons and property of the inhabitants of the county of Westchester from injury and abuse.

New Jersey.

March 15, 1777.
 An act for investing the governor and a council consisting of 12 with certain powers therein mentioned for a limited time.

April 4, 1778.
 An act constituting a council of safety.

June 12, 1779.
 An act for the removal of criminals for their more safe custody. . . .

Delaware.

March 20, 1778.
 A resolve of the Council to disarm the disaffected of Sussex County.

Virginia.

October, 1777.
 An act for indemnifying the governor and council and others for removing and confining suspected persons during the late public danger.
 (See October, 1779. "Hennings," X., 195.)

October, 1777.
 An act for better securing the commonwealth, and for the further protection and defense thereof.

May, 1780.
 An act for giving further powers to the governor and council and for other purposes.

October, 1783.
 An act prohibiting the migrations of certain persons to this commonwealth. . . .

North Carolina.

May 13, 1776.
Resolve of Provincial Congress to disarm and imprison all who aid Great Britain.

South Carolina.

October 17, 1778.
An ordinance to empower the President or Commander-in-Chief . . . with the advice of the privy council to take up and confine all persons whose going at large may endanger the safety of this State.

August 31, 1779.
(Same as above.)

Georgia.

September 16, 1777.
An act for the expulsion of the internal enemies of this State.

March 1, 1778.
An act to prevent the dangerous consequences that may arise from the practices of disaffected . . . persons within this State.

August 21, 1781.
An act for prevention of internal conspiracies and for the empowering certain committees therein named, to examine into the conduct of certain suspicious persons.

January 9, 1782.
An act to repeal an act entitled "An act to draw a line . . . between the good citizens of this State and the enemies thereof; and to prevent plundering and detect spies within the same."
(Original act January 29, 1780.)

August 5, 1782.
An act for preventing improper or disaffected persons immigrating from other places, and becoming citizens of this State, and for other purposes therein mentioned.

Laws Providing for the Crime of Adhering to Great Britain.

New Hampshire.

January 17, 1777.
An act against treason and misprision of treason and for regulating trials in such cases, and for directing the mode of executing judgments against persons convicted of those crimes.

Massachusetts.

———, *1777.*
An act against treason and misprision of treason. . . .
(A general law for treason in general.)

Connecticut.

May 8 (?), 1777.
An act to prevent traitorous conspiracies against this and the United States of America.

New York.

March 30, 1781.
An act more effectually to punish adherence to the king of Great Britain, within this State.

New Jersey.

October 4, 1776.
An act to punish traitors and disaffected persons.
(Supplemented October 3, 1782.)

October 2, 1778.
An act for apprehending and delivering up to justice all persons residing or taking refuge in this State, charged with crimes committed in any other of the United States, and for other purposes.

Pennsylvania.

February 11, 1777.
An act declaring what shall be treason and what other crimes . . . shall be misprision of treason.

March 6, 1778.
An act for the attainder of divers traitors, if they render not themselves by a certain day, and for vesting their estates in this commonwealth. . . .
(Amended November 26, 1778.)

March 8, 1780.
An act for the amendment of the law relative to the punishment of treasons, robberies, misprisions of treason. . . .
(See also November 27, 1778, and March 31, 1781).

Delaware.

February 22, 1777.
An act to punish treasons and disaffected persons. . . .

Maryland.

July 4, 1776.
Resolve of the Provincial Convention. Adherents to Great Britain to suffer death.

February, 1777.
An act to punish certain crimes and misdemeanors and to prevent the growth of Toryism.

Virginia.

October, 1776.
An act declaring what shall be treason. Followed by an act for the punishment of certain offenses.
(See acts of pardon, May, 1782, October, 1782, May, 1783.)

North Carolina.

April 8 (?), 1777.
An act declaring what crimes and practices against the State shall be treason and what shall be misprision of treason . . . and for preventing the dangers which may arise from persons disaffected to the State. (Amended later in 1777.)

September 15, 1777.
(Heading is same as above.)

South Carolina.

February 20, 1779.
An ordinance to prevent persons withdrawing from the defense of this State to join the enemies thereof.

Laws Amercing, Taxing or Confiscating the Estates of Loyalists or Anticipating such Action.

New Hampshire.

November 29, 1777.
An act to prevent the transfer or conveyance of the estates and property of all such persons who have been or shall be apprehended upon suspicion of being guilty of treason, misprision of treason, or other inimical practices respecting this State, the United States, any or either of them, and also for securing all lands within this State as well of such persons as have traitorously deserted, or may hereafter desert the common cause of America, and have gone over to, or in any way or manner joined our enemies, as of those who belong to, or reside in Great Britain.

November 26, 1778.
An act to prevent trespass upon the waste lands within this State.

November 28, 1778.
An act to confiscate estates of sundry persons named.
(Supplemented June 25, 1779.)

December 26, 1778.
An act to make void all attachments which have been or hereafter shall be laid or made on the estates of persons who have left this State or any of the United States, and have gone over to the enemies of the said States since the commencement of hostilities by Great Britain; or on the estates of any inhabitant or subjects of Great Britain.

Preamble.—Whereas such attachments may be made by the collusion of the parties in order to defeat this State of the benefit which may arise from the confiscation of such estates, and to defraud just creditors of their honest demands against such *persons.*

Massachusetts.

April 10 (?), 1777.
An act to prevent the waste . . . of goods or estates of such persons who have left . . . fled to our enemies for protection. . . .
(Amended May–June, 1778.)

April 30, 1779.
An act for confiscating the estates of certain persons commonly called absentees.

April 30, 1779.
Act to confiscate the estates of certain notorious conspirators against the government. . . .

Rhode Island.

October, 1775.
Act to confiscate and sequester estates and banish persons of a certain description.
(Special acts confiscating special estates are to be found in the Rhode Island records from this date to October of 1783.)

October, 1779.
An act for confiscating the estates of certain persons therein described.
(See "Records of Rhode Island," Vol. IX., p. 461.)

Connecticut.

June 14, 1776.
An act in addition to an act . . . entitled an act for restraining and punishing persons inimical.

May 14 (?), 1778.
An act for confiscating the estates of Persons inimical to the independence and liberties of the United States. . . .
(Amended May 15 (?), 1779.)

New York.

March 7, 1777.
(See Proceedings of the New York Provincial Congress.)

October 15, 1779.
An act more effectually to prevent robberies within this State.
(Revived July 30, 1780.)

October 22, 1779.
Act for forfeiture and sales of the estates of persons who have adhered to the enemies of this State. . . .

March 10, 1780.
Act for the immediate sale of part of the confiscated estates.
(Amended October 7, 1780.)

June 15, 1780.
Act approving the act of Congress of March 18, 1780, relative to finances of United States and making provision. . . .

October 7, 1780.
Act to procure a sum in specie. . . .
(Amended March 31, 1781.)

March 15, 1781.
An act for relieving such persons . . . whose sons have joined the enemy from the penalties of a law therein mentioned.
(Law of October 9, 1780.)

April 14, 1782.
An act for the further relief of the tenants of forfeited lands. . . .

March 4, 1783.
An act to enable certain persons whose buildings have been destroyed . . . to procure timber for building.

April 6, 1784.
An act for the immediate sale of certain forfeited estates.

May 12, 1784.
   An act for the speedy sale of the confiscated estates. . . .

New Jersey.
April 18, 1778.
   An act for taking charge of and leasing real estates and for forfeiting personal estates of certain fugitives and offenders. . . .

December 11, 1778.
   Act for forfeiting to and vesting in the State the real estates of certain fugitives and offenders. . . .
   (June 26, 1781, an act to suspend the sales, and December 16, 1783, an act to continue the sales.) (Supplemented, December 23, 1783.)

December 23, 1783.
   An act to appropriate a certain forfeited estate . . . to the use of Major General Baron Steuben during his life.

Delaware.
February 5, 1778.
   Act declaring the estates of certain papers forfeited. . . . (?)

Pennsylvania.
March 6, 1778.
   (See under "Laws providing for the crime of adhering to Great Britain.") (Supplemented April 9, 1779.)

March 18, 1779.
   (Provides for the disposition of Joseph Galloway's house.)

Maryland.
April 25–June 15, 1782.
   An act for the liquidation and payment of debts against persons convicted of treason.

October–December, 1780.
   (Relates to treble tax on non-jurors.)

Virginia.
December, 1775.
   An ordinance for establishing a mode of punishment for the enemies to America in this colony.
   (Amended, May, 1776.)

May, 1779.
An act to secure the movable property of those who have joined or hereafter may join the enemy.

October, 1779.
An act concerning non-jurors.

October, 1784.
An act respecting future confiscations.

North Carolina.

May 13, 1776.
Resolve of Provincial Congress—estates of refugees to be seized.

November, 1777.
An act for confiscating the property of all such persons as are inimical to the United States, and of such persons as shall not within a certain time therein mentioned, appear and submit to the State whether they shall be received as citizens thereof and of such persons as shall so appear and shall not be admitted as citizens. . . .

October, 1779.
(Act to carry above into effect; suspended, September, 1780.)

September 5, 1780.
An act for securing the quiet and inoffensive inhabitants of this State from being injured, and for preventing such property as hath or may be confiscated from being wasted or destroyed. . . .

April 13 (?), 1782.
An act directing the sale of confiscated property.

April 18 (?), 1783.
An act of pardon and oblivion.
(For similar laws see November, 1786, and November, 1788.)

———, 1783.
(An act relating to the Commissioners of confiscated property.)

October 22, 1784.
An act directing the sale of confiscated property.

November, 1785.
(An act to secure the buyers of confiscated estates.)
(Amended November, 1786.)

South Carolina.

February 26, 1782.
An act for amercing certain persons therein mentioned.

February 26, 1782.
Act for disposing of certain estates and banishing certain persons therein mentioned.
(Amended March 16, 1783, and March 22, 1786).

February 26, 1782.
An act for pardoning the persons therein described on the conditions therein mentioned.

March 17, 1783.
An ordinance for disposing of the estates of certain persons, subjects and adherents of the British Government. . . .

March 26, 1784.
An act for restoring to certain persons . . . their estates, both real and personal, and for permitting the said persons to return to this State. . . .

March 26, 1784.
(Ordinance amending Confiscation Act.)

March 11, 1786.
(Concerning the debts due forfeited estates.)

March 24, 1785.
An act to secure the payment of the amercements imposed by . . . this State and finally to close the business of confiscation and amercement.

Georgia.

March 1, 1778.
An act for attainting such persons as are herein mentioned, of high treason and for confiscating their estates . . . for establishing boards of commissioners for the sales of such estates. . . .
(Amended October 30, 1778.)

November 15, 1778.
An act to compel non-residents to return within a certain time, or in default . . . their estates to be confiscated. . . .

January 11, 1782.
An act for the confiscating of the estates of certain persons . . . and for providing funds for defraying the contingent expenses of this State.

May 4, 1782.
  An act for inflicting penalties on, and confiscating the estates of such persons as are declared guilty of treason. . . .

August 5, 1782.
  An act for amercing certain persons therein named. . . .

February 8, 1783.
  (Act changes the number of commissioners of confiscation.)

February 17, 1783.
  An act to point out the mode for the recovery of property unlawfully acquired under the British usurpation and withheld from the rightful owners.

July 29, 1783.
  An act for releasing certain persons from their bargains, and again selling and disposing of the same premises, etc.

February 7, 1785.
  An act for amercing certain persons therein named and admitting others to the rights of citizenship. . . .

February 10, 1787.
  An act for taking certain persons out of the act of confiscation and banishment. . . .

INDEX.

ACTION, freedom of, denied the Loyalist, 203, 204, 205, 207, 208, 209, 210
Adams, John, 2; his theory of the Loyalist party, 3; his opinion of "committees of correspondence," 62; fear of unsettled conditions, 92; supports independence, 100, 101; anecdote of, 202; favors compensating Loyalists, 287; on reasons for toleration, 297
Adams, Samuel, 2, 7; his addresses, 8, 14, 15; his opinion of the Regulating Act, 22; bold measures of, 34; arrest ordered, 45; his belief in independence, 93, 94
"Addressers," (see addresses); names published, 33; persecuted, 40, 41; asked to recant, 46
"Addresses," by the Loyalists, 27, 28, 29, 30, 31, 96, 128, 245, 246
Aid rendered by the Tories to the British (see Services), 126, 127
Allegiance, oath of, Washington demands, 129; effect of, 130; phraseology of, 130, 131; persons obliged to take, 132, 133; as a *privelege*, 133; place where taken, 134; administered by whom, 135; penalties of refusal, 136, 239, 240; attempts to enforce, 137, 138; failure of, 139; evasion of, 139, 140, 301; demanded by both British and Patriots, 141; result of refusal, 192; Whig objections to, 219, non-jurors not allowed to buy confiscated properties, 279
Allen, James, 142, 208, 217
Amory, Jonathan, 20
Amusements of the Tories in exile, 56,264, 265, 266, 267
Anglo-mania, 42, 49, 104
Aristocracy of the Loyalists, 4, 5, 25, 26, 33, 87, 91, 92, 280
Army, Patriot, Tory epithet for, 103, 105, 161; ridiculed, 157; accusation of, 157-8; the soldiers of, sell accoutrements, 162; Tory militia greater than, 172; Arnold's proclamation to, 188; not to be discountenanced, 200; starving, 206; aids in seizing the dangerous Tories, 223
Arnold, Benedict, 188; Whigs did not distinguish, from other Tories, 190
Ashe, "Colonel," 79
Association, beginning of, by the Loyalists, 27, 55;; resolved upon by the Continental Congress, 69; opposed by the Tories, 70, 71, 72; counter, by the Loyalists, 73; of Tories, combated by Whigs, 74; Whig more successful than the Tories in,74; Tories protest against in Georgia, 75; in arms, 75; in North Carolina, 76; phrase-

343

ology of armed Associations, 77; methods of enforcement, 78, 79, 80; active organization by Loyalists, 82; secret methods of, 82, 83; reasons for failure of Tory, 83, 85; of Tories destroyed by Whig militia, 84, 85; places where successful, 86; nature of, 129; of Refugees, 177; Board of Directors of the, of Loyalists, 262

BAHAMAS, as a refuge for the Tories, 243
Banishment, of Loyalists, 137; kind of Tories who suffered, 237; time and manner of, in the several states, 237–240; accomplished by social means, 241; place of, 243; life during, 244–267; laws for the purpose of, 331–333
Battles, in which Loyalists were prominent,—Moore's Creek, 97; Fort Stanwix and Oriskany, 166; Newtown, 167; Savannah, 185; Camden, 186; King's Mountain, 187; Cowpens, 188
Bernard, Governor, 8
Billeting, of British soldiers on Loyalists, 248, 249
Bishops, attempt to send them to America, 109
Boston, Action of, on the Townshend measures, 7, 8; the massacre, 9; the center of rebellion, 14, 15; tea party, 16; Port Bill, 19; four regiments for, 20; aid sent to, 24; Loyalist activity in, 27, 29; Whig League in, 31; measures for relief of, 34; as a haven of refuge for the Tories, 43, 46; British army beseiged in, 45; the seige of, 52–56;

Evacuation of, 56–59; conduct of Whigs in, 107
Boucher, Jonathan, on the divine right of Kings, 21, 22; opposes sending aid to Boston, 24
Boycotting, of the Tories, 39, 40, 72, 234
Branding, Loyalists punished by, 274
Brandt, the Indian ally of the Tories, 167
British Government, action of, 3, 11, 16, 18, 20, 45, 94; relied upon by the Tories, 81; compensates the Loyalists, 288; care for the refugee Loyalists, 288, 292, 298, 299, 300; compensates Loyalists, 300–303; costs of Loyalists to, 303
Bunker Hill, 50, 51
Burgoyne, the defeat of, effect of, 156; aided by Tories, 183, 299; defeat pleases Curwen, 257
Burke, Edmund, 16
Butler, Walter, a Tory leader, 166
Camden, battle of, 186
Campaigns in which the Loyalists aided the British, 183, 184, 185–189
Campbell, Duncan, 166
Campbell, General, 67
Canada, extended to Ohio River. 20; as a place of refuge for the loyalists, 243, 298, 299
Carlisle, a Philadelphia Loyalist, 270, 271
Caswell, Richard, 97
Catharine, Empress, 94
Catholicism, Tory denunciation of, 154, 188
Centers of Loyalism, 85, 96, 97, 98, 101, 102, 103, 108, 116, 117, 118; in Pa., N. J., Del., Md., Va., 160, 224, 225; in Conn., 226, in general, 302, 303

INDEX. 345

Certificates, travelers, obliged to carry, 132, 135, 149; issuing of, based on confiscated property, 279
Charity, for Loyalist poor, 171, 260, 261, 262
Charleston, Tories at, 185; evacuation of, 288, 289
Charlestown, demolition of, 53
Chatham, 11, 18, 20
Cherry Valley, 166, 167
Church, English or Established, 5, 21, 24, 25, 27, 108-115
Civil government, Loyalists urge the British to establish, 249
Clark, George Rogers, 184
Classification of the Loyalists, 26, 33, 92, 210, 240
Clergy, as Loyalists, 5, 21, 24, 25; of Boston address Hutchinson, 27; in New York, 108; in American revolutionary politics, 109-115; refuse to celebrate Whig fast day, 209
Clinton, Sir Henry, 185; importuned for aid by the refugees, 254
Colden, Lieut. Governor, 70, 89
College of Philadelphia, Whig attack upon, 196
Commercialism, of Tories, 9, 12, 13, 20, 21, 32, 33, 59, 70, 71, 73, 79, 108; of Whigs, 112, 117, 204
Commission, British, for enquiring into the Loyalists' claims, 82, 203, 301-303
Commissioners, tea, 13; resignation of, 14
Committee of safety, activity of, 46, 60; complaints made to, 47; organization of, 63; powers given, 64, 65, 66; tyranny of, 66; action in New York, 121; enforce fast day, 208, 209; treatment of prisoners, 237

Committees, organization of, 62-64; Tory protest against, 65; compared with those of French Revolution, 66; Tory hatred of, 67, 68; bounty offered for the members, 67; difficult position of, 68; importance of, 69; enforce the Continental Association, 71, 72; ordered to combat the Tory association, 74; draw up the "association," 77; proselyting by, 78, 79; demagoguery of, 81; methods of coercion, 82; attempt to capture Whigs, 84; of correspondence in New York, 116; of safety in New York, 119, 120, 123; members captured by Tories, 175; ostracise the Tories, 214; activity against Tories in New York, 271
Compensation, of the Loyalists, by the British Government, 260; discussion of, by treaty commissioners, 287; by the British government, 288; demand for, 299; history and method of, 300-303
Conciliation, attempts at, 127, 128; Tory attempt to bring about, 283-285
Confiscation, threats of, 80; authorized by Parliament, 96; early intended by the Whigs, 194, 239; in North and South Carolina, 241; of household goods, 276; urged by Paine, 277; Congress approves, 277, 278; method of, 278; results of, 280; defended, 280, 281; denounced, 281; threats against, 282; repeal of the laws asked by Tories, 284; treaty provision as to, 286, 295; laws for the purpose of, 335-341

Congress, the Continental, 34, 35, 41; action of the second, 50; resolves upon an association, 69, approves of committee activity, 76; imprecated by Tories, 83; nature of Tory opposition to, 87; how the delegates were chosen, 87, 88, 89; its remarkable hold upon the colonists, 89, 90; Tory invective against, 91, 96; struggle in for independence, 94, 95, 96; no Georgia delegates to First, 97; delay Declaration of Independence, 100; election of delegates in New York, 116; objections to its measures in New York, 117; New York's delegates to the second, 118; interferes in New York, 119; recommends disarmment, 122, 163; advise states to seize suspects, 149; finance of, 152; action in the French alliance, 153, 154; a plot to capture the, 161; denounced by Arnold, 188; by Tories, 193; urges attack on Tories, 198, 199; protected from defamation, 199, 200, 201; urges states to stop the depreciation of its money, 202; proclaims a fast day, 208; ostracizes Queens County, New York, 215; requests seizure of Tories in Maryland and Delaware, 224, 225; tardy action of, criticized, 225; denounced, 258, 259, 265; approves of confiscation, 277, 278; recommends revision of confiscation laws, 286, 289, 295

Congregationalists, in American politics, 109

Connecticut, special committees in, 64; independence in, 101; clergy of, 110, 113; "test laws" of, 132; laws against aiding the British, 150, 204; Tory raids in, 174; laws against freedom of speech, 199; laws against spies, 204; Tories from New Jersey and New York sent to, 226

Connolly, John, the seizure and imprisonment of, 228–231

Cornwallis, General, 186, 189, 247

Correspondence, committees of, 14, 31, 32; organization of, 62

Corruption, England's use of, 4; that of the English court reproduced in America, 4; charges of, 27; in the confiscation of Loyalists' estates, 280

Courts, civil, denied the Tories, 193, 194, 195; Tories tried in, 271; impossibility of fair trial in, 272

Covenant, the solemn League, and, 31, 32; the fate of, 69

Cowpens, defeat of Tories at, 188

Criminals, treatment of Tories regarded as, 235–237

"Cropping," Loyalists punished by, 205, 274

Cross Creek, 96, 97

Cunningham, the British jailer, 237

Curwen, Samuel, 46, 51, 102, 256; patriotism of, 257; philosophy of, 257, 258

DELANCEY Party, 109, 115

Delaware, test laws of, 132, 133; laws against aiding the British, 150; Loyalist centers in, 160; uprising of Tories in, 167; seizure of Tories in, 224, 225

Democracy, Whig belief in, 63; value of, appreciated by Congress, 76, 95; strength of, 89;

INDEX. 347

Tory disdain of, 91, 92, 229; take control in Pennsylvania, 102; ridiculed by Tories, 105, 254; furthered by confiscation, 280

Demagogues, revolutionary, 62, 63, 79, 80, 81, 87, 88, 91, 110

Denunciation, public, of Tories, 80, 190, 191, 192

Dependence, of Loyalists, 125, 146; fatal result of, 167; shown by their confidence in the British Gov't, 245, 259

Deserters, to the British, 157, 159, 160, 185; Loyalist's scorn for, 263

Directors, Board of, the Associated Loyalists, 262

Disarming, of Tories, 96; in N. Y., 121, 122–126; recommended by Congress, 122; effect of, 159; reason for, 163; agents employed in, 163

Disfranchisement, of Tories, 192, 199; laws aimed at, 330; after the treaty of peace, 295

Disqualification of Tories to hold office, 193; to sue in the courts, 193, 194; to practice in courts, 195; to practice professions, 196, 197, 209; of Tory merchants, 198; laws aimed at, 330

Dorchester Heights, 56

Dunmore, Lord, 82, 83, 84, 98, 99

Dutch as Loyalists, 102, 117

Dickinson, John, opposes independence, 94

EDEN, Robert, Governor of Md., 103, 255

Edson, "Deacon," 38

England as a place of Refuge for the Loyalists, 243, 256, 257, 258, 259

Employment of the Loyalists by the British, 55, 56, 146–148, 168

Enlistment of Loyalists in the British army, 147; delay in, 165; under Tory leaders, 166; delay in explained, 167; criticised, 168; encouraged by Howe, 168; urged by Loyalists, 169; new inducements to, 171; of refugees as privateersmen, 179; in the regular army, 182; total number of, 183

Episcopalians (see Church, English), identity with the Crown officers, 110

Evacuation of Boston, 56–59; of Charleston and Savannah, 288; of New York, 289, 291–296

Execution of Loyalists by Whigs, 176, 184, 269–272; actual number small, 273

Exile, of Tories, into neighboring states, 123; of Van Schaack, 142; of North Carolina Tories, 217–219; manner of, 225, 226, 227, 228; treatment in, 231; life of the Loyalists in, 243–267; laws intended for the purpose of, 331–333

Expatriation, 288–307

FACTION, among the Loyalists, 262, 263

"Fair American," a privateer fitted out by loyal women, 178, 179

Fairfield, burning of, 177

Falmouth, the burning of, 95

Famine, loyalists suffer from, 52–56

Faneuil Hall, 8, 14, 15, 32, 56

Farmers, interests of, 70, 117, 150, 151

INDEX.

Ferguson, Colonel, defeat at King's Mountain, 187
Fining the Tories, 121, 192, 194, 196, 198, 199, 200, 205, 206, 241; laws for, 335–341; general subject of, 273–275; compensation for, 302
Fiske, John, his theory of the Revolution, 158, 159
Foraging by the Tory bands, 174, 175, 182
France, alliance with, 152; abhorred by the Loyalists, 153–156; denounced, 266; urges compensation of the Loyalists, 287
Franklin, Benjamin, 11, 93, 154, 156, 251
Franklin, "Governor," 101
French Revolution, the committee-men of, compared with Whig committee-men, 66

GAGE, General, 8; temporary governor of Massachusetts, 20; addressed, 28, 29, 31; proclamation by, 32, 33, 34, 40; convenes Massachusetts Assembly, 34; shut up in Boston, 43; urged to be severe with Whigs, 43; denounced in England, 45; his action and the result, 45, 48; opinion of Whig government, 49
Galloway, Joseph, his testimony before the House of Commons, 85, 87, 247; employment by British, 157; urges British to arm the Tories, 159, 160; plots to seize the Governor and Council of New Jersey and Congress, 161; his relations with the British commander, 246; employment and salary of, 255
Gates, Horatio, defeat of, 186

George III., loyalist opinion of, 21; epithets for, 94; destruction of statue of, 107; celebration of birthday by Loyalists, 264, 265, 266
Georgia, strength of Loyalists in, 75, 88, 96, 97; internecine war in, 184; Tory power restored in, 185; passes proscriptive act, 240
Gerard, the French minister, 153
Germain, Lord, 94, 181
Germans, as mercenaries, 94, 95; as Loyalists, 102
Gilbert, Thomas, 39, 74
Government, local, in America, 48
Gray, Harrison, Loyalist, 258, 259
Graydon, Alexander, 66
Greene, General, 167
Guerilla warfare, carried on by Tories, 184–189

HALIFAX, claim commissioners in, 302; Shelburne Loyalists flee to, 306
Hallowell, Benj., 38, 58
Hamilton, Alexander, 296
Hancock, John, 45, 219
Henry, Patrick, on toleration for Tories, 297
Higginson, Madame, 43
Howe, Lord, 55, 57, 124, 127, 128, 141, 152, 158, 168, 217, 246
Hutchinson, Governor, 9; superseded by Gage, 20; addressed, 27, 28, 29, 30

IMPRISONMENT, of Tories, 123, 136, 192, 194, 199, 205, 216, 217; in Virginia, New York and Massachusetts, 220; in South Carolina and Connecticut, 221; of Connolly, 228–231; in the Sims-

bury mines, 235-237; treaty provision for freeing Loyalists, 287; no compensation for, 302
Independence, the idea flattered the people, 92; Whig leaders slow to embrace idea, 93; struggle for in Congress, 94, 95, 96; struggle in North Carolina for, 96, 97; struggle in Georgia for, 97, 98; in South Carolina, 98; in Virginia, 98, 99; in Rhode Island and Massachusetts, 99, 100; action on in Congress, 100; in Connecticut, New Hampshire, New Jersey, Pennsylvania, Maryland and New York, 101; opposed by Quakers, Dutch and Germans, 102; campaign for in Maryland and New York, 103, 104; denounced by Tories, 105, 106; not in favor in New York, 108, 120; king's oath concerning, 170; not to be denounced, 200; Quaker disapproval of, 210; loyal sentiment on, 265; the Loyalists' declaration of, 309-317
Indians, Tories act with, 167, 184
Inquisition, 60-86
Insurrections of Tories, the Whig terror of, 213, 162; methods of preventing, 163; between the Chesapeake and Delaware, 166
Interdict, Congress declares, against Queens County, 215; against Richmond County, 216

JACOBINISM, compared with Whigism, 66
Jay, John, on toleration of the Tories, 296
Jefferson, Thomas, on independence, 93; attempted capture of by Tarleton, 189

Johnson, Guy, a Tory leader, 165
Johnson, Sir John, 126; organizes refugee Loyalists, 166

KELLY, Hugh, 82
Kingship, love of in America, 2, 21, 22
King's Mountain, defeat of Tories at, 187

LAFAYETTE, 155
Laurens, Henry, 202
Lawyers as Loyalists, 28, 30, 111; disqualified to practice, 195
Lee, Charles, 126, 131, 225
Lee, Richard Henry, his resolution of independence, 100
Leonard, Daniel (see "Massachusettensis"), 21; attacked by mob, 36; on committees of correspondence, 62
Lexington, 45; Whig reports of, 48; political results of, 119
Liberty, the Sons of, 8, 34; a Tory epithet for, 60, 61, 62; action of, 75; denounced, 112
Livingston Governor, of New Jersey, 150; plot to seize, 161
Livingston Party, 109, 115
Lloyd's Neck, station for the loyal privateersmen, 182
Long Island, committee rule opposed in, 68; loyal majority in, 88; attack on church property in, 113; "protesters" in, 117; Tories harried in, 124; defeat of Patriots, 128; Tories seized on, 223; confiscation on, 280
Lotteries, use of, to obtain relief for refugees, 262
"Loyal Greens," 166
Loyalist, a typical, 1
Loyalists, persecution of the, 1; creation of the party, 3; their

number as compared with the Patriots, 3; colonial officers, the leaders, of the, 4; social position of, 5; failure to act in the early period, 6; wait for Parliament to act, 7; political philosophy of, 9, 10; difference between English and American Tories, 11; their defence of the tea tax, 12; abuse the tea commissioners, 13; threaten the Whigs, 16; complain of the British government, 16; fear to use tea, 17; reasons for joining the party, 17; urge the British Government to act, 18; attitude toward the Port Bill and Regulating Act, 20, 21; the patriotism of, 22; oppose sending aid to Boston, 24; the classes of, 25, 26; deprived of free speech, 27; address the king's officers, 28, 29, 30, 31; protest against Whig measures, 31, 32; the social status of, 33; leaders attacked by mobs in Massachusetts, 35-38; social reprobation of, 38, 39; boycotted and ostracised, 40-42; rash talk of, 43; urge soldiers to punish Whigs, 44; general persecution of, begun, 45, 46; their property destroyed, 47, 48; opinion of British power, 49; at Bunker Hill, 50, 51; beseiged in Boston, 52-56; evacuate Boston with the British, 56-59; threatened by Whigs, 60; tarred and feathered, 61; attacked by the revolutionary committees, 62; powers of committees over, 64, 65; protest against committees, 65; accuse Whig of tyranny, 66; hatred of Whig committeemen, 67, 68; oppose the non-importation association, 70, 71; suffer more than the Whigs, 72, 73; organize a counter-association, 73; their efforts denounced, 74; strength of, in certain parts of America, 75; coercion of, 78, 79, 80; prone to await British action, 81, attempt to associate in Maryland, 82, 83, 84; general reason for failure, 85; aristocracy of, 87; strength in New York, 89; combat in Congress the move for independence, 94, 95, 96; their disarmment ordered, 96; their strength in North Carolina, 96; their overthrow in North Carolina, 97; in Georgia, 97, 98; in South Carolina, 98; in Virginia, 98, 99; status of, after independence, 100; strength in New York and Pennsylvania, 101, 102; strength in Maryland, 103; new status of, after independence, 104, ridicule independence, democracy, etc., 105, 106; Episcopalians as, 109-115; liberal and ultra-tories in New York, 116, 118, 120; seized and disarmed in New York, 121; ordered disarmed by Congress, 122; exiled, 123; harried by militia, 124; without arms, 125; seizure of, 125, 126; plot against Washington's life, 127; joy at the coming of Howe, 128; compelled to take oath of allegiance, 129, 130, 132-134; denounced as perjurers, 140; between two fires, 141; criticise the test laws, 142-144; as refugees in New York, 146; employment by British, 147-149; services, 150, depreciate

INDEX.   351

Whig money, 151; abhor French alliance, 152-156; their political struggle with the Whigs, 158; as deserters to the British, 159, their eagerness to arm against Whigs, 160; plots of, 161; corrupt the Patriot soldiers, 162; agents who disarmed the, 163; thorough work disarming the, 164; delay in giving military aid to the British, 165; activity in frontier warfare, 166; defeated at Newtown, 167; a British commission urged the employment of, 168; urge fellows to enlist, 169, 170; to have their own officers, 171; compulsory military service for, 173; nature of their military duty, 173, 174; licensed to prey on the Whigs, 174, charged with murder by the Whigs, 176; resolve on retaliation, 177; as privateersmen, 178, 179, 180; their Board of Directors, 181; nature of their marauding expeditions, 182; number of in the British service, 183; aid Burgoyne, 183; active in border warfare, 184; in the south, 184-189; method of escape from Yorktown, 189, rabid denunciation of, 190-192; disfranchisement of, 192; disqualification to use the courts, 193, 194, 195; disqualified to practice their professions, 196, 197; merchants forbidden to sell, 198; forbidden the freedom of speech and press, 198, 199, 200, 201; depreciate Continental money, 202; ruined by Continental currency, 203; the scapegoats for Whig laws, 204; as spies, 204, 205; compelled to military service, 206, 207, 208; persecuted for failure to fast, 208, 209; Quakers as, 210; Whig desire to convert, 212; social ostracism, 213, 214, 215; confined to their houses, 216; exiled from North Carolina, 217; seizure of in several states, 218-222; Whig fear of, 222; seized and exiled by the army, 223; seized in Maryland and Delaware, 224, 225; places to which they were exiled, 226; manner of exile, 227; treatment of, when driven from home, 227-230; in prisons, 231; under parole, 232, 233; life of, in exile, 234, 235; in prison, 236, 237; banishment of, 237-242; their places of refuge, 243; summary of persecution of, 244; life in New York, Philadelphia and Newport, 244-255; civil government for, 249, 250; support of, by British, 255, 256; patriotism of, 256, 257; despair of, 258; confidence in British Government, 258, 259; care of, in New York, 260-262; faction among, 263; pleasures and pastimes of, 264-267; how they received the treaty of peace, 267; regarded as traitors, 268, 269; tried and executed for treason, 270-273; fined, 274; property amerced, 274, 275; treble-taxed, 275; their household goods seized, 276, 277; confiscation of their property, 278-282; threaten the Whig confiscators, 282; attempt reconciliation with the Whigs, 283, 284, 285; disposition of in the treaty of peace, 286; denounce the treaty, 287; compelled to leave with the British troops, 288; evacuate Charleston and Savannah, 289; begin to leave New York, 289; removal undertaken by British government, 292; 29,000 leave New York, 293; accused of outrages when leaving New York, 294; persecuted after peace, 295, 296; reasons for toleration of, 297; remain, in part, in the United States, 298; routes taken by the fleeing, 298; dispersion of, 298, 299; temporarily supported by British Government, 299, 300; history of the compensation of, 300–303; life in Nova Scotia, 304–307; United Empire, 307

Loyalty (see "Reasons") the normal condition, 2; of influential Americans, England's attempt to retain, 3; of the aristocratic elements of society, 5; due to religious reasons, 25, 27; economic reasons for, 70; proclamations of, 73, 75; extravagant expressions of, 264, 265, 266, 267

M ANDAMUS Council, 19: members persecuted, 35–39; boycotted, 41; activity of its members, 73; not allowed to take oath, 133

Marauders, Tories as, 174, 175, 176, 177, 182

Marblehead, citizens of, address Hutchinson, 28; addressers rebuked, 29

Marion, the Patriot leader, 185, 186

Martin, Governor, 79, 80, 88, 96, 204

Maryland, committee system in, 64, 82; Loyalist association in, 83, 84; political campaign in, 101, 103; exemptions from its test law, 133; Loyalist centers in, 160; uprising in, 167; defends severe laws against the Tories, 211; seizure of Tories in, 224; treble-taxes the Tories, 275

Massachusetts, 8; charter annulled, 19; political parties in, 26; assembly convened, 34; resolve of its provincial congress, 41; declared in rebellion, 45; Tory property destroyed in, 47; committees of correspondence organized in, 62; Provincial Congress of, denounces loyal association, 74; forms the first independent government, 93, 99, 100; test laws, 133, 135; laws against Tories in, 194, 200; seizes the Tories, 220; banishes Tories, 237, 238, 239

"Massachusettensis," denounces rebellion, 42; shows the power of England, 49; sneers at Whig pretensions of loyalty, 93

Maximum, the law of the, 71, 73; established by the British in New York, 250

McDonald, Donald, 96

McLean, Allan, a Tory leader, 165

Militia, Tories organize, 54, 55, 74, 81, 83, 84; of Whigs destroy Tory associations, 85; in North Carolina, 96, 97; service of Tories not appreciated by British, 147; attempts to organize, 159, 160; Loyalists urge the formation of, 169, 170; method of organizing, 171, 172, 173; first appearance

INDEX.   353

and number of, 171, 172;
compulsory service in, 173;
work of, especially angers the
Whigs, 173, 174; number of,
183; their campaigns with the
British, 184-189
Militia, Tories organize, reasons
for delay in so doing, 246
Military service, compulsory,
206, 207, 208; by the British,
250; by the Whigs, 273
Mobs, early action of, 6, 7;
attack tea commissioners, 14;
attack Mandamus Councillors,
35-39; persecute Tories, 46,
47, 75; in Boston, 107; in
New York, 107; in Philadelphia, 210; their treatment of
exiled Tories, 228, 230
Mohawk Valley, Tory reign of
terror in, 167
Money, the Continental, depreciated by the Tories, 149, 151,
152; depreciation prohibited,
200, 201, 202, 203
Montreal, as refuge for Loyalists,
298; claim commission at, 302
Moore's Creek, 97, 166, 217
Morgan, Daniel, 188
Morris, Robert, 251
Murray, James, 6, 7

NANTUCKET, a refuge for
Tories, 46
Nationality of Loyalists, 33, 79;
of deserters to the British, 157;
the proportion of foreign born,
303
Neutrals, the proportion of, 158,
159, attempts to force them
from their position, 275
New England, religion in the
politics of, 109, 110; coast attacked by loyal privateers, 182
New Hampshire, 95, 101, 240
New Haven, ships burned in the
harbor of, 177

New Jersey, destruction of Tory
association in, 84, 85; independence in, 101; test laws of,
132; laws against aiding the
British, 150; Loyalist centers
in, 160; Loyalists in, abandoned by British, 167; Tory
raids in, 174; legislature of,
denounces Tory marauding,
176; disqualifies Tory lawyers,
195; and teachers, 196, 197;
laws regulating travellers, 205;
laws to stop trading with the
British, 205; exiling of its
Tories, 222; sends Tories to
Connecticut, 226; law against
treason, 268, 269
Newport, R. I., treatment of the
Tories in, 247
Newspapers, the political work
of, 9, 12, 13, 16, 17, 21, 23,
42, 70, 93, 104, 105, 113, 114,
140, 150, 151, 152-155, 253,
254; virulence of, 175, 176,
182, 190; canards of the loyal,
251, 252
New York, 12; Whig mobs in,
14, 107; political parties in,
26; special committees in, 64;
difficulties of its committeemen, 68; strength of Loyalists
in, 75, 88, 89; representatives
in Congress oppose independence, 100; continued struggle
in, 101, 103, 104; details of
the political struggle in, 108,
116, 120; religion in the politics of, 109, 113; authorizes
the punishment of Tories, 121;
disarms, 122-126; refuge, 128;
test laws of, 132; effect of the
loss of the city of, 156; the
frontier terrorized by Tories,
166; furnishes British army
15,000 men, 182; 8,000
militia, 183; Arnold's regiment organized in, 188; at-

24

tacks Tory lawyers, 195; threatens death to those acknowledging King George, 200; urged to stop the trading with the British, 205; seizure of Tories in, 220, 221; removes the families of refugees, 223; Lee sent to, 225; sends its Tories to Connecticut, 226; proscribes 60 Tories, 240; as a city of refuge, 243; treatment of Tories in, 248-251; trial of Tories for treason in, 271; Loyalists compelled to make good the robberies in their vicinity, 274; proceeds of confiscation in, 280; Loyalists concentrate in the city, 289; evacuation of, 289, 293-296; "Trespass Act" in, 295; many Tories remain in the city, 298; greatest number of Tories come from, 302
Niagara, as Tory refuge, 298
Non-associators, treatment of, 78, 79, 121; to be disarmed, 122
Non-importation, 31, 32, 34; resolved upon by the Continental Congress, 69; opposed by Tories, 70; approved by the Livingston party, 115
Non-jurors, 136, 138, 139
Norfolk, Va., 99
North, Lord, 18, 152
North Carolina, 65, 76, 79, 80, 81, 82, 88; takes decisive action for independence, 96, 97; test laws of, 132, 134; uprising of Tories in, 167; Tories defeated in, 184; social ostracism of Tories, 214; exile and imprisonment of Tories captured at Moore's Creek, 217-219; sends Tories to South Carolina, 226; banishes Tories, 237, 240

Northwest, Tories aid in defence of, 184
Norwalk, burning of, 177
Nova Scotia, 59; described by derisive Whigs, 281, 294; Loyalist's description of, 293, 294; as place of refuge, 299; the English claim commissioners go to, 302; Loyalists refugees in, 304-307

OLIVER, Thomas, 36
Organization, by the Tories, (see association), 54, 55, 81; under loyal leaders, 165, 166; mistaken delay in, 167, encouraged by British concessions, 168; for mutual aid, in New York, 244, 262
Ostracism, social, of the Loyalists, 38, 39, 41, 42, 82, 213, 214, 215, 241
Outlawry of Tories, 193

PAINE, Thomas, 95; advises confiscation, 277.
Paine, Timothy, 38
Parliament, passes Townshend measures, 8; question of sending representatives to, 9, 10; complaints against, 16; passes the five acts, 19
Pamphleteers, work of, in arousing party spirit, 9, 12, 13, 16, 17, 21, 23, 42, 49, 61, 65, 70, 89, 91, 93, 113
Parole, of Tories, 216, 232-237
Particularism, 118, 244, 262
Partizan feeling, causes of, 43, 44, 67, 78, 79, 98, 99, 107, 109-115, 122, 152-156, 173, 174, 175, 182; intensity of, 190-192, 197, 234, 297; persistence after war, 297, 298
Patriots, see Whigs
Peace, the treaty of, 267; terms of, as to the Loyalists, 286;

compromise in the making of, 287; denounced, 287, 288
Penn, Richard, 94
Pennsylvania, no Tory associations in, 85; its delegates in Congress oppose independence, 100; political campaign in 101, 102; test laws in, 133; exempts, 133; few signers in, 139, 142; Loyalist centers in, 160; "Volunteers of Ireland" raised in, 186; laws against Tories in, 194, 195; attacks the College of Philadelphia, 196; and professional men, 197; compulsory military service in, 207, 208; Council orders seizure of Tories, 217; sends Tories to Virginia, 226; banishmemt of Tories in, 240; law against treason, 269; the famous "Black List" of, 269, 270; trial and execution of Roberts in, 269, 270
Pensions, granted Loyalists by British Gov't, 255, 260
Pepperell, Sir William, 39
Persecution, of Tories, 46, 47; nature of, 48, 60–62, 78, 79; in New York, 121–128, 192–200; general, 203, 204, 206–212, 226–242; summary of, 243, 244, 274; by attacks on property, 276, 277; after the treaty of peace, 295, 296, 297
Peters, "Parson," 61, 110
Philadelphia, Loyalists in, attacked, 196; British in, 206; Tories quarantined in, 219; Loyalists executed in, 270, 271
Pickens, Colonel, 184
Pickering, Timothy, 102
Pillory, Loyalists punished in, 205, 274
Pitt, William, Tory hatred of, 265; plan of compensation, 303

Political ideas of Loyalists, 21, 22, 42, 70, 91, 104, 105, 143, 245, 252, 253, 254
Politics, revolutionary, 87, 88, 89, 91, 97, 98, 99, 101, 102, 115; in New York, 116–120; in general, 152–156, 158, 159
"Poplicola," 12
Port Bill, the Boston, 19, 22, 23, 25; Loyal criticism of, 30
Presbyterians, in revolutionary politics, 112, 113, 114, 115
Press, the use of, by the Loyalists, 27; lack of freedom of, 66, 198, 199, 200
Prevost, General, 185
Prisons, where Tories were confined, 230; treatment of Tories in, 231; in Simsbury mines, 235–237
Privateering, by the Tories, 178, 179; inducements to, 180; approved by the British government, 181
Property, destruction of the Tory, 47, 48; attacks upon in New York, 121; attacks in form of fines, 136; by denial of legal redress, 194; greed for the Tory, 275; seizure of, 275–278; compensation for loss of, 300–303
Proscription of Tories, 239, 240; continues after peace, 295
Proselyting, by Whigs, 78, 79, 81, 82; by Loyalists, 83, 84, 148, 152, 157, 198
"Protesters," 31; names published, 33, 40, 42; in Georgia, 75; in New York, 117
Provision, for refugees, by British Government, 292, 293, 294, 298; generosity of the, 299; cost of, 303; in Nova Scotia, 305
Puritanism, 71, 72, 110, 114

QUAKERS, as Loyalists, 102; favors granted, 133; aid loyal militia, 171; driven to military service, 207, 208; accused of Toryism, 210; exiled to Virginia, 226, 227, 228

Quarantine, political, 213; by confinement in the Loyalist's own house, 218; in prison and other states, 217-219; reasons for, 218, 219, 222; in Massachusetts, Virginia and New York, 220; in South Carolina and Connecticut, 221, 222; seizure and, of Tories, 223, Washington approves of, 224; in Maryland and Delaware, 225; principal places of exile, 226; treatment on the way to, 227-231; life of Tories in, 232-235; Rivington's comment upon, 262; laws for the purpose of, 331-333.

Quebec, as a Loyalist refuge, 298; claim commission in, 302

Queens County, N. Y., 89, 119, 123; intercourse with, cut off, 215

RAWDON, the Tory leader, 186

Reasons, for loyalty, 3, 6, 10, 12, 17, 20, 21, 22, 25, 26, 32, 33, 70, 71, 73, 89, 107, 112, 150, 185, 186; nationality as one of the, 303

Recantation, demanded of the Tories, 46; effect of, 66

Reconcentration camps (see quarantine)

Recruiting, of Loyalist, 165-168; advertisements of officers, 170, 171; of privateersmen, 180, 181; by Benedict Arnold, 188

Refugees, 43, 46; their pride in America, 51; protected in Boston, 52; leave Boston, 57-59; list of, 59; to New York, 128; not allowed to take oath, 133; on account of oath, 140; to New York, 146; join the British army, 165, 242; organize under loyal leaders, 166; urged to enlist, 169; as marauders, 174-176; the Loyal associated, 177; value of, as marauders, 178; enlisted as privateers, 179, 180; at Camden, 186; from Yorktown, 189; societies, of 244; rendezvous of, in New York, 245; sufferings in New York, 254, 255; provision for by the British Government, 255; in England, 256-259; charity work for, 260, 261

Regulating act, 19; Whig opinion of, 23; Loyal criticism of, 30; attempt to inaugurate, 35, 39

Relations between the British and Loyalists, 246-251

Religion, in revolutionary politics, 25, 27, 71, 102, 109-115; as an excuse from military service, 206, 207

Renegades, Tories as, 161

Representation, Loyalist view of, 9, 10

Restitution of Loyalist property, provision in treaty for, 286

Retaliation, Loyalists and Patriots resort to, 175, 176, 182, 184, 187

Revolution, the American, theory of, 158, 159

Rhode Island, 99, 125, 132, 135, 150, 153, 177; laws against Tories in, 194; urged to stop the trading with British, 205; law for the relief of tender con-

INDEX.   357

sciences, 206, 207; experience of a Tory in, 233-235; passes proscriptive act, 240
Richmond County, N. Y., 119, 216
Rivington, James, 12, 13, 151, 156, 161; defends the Tory delay in arming, 167; publishes Tory letters, 169; comments on Tory militia, 172; "yellow journalism" of, 175, 176, 178, 251; denounced, 252, stimulates the Loyalists, 253; praises the charity for refugees, 262; on the amusements of the Loyalists, 264; reports treaty of peace, 286; his apology ridiculed, 290, 291
Roberts, a Philadelphia Loyalist, executed, 270, 271
Robertson, General, 173, 250
Rotch, the owner of the tea-ships, 15
Ruggles, Timothy, 35, 55, 73, 74

ST. JOHN, the island of, as a place of refuge, 292, 306; claim commissioners at, 302
St. Leger, with Tories, defeated, 166
Savannah, 184, 185; evacuation of, 288, 289
Schuyler, General, 125
Scotch, the, as Tories, 79; the Highlanders of North Carolina, 96; in Georgia, 96; in Virginia, 99; a Tory regiment of, 165
"Scotus Americanus," 169
Seabury, the Tory pamphleteer, 116
Sears, Isaac, 136
Services of the Tories to the British, 148, 149, 150, 151, 152, 157, 159, 160, 161, 162, 174, 175, 179, 180, 190-192, 204, 205
Sewell, Jonathan, Loyalist, 258, 259
Shelburne, Nova Scotia, Loyalists in, 304
Simsbury mines, 235-237
South Carolina, 95; struggle for independence in, 98; clergy in, 111; test laws of, 132, 134; internecine war in, 184; effect of Clinton's proclamation in, 186; Ferguson's defeat in, 187; governor given power to seize Tories, 221; sends Tories to N. C., 226; banishment of Tories from, 240; Tory restitution for robbery in, 274; second state in number of Loyalist claimants, 303
Speech, freedom of, denied Tories, 198, 199, 200, 201; laws against freedom of, 327-329
Spies, Tories as, 204, 205
Stamp Act, 7, 108
Statistics as to the Loyalists, 29, 30, 33, 59, 82, 88, 96, 111, 157, 160, 172, 173, 182, 183, 186, 188, 255, 261, 269, 271, 280, 288, 289, 293, 299, 300-303
Suffolk County, resolves of, 41
Sumter, the Patriot leader, 185, 186, 187
Support, of Loyalists by British, 181; necessity for, 254; cost to the British, 255; unjust apportionment, 260, 292, 298, 299-303

TARLETON, the Tory leader, 185, 186, 187, 188, 190, 297
Tarring, and feathering, 2, 61, 80, 208, 241; after the treaty of peace, 295

Taxation, Loyalist position in regard to, 9, 10, 70; in New York, 115, 116; under the Whig regimé, 252; Tories double and treble taxed, 275
Tea, duty on, 9; ruse to get it used in America, 11, 12; commissioners, 13, 14; agitation over, in Boston, 15, 16; danger of using, 17; Tories propose paying for the "Party," 20, 93; burning of, 60; importation prohibited by Congress, 69; tax on, condoned, 70; attitude toward, in New York, 115; ridiculed, 252
"Test laws," purpose of, 130; evolution of, 131, 132; methods of executing, 133-138; difficulties of administration, 138, 139; evasion of, 140; changing fortunes of, 141; criticisms of, 142, 143; justification of, 144, 145, analysis of all passed in America, 318-326
Tory (see Loyalist), popular definition of, 192
"Tory Rangers," 166
Townshend, measures of, 8
Trade, with England forsworn, 32, 34, 69, 70
Treason, Whig definition of, 100, 176; of Arnold, 188; Tories charged with, 268, 269; Roberts and Carlisle tried and executed for, 270, 271; Washington's attitude, 272, Whigs disapprove trying for, 272, 273; laws against, 333-335
"Trespass Act," 295, 296
Tryon, Governor, opinion of Whig committees, 67; laments anarchy in New York, 119; a refugee, 120; urged to aid Tories, 125; schemes and plots of, 160, 161; Major Gen'l of the Loyalist forces, 168; supports the refugee resolves, 177; asks for letters of marque and reprisal, 179; opposes civil government for Tories in New York, 250
Tyranny of Whig committees, 66, 79, 80, 121, 125, 221

UNION, Tory desire for, 106, 307
United Empire Loyalists, 307

VALLEY Forge, 206
Van Schaack, Peter, 142-144
Vernon, Thomas, life of, in exile, 233-235
Vincennes, 184
Virginia, 65, 95; independence in, 98, 99; religion in the politics of, 112; test laws of, 132, 134; Loyalist centers in, 160; Arnold in, 188; seizure of Tories in, 220, 223; Tories exiled to, 226; treble-taxes the Tories, 275; defends confiscation, 280

WARREN, Joseph, 31
Washington, George, chosen commander-in-chief, 50; comment on Tory refugees, 56, 57; uncertain of the wisdom of independence, 93; urges the seizure of Tories, 125; approves disarmment of Tories, 126; moves to New York, 126; plot against the life of, 127; demands oath of allegiance, 129; denounced for demanding an oath, 141, 142; complains of Tory proselyting, 149; the Lieut. General of France, 155; plot against, by Tryon, 161; at Yorktown, 189, approves severe laws

INDEX.   359

against Tories, 211; retreat of, 217; orders Putnam to seize Tories on Long Island, 223; approves of seizure and imprisonment of Tories, 223, 224; canards concerning, 251; opinion of trying Tories for treason, 271; orders protection of Tory property, 277; approves confiscation, 281
Watson, George, 38
"Westchester Farmer," 70
West Indies, as a refuge for Tories, 243
Whigs, necessity of action by, 2, 3; intolerance of, 6, 14, 15, 77; on the subject of taxation, 10, 16, 17; their opinions of the Regulating Act and Port Bill, 22, 23; use of the press by the, 27; rebuke the "addressers," 29; League of, 31, 32; publish names of "addressers," 33; persecute the Tories, 35-42, 45-48; gain confidence, 49, 50; Tory opinion of, 52; threaten the Tories, 60; invent the committee system, 62-64; compared with Jacobins, 66; their committee-men hated, 67, 68; association of, 69, 70; not bound by association as were Tories, 72, 73; intolerance of, 74, 190; armed association of, 75, 76, 77; force the Tories into the association, 79; methods of, 80; reason for success, 81, 85; disdained by the Tories, 87; their method of appointing the delegates to Congress, 87, 88; appoint delegates from New York, 89; their reliance on Congress, 90; reason for success in getting people to approve of independence, 92; leaders of, late to approve independence, 93; their struggle in Congress, 94, 95, 96; in North Carolina, 96, 97; in Georgia, 97, 98; in South Carolina, 98; in Virginia, 98; define "treason," 100; gain adherents for independence, 101; act strenuously in Pennsylvania, 102; their active campaign in Maryland, 103; alarmed at idea of independence, 106; disregard of conservatism, 107; the religion of, 110-115; their campaign in New York, 116-121; exile the Tories, 123; success in New York, 127; make test laws, 129-139; refuse test oath, 139; oppose test, 140; defend test laws, 144-145; ridicule Tory service to the British, 147, 148; denounced for making the French alliance, 153-156; not a "desperate minority," 158, 159; cause of their victory, 159; enraged because of Tory services to the British, 161; their fear of Tory insurrections, 162; raids on, 174, 175, 182; carry on internecine war with Tories, 184; bitterly denounce the Tories, 190-192; nature of the patriotism of some, 204; mercenary traits of, 206; defend severe laws against Tories, 211, 212; ostracise the Tories, 214; quarantine the Tories, 216-223; their treatment of exiled Tories, 224-237; banish the Tories, 237-242; better treated by the British than the Tories, 248; denounced by Tories, 252; Tory characterization of, 253, 254; on the trial of Tories for treason, 271, 272; charge Tories with out-

rages, 294; persecute the Tories after the war, 294; pass "Trespass Act," 296, 297
Williams, Colonel, 186; Israel 35, 36
Wilmot, commissioner on Loyalist claims, 302

Wright, "Governor," 97, 98, 185
Wyoming, the valley of the, 166, 297

YORKTOWN, surrender at, 189

Printed in the United States
2668